The Roots of Normativity

'This book, skillfully edited and introduced by Ulrike Heuer, is the final volume of essays published by Joseph Raz before his passing in May 2022. Like all of Raz's work, these twelve essays leave an indelible mark on the reader. They address the weightiest foundational questions in normative theory (What is normativity? What are its roots?), yielding powerful insights on the nature of reasoning; the role and rationality of intentions; the nature of value, morality, and action; and indeed how to live. (…) These essays are a fitting finale to Raz's monumental contribution to moral, political, and legal philosophy, a contribution that concludes generously by mapping out innumerable intellectual paths for normative philosophers to explore.'

Kimberley Brownlee, *Ethics*

'The book "displays a Raz who will be familiar to many of us, with his very individual mixture of ferocity and generosity and his eye for the telling detail.'

Jonathan Dancy, *Mind*

'The essays in this collection "exemplify [Raz's] strength and originality as a moral philosopher: his wisdom, care in working through an argument, suspicion of merely fashionable claims, and intentness in arriving in his own way at his own view.'

John Skorupski, *Philosophical Quarterly*

The Roots of Normativity

JOSEPH RAZ

Edited with an Introduction by

ULRIKE HEUER

Great Clarendon Street, Oxford, OX2 6DP,
United Kingdom

Oxford University Press is a department of the University of Oxford.
It furthers the University's objective of excellence in research, scholarship,
and education by publishing worldwide. Oxford is a registered trade mark of
Oxford University Press in the UK and in certain other countries

First published 2022
First published in paperback 2024

Published in the United States of America by Oxford University Press
198 Madison Avenue, New York, NY 10016, United States of America

British Library Cataloguing in Publication Data
Data available

Library of Congress Cataloging in Publication Data
Data available

ISBN 978–0–19–284700–3 (Hbk.)
ISBN 978–0–19–891366–5 (Pbk.)

DOI: 10.1093/oso/9780192847003.001.0001

Printed and bound by CPI Group (UK) Ltd, Croydon, CR0 4YY

Contents

Notes on Previous Publication

Chapter 1: 'Intention and Value', in *Philosophical Explorations* 20 (2017) Supp. II, pp. 109–126. Reproduced by permission of Taylor and Francis.

Chapter 3: 'Normativity: The Place of Reasoning', in *Philosophical Issues* 25 (2015), ed. Ram Neta, pp. 144–164. Reproduced by permission of John Wiley and Sons.

Chapter 5: 'Value and the Weight of Practical Reasons', in *Weighing Reasons*, eds. E. Lord and B. Maguire (OUP, 2016). Reproduced with permission.

Chapter 6: 'The Guise of the Bad', in *The Journal of Ethics and Social Philosophy* 10, (2016), n.p.

Chapter 8: 'Is There a Reason to Keep a Promise?', in *Philosophical Foundations of Contract Law*, eds. G. Klass, G. Lestas, and P. Sarpai (OUP, 2014). Reproduced with permission.

Chapter 9: 'The Role of Well-Being', in *Philosophical Perspectives* 18, 'Ethics', (2004). Reproduced by permission of John Wiley and Sons.

Introduction

Ulrike Heuer

This book contains 12 essays by Joseph Raz, mostly written in recent years, some already published in more remote places, some published here for the first time. The three Parts of the book break up the themes covered in the essays roughly, but there is a common thread running through them all. They centre around the explanation of normativity. Jointly, they present Joseph Raz's account of practical normativity, and the role of values and reasons therein. While the papers have been written independently, and for different occasions, they form a closely knit web of related arguments, and concerns. In the following, I will try to highlight some of the ways in which they illuminate each other and various central themes of Raz's work on the explanation of normativity.

Raz's work is guided by a methodological assumption: the aim of much of philosophy, and, at any rate, his, is to elucidate practices and concepts as we find and already understand them. The complexity of his work is owed to the complex structures of the phenomena he seeks to explain. The attempt is to understand them individually but also as part of a larger picture.

Take a claim which reappears in many of the chapters as an example: practical reasons, which are the small currency of practical normativity, are in some sense always based on values. But this claim will need refinement when the reasons in question are (e.g.) reasons created by the exercise of a normative power, as, for instance, reasons for keeping promises (Chapters 7 and 8). But then, why not at least round the account up, and claim that all normativity is grounded in values, practical and epistemic alike? That would make for a cleaner theory. Well, the reason is simple: because it is false. To understand practical reasons and their particular way of justifying actions and of presenting us with options, we need to understand that each reason is based on value. This has no parallel when it comes to epistemic reasons: whether or not following them leads, for the most part, to having true beliefs, and whether or not having true beliefs is generally of value, it is simply false that each epistemic reason is a reason because following it has value. As a consequence, it

The Roots of Normativity. Joseph Raz, Edited with an Introduction by Ulrike Heuer, Oxford University Press.
 DOI: 10.1093/oso/9780192847003.003.0001

is also false that there are epistemic options in the same way as they exist with regard to practical reasons. Bringing out these differences and nuances leads to Raz's distinctive view of practical normativity, the crucial role of values in the explanation of reasons, and his account of practical conflicts which often arise from the incommensurability of options.

Thus, this book concerns one of the most basic philosophical questions: the explanation of normativity in its many guises. It lays out succinctly the view of normativity that Raz has sought to develop over many decades and determines its contours through some of its applications. In a nutshell, it is the view that understanding normativity is understanding the roles and structures of normative reasons which, when they are reasons for actions, are based on values. That is, there is a reason to act in a certain way when the action has value—at least in some respect. Raz avoids the current 'reasons first' discussion. Reasons may be first or basic in some contexts, for example when we try to understand the rational functioning of beings like us (Chapters 1–3), but they depend for their existence on values. 'Values first' then? Well, for some purposes, but not for others.

The book aims in part at clarifying the ways in which normative reasons are made for rational beings like us (don't mishear me: they are not made at all, but they fit and perhaps even depend on rational capacities). It brings the account of normativity to bear on many aspects of the lives of rational beings, most abstractly, their agency, more concretely their ability to form and maintain relationships, and live their lives as social beings with a sense of their identity.

With these remarks in place, let me say something about the Parts and the essays in them. The first Part, *Normativity in Action*, looks to explain how in functioning rationally we respond to our reasons, beginning with the role of forming intentions (which is discussed in Chapters 1 and 3).

Chapter 1, 'Intention and Value' argues for two claims: (i) intention 'is a stage in moving to act' and (ii) intentions reflect the reasons an agent believes to have when she guides herself in accordance with the (believed) value of the intended action. (ii) invites an immediate objection: forming intentions is not the unique province of rational (human) agents. Non-human animals too have intentions and act with intentions. But presumably they do not act for reasons. Are these intentions in a different sense then? Yes and no. Raz explains that what is common to all intentions is (i): an agent who forms an intention is 'set to act' as intended. This much is true for human and non-human intentions alike. But depending on the agent's psychological functioning, other features of the intention can be different. Not denying that some non-human animals too respond to certain kinds of reasons and act in light of their beliefs, for rational human agents acting with an intention takes a specific form: intentions are the result of assessing one's situation in the light of one's reasons and resolving what to do. Acting with an intention is being guided by the (believed) value of the action one is set to perform. Thus (ii) applies only to rational human agents.

The main argument of the paper seeks to establish this crucial claim, the claim that the way in which human agents are reason-responsive when forming an intention is by being guided by the believed value of the intended action. This is what is often called the Guise of Good Thesis regarding intentions. The first part of the argument addresses a number of objections and purported counterexamples to the idea that intention involves a belief in the value of the intended action. The second part concerns questions about the relation of intentions, motivation and the will. It is (i), the fundamental role of intentions in moving us closer to action, which requires the participation of the will. After all, we always face options when considering what to do. Resolving what to do is an exercise of the will. Raz explains that, while resolving conflicts of reasons in the case of practical reasons involves the will, in the epistemic case (the case of reasons for belief), it does not. (I will not rehearse the argument for this claim here). The will then concerns resolve and perhaps 'steadfastness', but, Raz says, it has nothing to do with motivation. Human motivations are often seen as rooted in our biological functioning: hunger, aversion to cold, desire for sex, etc. They occasionally trigger behaviour which bypasses rational agency (e.g. in the cases of blinking, breathing, or recoiling from heat). But their relation to action can also be less direct and can be transformed by the human form of rational agency. Hunger, for instance, typically leads to intentional agency, which involves considering reasons for when and what to eat. Not only that, but the knowledge that we need food leads to planning and preparing meals quite independently of the promptings of hunger. In addition, the reasons for our meals rarely concern the bare need for food. Instead, they are reasons of enjoyment and sociality, they may involve environmental, religious, and ethical concerns, etc. Our intentions to eat are formed in response to all those reasons. It is in this way that rational human agency becomes the kind of agency of which (ii), the claim that intentions reflect the reasons for acting (as the agent sees them) is true. For non-human animals, the relation between biological needs and intentions takes somewhat different, but varying, forms.

Chapter 2, 'Intention and Motivation' attempts to locate actions done with an intention or with a purpose within the array of the things people do—both within the broader class of intentional agency and the range of things we do unintentionally. But it also continues, expands, and deepens the exploration which began in the final parts of the first chapter about the relation of motivation and intention in the explanation of action. Both contribute to the causal explanation of actions, but in different ways. The 'simplified' view of their mutual contribution is 'that motivation and intention are seamlessly aligned, in that their motivations move agents towards their intended actions, while their intentions monitor that they are on course towards these actions so long as they are motivated to perform them' (p. 67). Thus the (believed) reason to pursue a purpose typically provides the motivation for acting, as explained in the previous chapter. If the agent decides to pursue a purpose, she has an intention to do so, which will guide her through the process of achieving her end.

Here, as in the previous chapter, Raz treats having an intention as a stage towards action, while rejecting the view that intending is itself the beginning of an action or an activity. Instead, having an intention to do something involves believing that there is a reason for pursuing a certain purpose, and being alert to changes to the opportunity and one's ability to perform the action. But especially in the case of future-directed intentions, none of this needs to involve the beginning of acting. Finally, the chapter asks whether intentions are themselves reasons, that is, content-independent reasons for acting as intended independently of the reasons for so acting on which the intention is based. Raz argues that decisions, and decision-based intentions, are under suitable conditions reasons not to revisit the decision. But they are not reasons for acting as intended. However, isn't there at least a reason to take actions that are necessary for reaching the intended purpose once one has an intention to do so? As Raz sees it, the reason for taking such steps towards realizing one's purpose (e.g. taking means to realizing it) *is* the reason for pursuing the purpose itself. There is no further reason, provided by the intention or otherwise. (This is only the gist of a more nuanced discussion of the normativity of intentions which is one of the recurring themes of the book, especially in this chapter and the next.)

Chapter 3, 'Normativity: The Place of Reasoning', puts one more piece into this picture. One manifestation of rational functioning is reasoning. '[R]easoning is an activity in which we engage for a reason. And typically the reason is to find an answer to a question. More accurately, reasoning is… an activity aiming to establish the justification of, the case for, its conclusion, undertaken in order to establish whether the conclusion is a correct answer to its question' (p. 73). On this view, reasoning is an intentional activity with the aim of answering a question, rather than a way of establishing that a conclusion follows from certain premises. Idly performing logical deduction, say, would not count as reasoning on this view. But does it matter whether we call training one's logic muscles reasoning or not? It does, and it has a number of implications. Here is the first: 'the "real" conclusion is a proposition that is taken by the reasoner to be an answer to the question' (p. 74). Thus, reasoning which doesn't end with the reasoner's answer to their question hasn't (yet) concluded. Understood in this way, the conclusion of reasoning 'can only be a belief or a proposition believed' (p. 80). In Parts 3–5, Raz defends this implication against objections. In particular, he addresses the view that the conclusion of practical reasoning is (or can be) an action, or that it is an intention, as well as the generalized claim that reasoning is just responding to reasons. On Raz's own view, reasoning is a specific response to reasons, but there are others (e.g. performing an action). Thus there are ways of responding to reasons that are not reasoning, and ways of failing to do so (as well as failing to act or to form intentions) when this is not a failure of reasoning.

But isn't there a further question to be considered here: if the conclusion of all reasoning is a belief, what, if anything, is practical about practical reasoning? Well, the question it answers is a practical one. In all other respects, it is just ordinary reasoning. The chapter provides a number of interesting arguments for this conclusion, in particular for the claim that it is possible to have a reason to conclude that one should ϕ, while having no reason to intend to ϕ, and even an adequate reason not to form such an intention.

But even if the conclusion of practical reasoning needn't be an intention, couldn't it be one? The final section sets out to answer this question. Raz argues in detail that any valid reasoning whose conclusion is an intention to ϕ (= AC) would have to include the proposition that there is a conclusive reason to ϕ (= IC) as a premise. Even then, 'the argument from (IC) to (AC), if valid, is valid in virtue of an inference rule [= the Intention Derivation Rule, IDR] sanctioning that transition' (p. 89). But, Raz argues, the step from IC to AC is not reasoning. This is just the briefest glance at an intricate argument which has many repercussions for recent discussions about the rationality of intentions, reasons to intend, and the unity of practical and epistemic normativity. It draws on the view of reasoning described above as well as Raz's account of the role and rationality of intentions. This is a fascinating part of the paper, whose observations and arguments, while not fully worked out, are the nucleus of a new way of understanding reasoning and the role of intentions. The chapter also contains a sustained discussion of the differences between practical and epistemic reasons, the ways in which they are different domains and support different kinds of conclusions, as well as an account of reasoning as one, but only one, of the ways in which we respond to reasons.

The first three chapters sketch a complex view of the ways in which the rational functioning of human agents can be understood as a response to reasons. Chapter 4, 'Can Basic Moral Principles Change?', reverses the perspective by looking at the question what reasons are and in what way their existence depends on the rational abilities of beings like us. The guiding question of the paper, whether moral principles can change concerns only basic moral principles. What (e.g.) avoiding unnecessary harm to people consists in can vary in different historical contexts and change with the development of new technologies, for instance. But that there is a reason to avoid unnecessary harm does not change. Or does it?

Raz's answer to the title question is a cautious yes, moral change is possible. Moral change would be impossible if any explanation of a seemingly new moral reason must be 'subsumptive'. But if there are ways of establishing that there are reasons to do something that don't draw on existing principles in this way, change may be possible. But first of all, why does the answer turn on the explanation of reasons? Because, Raz tells us, normative considerations are intelligible. Those who are subject to them can in principle understand why that is so, at least on reflection. If this weren't so, reasons couldn't guide us in the way they do. We wouldn't be able to extrapolate, or to understand their point which is crucial when there is a conflict with other reasons. Therefore, if there were no explanation of any kind, the purported new reason would seem arbitrary, unintelligible, and therefore not a reason at all. One way in which a purported new consideration can be made intelligible is by showing that it is an instance of a more general principle. This is explanation by subsumption. But is subsumptive explanation the only way of making a new reason intelligible? The alternative that Raz explores in the paper is that of analogical explanations. They too draw on what is known already, but as opposed to the 'vertical' explanation that subsumption delivers, it provides a 'horizontal' one. It thereby allows that there can be genuinely new reasons, which are not derived from known ones.

The final part of the paper urges caution though: the analogical way of explaining reasons allows for the possibility of normative change and it seems quite common. But the differences between subsumptive and analogical explanations are perhaps not all that deep after all.

In the first Part, Raz develops an account of value-based reasons and the various ways in which reasons guide us insofar as we are rational. The second

Part, *Reasons and Values*, goes deeper into developing the value-based view. In particular, it advances a number of considerations which show that it would be a misunderstanding to think that we have reason to promote or maximize value. The value-based account, as Raz sees it, is not committed to consequentialism. Both the reasons for doubting this familiar tenet of value-based views and the alternative of value-based reasons, as Raz understands them, are explored from a range of different angles.

Chapter 5, 'Value and the Weight of Practical Reasons', starts by laying out the value-based account of reasons. When something is of value, it provides reasons for those who can be guided by reasons, that is, for beings who have rational powers. But saying that something is good for someone is not the same as saying that there is a reason. 'A good car can be good for people, and a good banana can be good for a baboon, and these goods indicate something of value because the good of people and baboons matters, because the life of people and baboons is of value' (p. 129). While all of the things that are good for beings whose life is of value provide reasons for us, they may not, or not in the same way, provide reasons for non-human animals whose rational powers are different or who lack them altogether.

The value-based account on which Raz relies here has been introduced and explained in the first Part. This paper addresses, in greater detail, a question that the value-based account faces: what determines the relative strength of reasons? Recognizing something of value as a reason does not, by itself, involve gauging the strength of the reason. What we have reason to do doesn't always depend on the strength of our reasons. It doesn't when there is no conflict with other reasons, for instance (as in the rare instance where there is only one reason). But how can one measure the relative strengths of reasons in those cases where there is a conflict? We should always get as close as possible to full compliance with all the reasons that apply to us. In many cases of conflict, full compliance is impossible, but one available option may be closer to it than another (e.g. in aggregation cases). In cases of conflict, we have strongest reason to perform the actions that come closest to full compliance.

But approximating full compliance with the reasons that apply to one doesn't consist in promoting or maximizing value. Showing this is one aim of this paper. Raz argues for this claim by explaining (i) what determines that something or some option is best, and (ii) what determines what a person has most (or sufficient) reason to do. (ii) isn't simply a consequence of (i). Raz carefully analyses a number of examples showing that being guided by what is best is not only not required, but sometimes even inappropriate. There is a reason to pursue an option or engage with something only if it is good in some respect. That much follows from the value-based account. But it needn't be the best (of its kind)—and this is not (or not only) because there may be reasons bearing on the value of an action which do not concern the value of what is pursued. As Raz sees it, there simply isn't even a *pro tanto* reason to pursue what is best.

Chapter 6, 'The Guise of the Bad', continues the exploration of the value-based account of reasons by focusing on a somewhat unusual question: could a person do something because she believes it to be bad, and could the content of her belief ('that it is bad') provide a normative explanation, an explanation of the action by what the agent took to be a normative reason for acting as she did?

The paper does not consider the question whether badness could in fact be a reason for action. Raz makes clear at the outset that he takes that to be impossible. Thus, the paper presupposes the value-based view, and explores its implications for normative explanations of actions.

Raz contrasts the question whether the belief that an action is bad can furnish a normative explanation with the question whether it can be the motive for the action (coming back to the contrast between explanatory reasons and motives which has already been introduced in Chapter 2). A crucial step in the argument is 'that acting for a bad or worthless motive is a distinctive phenomenon, different from taking the fact that an act is bad or worthless to be a reason to perform it' (p. 150). One further assumption is the one argued for in Chapter 1: namely the Guise of Good Thesis for intentional action (when this is understood as acting with an intention).

In the very short Part 4 of the paper, Raz states succinctly what the problem is: according to the Guise of the Good Thesis regarding intentional action, a person acts with an intention if and because she believes that the action is good (worthwhile, etc.) in some respect and is guided by the value of the action as her reason for performing it. The Guise of the Bad Thesis, explored here, states that a person can act intentionally in the belief that the action she sets out to perform is bad, regarding the badness as her reason and being guided by it in performing the action. This seems a straightforward contradiction. Furthermore, there is no easy conciliation. The insistence that intentional actions are guided by features of an action that the agent regards as good or worthwhile ensures that intentional actions are intelligible. Normative explanations provide a way of understanding why, from the agent's perspective, the action made sense. But if we find that actions done under the guise of the bad can be subject to the same normative explanations and thus can be intelligible in the very same way, then the Guise of the Good Thesis (= GG Thesis) of intentional agency must be false. But the GG Thesis is sound—as Chapter 1 has shown.

Raz explores various ways of understanding actions from 'Luciferian motives' as actions for what the agent takes to be reasons, but none seems to be successful. Doing so would involve ascribing a mistake to an agent that is hard to make sense of, a mistake about, or a desire to push, the boundaries of the concept of a reason. Some such mistakes or desires would undermine the possibility of acting for a reason, for example 'when the desire is to defy basic concepts: to produce an object that will not be an object, to add one to one without their sum being two or to take the badness of an action as something that is a reason for doing it' (p. 159). 'The Luciferian aspires to act for a reason by taking something that cannot be a reason for a reason...to break the mould.... In effect he is trying by his action to *make* the bad a reason for action, knowing that it is not, or has not been so far, or cannot be for beings lesser than he is' (p. 160). But the aspiration fails: there is a motive for the action which explains it, but that is not a normative explanation, and therefore none that conflicts with the GG Thesis. (Raz countenances a different way of explaining actions under the Guise of the Bad, which I will leave to the reader to discover for herself.)

Chapter 7, 'Normative Powers', looks at a different aspect of the value-based view of normativity, one which, at first blush, may seem to escape it: the having and exercising of normative powers. In the *wide sense* of normative powers, they are simply abilities to make a normative change. In the *narrow sense*, they are abilities of persons or institutions to make (or prevent) a normative change that the persons (or institutions) have because it is desirable (has value) that they have the power in question. The paper is concerned with the narrow sense only.

While exercising such a power may not be of value in particular instances, the exercise leads to a normative change as long as having the ability to make changes of this kind is of value. In this way, normative powers can be explained within the value-based view. However, often the exercise of such a basic normative power brings the creation of a 'chained power' in its wake. *Chained powers* are normative powers that a person has only as a result of an exercise of a more basic normative power. To give an example: we have the basic normative power to undertake an obligation by making a promise, and this is so, as long as it is of value that we should have this power. But a chained power that results from the exercise of the power to make promises is, for instance, the power of the promisee to release the promisor from her promise.

She has this power only as a result of the promisor's exercise of her power to promise. Is it true here too that the promisee's power to release exists only if it is good that she should have it? This is one of the questions Raz pursues in this paper.

To give the answer right away: it seems that the chained power cannot be related to value in exactly the same way in which basic normative powers are. The reason is that normative powers can be used well or badly. One way of using them badly is to grant someone or some institution a chained power when it would be better that they didn't have it. This doesn't, or at any rate, it needn't, invalidate the use of the basic power simply because its success in effecting a normative change does not depend directly on the value of using it in a particular situation. So what exactly is the relation of values and normative powers? This is the main question of this chapter.

On some accounts, there needn't be any such relation at all. Normative powers often involve acts of communication. For example, consent often consists in communicating an intention. Mightn't that be all we need to explain how consent effects a normative change? But how would such a communicative act do this? Perhaps consent is valid if and because it expresses the will of the consenting party. However, Raz shows that our common practice does not accord with this view. Instead he sets out to explain why the general account of normativity and normative powers applies here too: an act of consent is considered to be normatively binding when there is value in having the power.

The chapter concludes with an illuminating discussion which places the account of normative powers within the general account of value-based normativity as it has been developed in the previous chapters. Raz explains that '[t]he definition of normative powers does not stand or fall with the success of the view of value that [he] sketched in the previous section. However, if that view is correct it can apply to normative powers, and shows how their definition is but a special application of that general account of values' (p. 176).

Chapter 8, 'Is There a Reason to Keep a Promise?', takes a closer look at a prominent case of exercising a normative power, promising. Promises generate what Raz calls 'content-independent' reasons, that is, reasons for actions which arise from a valid promise independently of its content. Or, put differently, 'that I promised' can be the reason for an infinite number of different actions. The reason is always the same. Despite this content-independence, some promises are not binding, and that is so because of their content, the content of what is being promised. How is that possible? If the validity of a promise does not depend on what is promised, how can some promises fail to be binding because of what is promised? The reasons to comply with a promise may be defeated when their content is objectionable but that doesn't show that the promise wasn't valid to begin with.

As explained in the previous chapter, the explanation of normative powers is itself in terms of values: the value of having and being able to exercise the power. Applied to promises, the value that explains when and why promises are valid lies in their ability to enhance people's control over their lives. 'The power is grounded in the desirability of people being able to commit themselves by the relevant act of communication' (p. 184). Thus if a promise isn't valid, this is because 'there are some undertakings, ability to make which does not serve the value of having enhanced control' (p. 184). It is not the value of the promised action, but the value of the ability to commit oneself (even when the commitment itself is of no value) that explains why there is a reason to act as promised. In this way, the explanation why some promises are invalid, and thus don't create an obligation, does not contradict the claim about content-independence. 'Content-independence' should not be understood as saying that there is no restriction whatsoever on the possible content of a valid promise (in fact, there is)—but just as the claim that the promissory reasons created by *valid* promises aren't explained by the content of the promise.

With this account in place, Raz argues against a view of promissory obligations that has been developed by David Owens. Promissory obligations are, on this view, 'bare' reasons. The idea is this: the relative strength of all promises is the same as far as the promissory obligation is concerned, since the reason is always the same, namely that I promised. This leads to what Raz calls 'the puzzle': if the reason why promises are binding is that they enhance our ability to control our lives by making commitments, forging relationships with others, etc, why is there any reason to keep a promise? After all, keeping the promise does not enhance one's power to control one's life, on this view. Making binding promises does. So keeping them doesn't contribute to the value that explains why promises are binding. The question about the strength of promissory reasons and the puzzle join up: 'Without resolving the puzzle about the force of bare promissory reasons, one may claim, there is no case for holding that there are any reasons for keeping promises' (p. 191). 'Unless there are factors that determine the strength of a bare reason it is not a reason, and we have discovered no such factors. Indeed, if all promises have the same strength it is difficult to see what could determine it' (p. 193).

However, if the 'bare reasons' account is mistaken, how can we determine the strength of promissory reasons without abandoning content-independence? 'We need an account that shows how the exercise of the power changes the normative situation,...and...the value of the power to promise can explain why one has a reason to keep promises, the same reason, but possibly with a different strength on each occasion' (p. 195). And here then is his suggestion: promises create promissory reasons because they are exercises of a normative power (which in turn is explained by the value of enhanced control), but individual promises have a different point. They are not test exercises of a power which we exercise in order to see whether it works. Promises are always, as Raz puts it, 'for the promisee', that is, in some sense in their interest. They are given to provide the promisee with 'normative assurance' of an action (or an omission) and receiving this assurance has different value for the promisee, depending on what is promised. Receiving this kind of assurance is of varying importance to the promisee. The strength of the reason for keeping the promise then depends on the value of the normative assurance in a particular case.

In the third Part, *The Normative in Our Lives*, Raz explores the ways in which normative considerations either depend on our relationships with others or structure and guide them.

Chapter 9, 'The Role of Well-Being', explores the claim that when we care (or ought to care) about others, what we care (or ought to care) about is their well-being. Well-being, as Raz understands it, consists in the (somewhat) successful and wholehearted pursuit of activities or aims that are worthwhile. It is not the same as a happy life, but it is a condition of happiness: 'normally people can be happy only if they believe that their life, activities, etc. were worthwhile' (p. 211). Well-being, understood in this way, lines up with what is good for a person, because, Raz argues, what is good for a person is engaging in the right way with things that are good. When people engage with value in this way, it contributes to their well-being. At least, it does when the person embraces what she does, and isn't afflicted by self-hating or other destructive attitudes that undermine well-being. The qualification 'in the right way' is meant to exclude those undermining attitudes as well as ways of engaging with value that are not appropriate to the value it is. This kind of engagement is what Raz means by the pursuit of worthwhile activities, and thus by well-being. Raz argues that the contribution that episodes in a person's life make to their well-being is pattern-dependent, that is, 'the relevance, if any, of different episodes...to people's well-being cannot be determined independently of their relations to other episodes' (p. 219). For example, how much and in what way something matters depends on whether it is embedded into a person's projects and at which stage it occurs. Raz calls this 'the variable pattern view'. So far, this is just an explanation of the concept of well-being and its relation to happiness and to value. It is a consequence of the view that we normally do not pursue our own well-being. Well-being is the upshot of successfully pursuing worthwhile activities and relationships, and the reasons for pursuing them are the features that make them worthwhile. But has well-being no normative role to play then? Doesn't it provide any kinds of reasons? Raz explains how assigning it such a role fails to capture the most likely context where one would expect such reasons be relevant, namely the various ways in which we are partial to ourselves.

But that leaves him with the question he started with. What about the thesis that when we care about others, it is their well-being that we (ought to) care about? Raz shows that it follows from the argument regarding one's own well-being that at least certain attempts to establish that we have a duty to promote the well-being of others fail. Taking the argument into account the question becomes: 'if we do not have an independent reason to promote our own well-being why should we have any reason to care about the well-being of others?' (p. 230) Raz argues that our duties towards all others (special obligations apart) are duties of respect requiring us 'to protect their capacities as rational agents, and the conditions for their successful exercise' (p. 232). Doing so requires both more and less than promoting their well-being. It requires more because the reasons by which other people are guided in leading their lives may not concern their own well-being but should nonetheless be respected by us. It requires less for basically the same reason (i.e. when others are not concerned with their own well-being, then our respect and support for their successful pursuit of their reasons shouldn't be either)—and also because 'promoting' value is not part of respecting it (see also Chapter 5). The remaining link to well-being is that the duty of respect amounts to a duty to protect the abilities of others 'to forge a good life for themselves' (p. 231).

Chapter 10, 'Attachments and Associated Reasons', discusses whether there are reasons to be partial (e.g. towards one's children), and if so, whether there is a tension between reasons of that kind and moral reasons. Raz's view of partial reasons, while not endorsing a Kantian view of morality, is nonetheless congenial in its approach to Barbara Herman's reply to Williams' 'One Thought Too Many' challenge to Kantian morality. On Raz's interpretation, Herman's point is that there are many reasons which depend on the value of relationships, but like all reasons, they are defeasible. So it is possible that, on occasion, they are defeated by non-partial reasons.

But isn't there still a tension? If the reason for favouring someone is that I am partial to them, how are we to understand that reason? Is the reason the value of the relationship when it is a universal feature of relationships of this kind to have value, as in the case of friendships? If so, partial reasons might be unproblematic, but grounded in a universal value. But isn't this a misinterpretation of the reasons we have to favour our friends? '[P]eople have reasons for their choice of friends, but those reasons are not unique to the people they choose to be friends with, nor do they fully explain their choice of friends' (p. 249). As Raz sees it, the reasons that pertain to friendship and other relationships are in part indeed grounded in universal values. But we do not choose to spend time with a friend because doing so instantiates a universal value. When one's reasons concern options that are incommensurate, as they often are, deciding in favour of one's friend because one likes her is not introducing a further reason, but it is nonetheless a perfectly acceptable way of resolving certain kinds of conflict. That leaves us with conflicts between reasons—universal ones, mind you—that are grounded in the value of friendship and others that are, say, grounded in the value of persons qua persons (impartial reasons proper). Raz has a simple response to that kind of conflict: it reduces to the question when reasons of friendship are stronger than the competing ones. If we may assume that at least sometimes they are, there is no need to give a general answer to the question when that is. This is simply an everyday moral question. The answer will turn on the particular features of the case in question.

In a second part, Raz explores whether there is another kind of partial reasons, reasons to be partial to oneself. Distinguishing a number of different interpretations of what might be meant by this, Raz rejects in particular the idea that we have reason to further our own well-being. This part of the paper is an interesting application of the discussion of well-being in Chapter 9. It leads to the surprising conclusion that while there is an unproblematic sense in which we have reason to be partial to our friends and others close to us, there is no unproblematic sense in which we have reason to be partial to ourselves.

Chapter 11, 'Identity and Social Bonds', continues the discussion of the possibility of justified partiality, but from a different angle. Partiality, and the reasons that arise from it, are not a problem (as the previous chapter has perhaps shown already). But how about the particular kind of partial reasons, or even duties, that are thought to arise from features of a person's identity? Some identities are chosen. They are a matter of 'voluntary association'. But does that help with understanding why they give rise to reasons and duties?

'The mystery is why one is bound to act as one does not want to because of a past choice that does not prevent one from acting as one wants, but makes it wrong to do so' (p. 263).

Raz sets out to show, here again, that it is value that explains reasons, not choice, at least not choice per se. That something is chosen can make it valuable. If it does, but only then, is there a reason in virtue of its being chosen. Furthermore, belonging to a group as a matter of choice has value only if belonging to the group itself has value. But there can also be value in belonging to a group where membership is not voluntary. When it is, there can be related duties.

In the final part of this chapter, Raz argues that belonging to a group can be good—good for the member—even when the group itself is defective. Social groups often have a long and chequered history which makes it likely that they will be defective at least in some respects. Being a member can still be rewarding. Besides, it opens opportunities for reform which are not open to non-members. But it also gives rise to conflicts and problems. For instance, are all the alleged duties of membership binding, even when they issue from objectionable practices; and is participation in all of the group's practices required by one's identity as a member? Raz doesn't seek to answer these questions but only to provide a framework for thinking about them.

Chapter 12, 'Normativity and the Other', the final chapter of this book, returns to basic questions regarding the nature of normativity, in particular the question whether, or in what way, normative truths depend on what Raz calls 'participatory conditions': 'The distinctive constitutive element of participatory conditions is that conduct or attitudes, actual or hypothetical, of people other than those who have a reason, which express approval or the absence of disapproval of the reason in question, are a condition for the existence of practical reasons, or of large classes of them' (p. 271). Raz doubts the existence of such conditions, and this chapter offers his reasons. The aim is to restate the view of normativity that has been developed in the earlier chapters, and seen at work throughout this book, and to show that it can account for the features that motivate the introduction of participatory conditions without including any such conditions.

Arguments in favour of participatory conditions are many and they are diverse. Raz doesn't engage with any particular argument in great detail (with one exception that I will come back to). This is on the one hand to avoid being side-tracked into interpretative questions, and on the other to identify the contours of general and widely shared features of theories of normativity.

The general view of normativity that Raz endorses is the by now familiar value-based view: 'Features of the world that are desirable are valuable, and valuable features that meet certain conditions constitute reasons that agents are to be guided by in their thoughts and actions' (p. 275). If we accept this view, might the approval of others constitute a source of the justification or validation of reasons? Raz argues that it can't since others are no less fallible than I am when it comes to responding to reasons.

But might the reasons I have with regard to others (for their good) depend their choices and their reasons? They do (as we have seen in Chapter 9 for instance), but there may still be no room for a participatory condition. Our reasons to act for the good of others depend on their reasons, but it is not their approval that is needed, except in cases where consent is required. Those are special cases, since consent is not a general condition of having reasons with regard to protecting or supporting others.

But there are also reasons regarding others that are not reasons to act for their good and are not determined by the reasons that apply to them. Raz introduces the recognition principle (p. 281) which requires of us to respect the choices of others whether or not they are based on reasons. It applies to rational beings, 'beings whose life is valuable in itself [and who] have their own view of themselves and of the world around them' (p. 282). Rational beings like us have normative powers which they can use for better or ill. Having and exercising these powers is itself of value, and thus must be respected (cf. Chapters 7 and 8). One implication is that 'we have reason to enable others to pursue goals of their choice, even though their life would be less good than it could have been had they made different choices' (p. 282). This is one more way of showing how the value-based account of reasons can explain the reasons we have even when they are not reasons to do what is best. On the view Raz expounds here, we have (i) reasons to respect the reasons of others, as well as (ii) the value of their normative powers and their way of exercising them, (iii) even when their choices rest on mistakes, (iv) including mistakes about the reasons they have. (ii), (iii), and (iv) are just different ways of respecting the value of normative powers which are part and parcel of a rational being's exercise of their ability to respond to reasons (see Chapter 7) but none of these reasons require participatory conditions.

As mentioned at the beginning, Raz discusses one version of a participatory condition explicitly in the Appendix to this chapter, namely T. M. Scanlon's contractualism. According to it, an action or a policy is wrong if there is an individual who has a reason of a certain kind—a personal reason, as Scanlon used to call it—to reject it. As Raz sees it, this is a mistake. No one has a personal reason to reject the hunting of whales, but it is nonetheless morally wrong. Scanlon does not provide an account of moral wrongness (unless his is a stipulative use of the expression 'moral wrongness').

But might a person's ability to advance a personal reason against an action or a policy nonetheless introduce a reason of a special kind? It is the individual's ability to raise decisive reasonable objections on her own behalf which explains why Raz sees Scanlon as endorsing a participatory condition. But here too Raz is doubtful. There are such personal reasons, of course, but ordinarily they would just be defeasible (*pro tanto*) reasons. The contractualist account elevates them to being decisive—to having a kind of veto power. Thus it is a view about the stringency of personal reasons (of a certain kind) and as such, it seems unwarranted.

While weaving together the various aspects of this exploration of normativity to a general view of what normative considerations are, how they relate to values, and structure our relationships, Raz tries to stay at all times close to the phenomena as we know them. He relies on everyday examples throughout. The account's ability to make sense of them or to explain them is paramount to its success. In this way, the book delivers a non-revisionist understanding of normativity and its role in our lives. A recurring theme concerns the ways in which both reasons and values depend on us: on our nature as rational, reason-responsive creatures, and on the social practices which we create or find ourselves embedded in. Raz sometimes calls his view 'classical' because of a kinship to Aristotle in its emphasis on agency. But he is aware of the limits of our agency too, the contingent features of our social world that, to some degree, determine and constrain our options and our abilities to engage with them.[1]

[1] I am grateful to Felix Koch and David Owens for very helpful comments on an earlier draft.

PART I

NORMATIVITY IN ACTION

1
Intention and Value

In previous writings, I joined those who take the view that action with an intention is an action for (what the agent takes to be) a reason, where whatever value there is in the action is a reason for it. This chapter sketches the role of reasons and intentions in leading to action with an intention. Section 1 explains that though belief in the value of the intended action is not an essential constituent of intentions, nevertheless when humans act with an intention they act in the belief that there is value in the action. Section 2 explains the relative role of value and intention in 'producing' the action and relates their role to that of motivation.[1]

1. Intention and Belief

1.1 Intentions

For people, having intentions involves belief in the value of what they intend (to do or resolve or be, etc.).[2] This thesis, central to the development of my argument, encounters immediate and obvious questions and difficulties. Why, one may ask, does the thesis assert belief in the value of the object of the intention, rather than belief in the value of the intention itself? The answer is

[1] I am grateful to Ulrike Heuer who proposed the idea of this book and fashioned its conception, and to Penelope Bulloch who worked tirelessly on every part of it, improving its style and thought in innumerable ways.

[2] Throughout the chapter, 'actions' will refer to actions, omissions, or activities. The only intentions I discuss are intentions to do or omit something. In various locutions, 'intentions' refer to other conditions. I may, e.g., intend something to be the case, meaning expect or hope that it will be the case partly as a result of something I do (e.g. I intended you to be grateful...). The belief in the value of the intended that I refer to can be no more than belief that what is intended is better than the available alternatives. The relation of the action and the value it is taken to have can be complex: the action need not be of value in itself, but only because it was commanded by one's superior and it is good to act as commanded, etc. Some of the complexities will be examined later in the book. Note that the thesis is about 'belief in the value of...'. It is not about 'valuing...'. Valuing something is not to be confused with belief in the value of that thing. On valuing, see S. Scheffler, 'Valuing', Chap. 1 in *Equality and Tradition* (Oxford: OUP, 2010) 15–40 and N. Theunissen, *The Value of Humanity* (Oxford: OUP, 2020).

The Roots of Normativity. Joseph Raz, Edited with an Introduction by Ulrike Heuer, Oxford University Press.
 DOI: 10.1093/oso/9780192847003.003.0002

that normally intentions are not formed for their own sake, but to lead to the intended action. What constitutes this normality? How does it manifest itself? First, that the specification of an intention involves specification of its object (I intend to drink the water in this glass now, I intend to repeat my teachings next year, I intend to help my family during the recession, I intend to help the fight against discrimination in my country, I intend to dance all the way to the grave, etc.). Second, unfulfilled intentions, which were not revoked, that is that the agent did not decide to abandon, show some failure (though not necessarily a fault) in the agent who had them. Finally, even abandoned or revoked intentions may establish a failure in the agent if their occurrence is due to lack of resolve, to an inadequate ability to persevere, etc. There are occasions in which there is value in having an intention independently of any value there may be in its object. When agents think that this is the case the belief involved in their intentions would be, or include, that there is value in the intention itself. I will return to this point later in this chapter.[3] But there is another difficulty we need to attend to here: small children have intentions before they have the concept of something being valuable or of value. Furthermore, animals of other species that never have beliefs in values, and are incapable of such beliefs, have intentions.

I am thinking of the duck I watched in Regent's Park the other day. She was swimming in a shallow artificial pond, fed by water cascading down a gentle slope, bouncing down a flat ledge before flowing to the pond in a small waterfall. Some ducks were on that ledge, and my duck who was in the pond, swam near the ledge trying to mount it, and failed, slipping back into the pond. She turned back, swam a couple of metres away from the ledge, and then turning again swam towards it, approaching at a slightly different point, and tried again to climb the ledge, failing again and trying again, finally succeeding at her third attempt. My duck not only acted intentionally, that is she not only displayed an intention in action, she also had an independent intention, an intention that one can have even while not acting on it.[4] She intended to get to the place to which she eventually got. And that intention governed a number of her actions, guiding their choice and the manner of

[3] The question is discussed in detail in J. Raz, *From Normativity to Responsibility* Oxford: OUP, 2011) Chap. 3.

[4] The concept of an independent intention (discussed in Raz, *From Normativity to Responsibility*) is similar to 'future intentions' used in some philosophical writings, except that independent intentions, while they may be future directed, need not be so. They can be the intentions governing current actions. Unless otherwise indicated, I refer to independent intentions when writing of intentions.

their execution. But she had no belief in the value of being in, or of getting to, the place that she intended to get to.

Having a belief in the value of the object of the intention is not constitutive of having an intention. Yet, necessarily, those possessing full and unimpaired rational powers (namely those typical of adult humans) who have an intention do have that belief. I will try to explain why in the usual way: namely, as intentions are a distinctive kind of mental state, not consisting in a combination of some other states, or of some other states under certain conditions, they can only be explained by pointing in a general way to their connections to actions, beliefs, etc., even though the 'pointing' is not always perspicuous when taken in isolation.

Intentions are states in which the agent is set to act. Being in that state takes one some way towards the action. An example will help. It is of the way intentions bring people closer to the intended actions. And generally, when referring to people I have in mind people with unimpeded access to their rational powers, powers that are themselves undamaged. With people with limited rational powers, and with animals of other species, there will be different descriptions, appropriate to their psychology. The claim is that so long as we are dealing with a being who can have intentions we are dealing with a being who has mental states, or conditions of this generic kind.

My example concerns Jane, who is reading in her study. It is late afternoon, and the light is slowly fading, weakening. Being absorbed in her book, she does not want to interrupt her reading to go to the doorway to turn on the light. She intends to turn on the light when next she goes to the toilet, as she knows that she will before too long. Half an hour later, she goes to the toilet and when returning, she automatically, unreflectively turns on the light. She is not then conscious of her prior intention, and only marginally of her action. But she turned on the light intentionally because she had that intention and was guided by it. Compare the situation with another: Imagine that Jane was so deeply absorbed in her book that she did not form the intention mentioned. On her return from the toilet, she did not turn on the light as above, but just as she entered her study I said to her (or the thought came to her unbidden): would it not be good to turn on the light? She paused, however infinitesimally, and realizing that indeed the light was rather uncomfortably dim, turned on the light. It is this step, assessing the situation and forming an intention, which was absent in the first example, made unnecessary by the intention she conceived some time earlier. The absence of that step illustrates the way in which the intention set her to act, took her nearer the action.

Note that in the first example, the absence of the extra step was not necessary. It was possible. It is always (well, when we are not asleep, etc.) possible to review and revise our intentions. But their importance to our life lies in the fact that there is no need always to do so, and that we often do not. Also, while typically we are aware of our intentions when forming them (though not necessarily: self-deception and other conditions may obscure their formation from our minds), typically, we are not conscious of them for the entire duration of having them, and they can guide our actions even when we are not aware of the fact. Even though many of our intentions (like those in the examples above) are of short duration, they are, while they exist, like beliefs, like having goals and attachments, states constituting aspects of our settled, resolved, orientation to the world.

I repeated several times that intentions guide actions. They can of course fail to do so. I can unintentionally do something that I intend to do. I intend to turn on the light, when it suddenly comes on. 'Why did the light come on?' 'You turned it on.' 'Oh, I did not realize that I did that.' 'You moved the switch to the "on" position.' 'Oh, that is the light switch? I was looking for it and in doing so just leaned against it and accidentally turned it on.' It has become a familiar example: we can do what we intend because we intend, but unintentionally. While the intention plays a causal role in producing the action, it does not guide the action.

One can also intentionally do something in a way that is unrelated to one's intention to do it. Think of Jane again and vary the example yet again: she intends to turn on the light on her way back from the toilet. But as she returns, someone, gun in hand, threatens her: 'turn on the light or I will blow your brains out'. She intentionally turns on the light, but from the moment she encounters him her intention to do so anyway completely flies out of her mind in the shock of the encounter. She did not abandon it or forget it. It is common for our intentions not to be present in our mind when concentrating on other matters. As we saw, they may still guide our actions even then. But they may not. We may be so deeply immersed in some activity, or startled or shocked or otherwise diverted from our dominant frame of mind, that the intentions, though neither abandoned nor forgotten, are silenced, disabled for a while. That is what happened to Jane when encountering the gunman. Her action though intentional is not over-determined, as it were. It is not guided both by the new intention to avoid the threat and by the previous one. That previous intention is not guiding her at all. It was rendered temporarily inoperative. An intentional action is guided by a pre-existing independent intention when it is performed because of that intention, and the manner of its performance is governed by that.[5]

Three constitutive elements of intentions are relevant to our discussion. It is constitutive of intentions that: (a) They set the agent to act (as intended), resolve him so to act. Given that action with an intention is an action the agent resolved to take, forming intentions brings the intended action closer. One element of it is already in place. (b) They can both lead to and govern the intended actions, and other actions facilitating them. They play a causal role in the 'production' of the action, though as will be seen in the discussion of motives later on, it may be misleading to say that they 'cause the action'. (c) When they do lead to and govern the intended actions, they govern choice and manner of action through the operation of the rational powers of the agent. This last condition explains why it is wrong or misleading to give a purely dispositional analysis of the second condition. Whether the intention leads to the action depends on various contingencies, but also on the proper functioning of the agent's rational powers. Using their rational powers, agents identify the opportunity for the intended action, the advisability of preparatory or facilitative actions, and direct and adjust the action (trajectory of movement, speed, etc.) to fit the intention.

I will return to the three constitutive elements of intentions below. The remainder of Section 1 concerns the difference that human rational powers make. All these constitutive elements are true of my duck. The intention sets her to act and governs and guides her actions: she swims in the direction she does, etc. because of her intention. And the intention guides her through the functioning of her rational powers. Its guidance relies on her (perceptual) beliefs about the location of the ledge relative to her location, the conditions of the water, etc. and she relies on her knowledge of how to navigate herself and how to overcome certain obstacles, etc. That the duck has intentions entails that she has beliefs and other rational powers. It does not entail that her rational powers are the same as ours. They include, and they must include, given that she can have future-directed intentions, an ability to choose means directed at ends that she has, and whose pursuit she can intend. Where she can intend the end she can choose some means to that end. Crucially, this does not mean that the duck can choose among her ends (nor that she can recognize or choose all the means that would have served her end had she been able to choose them).

[5] Though we need to remember that agents can change in midperformance the intentions that guide their action.

Given that ends may themselves also be means to other ends, the duck may be able to choose among some ends one suitable to a further end of hers. What is not assumed is that to be able to intend an end she must have the rational capacity to approve, revise, or jettison that end.[6] But is not that power part of, or at any rate a necessary concomitant of the power to choose a means (namely to choose facilitative steps) to the end? The doubt is not based on the thought that if we have some rational powers we have them all. There is plenty of evidence that that is not so. The doubt is more specific: can I intend to do something without knowing that I intend to do so? Can I φ in order to secure E, without knowing that I intend to secure E? And if I know that I intend E, can it be the case that I cannot approve or disapprove of having that intention?

I think that those who intend to φ know that they do. But that knowledge consists in their seeking for ways of making it the case that E, in their inclinations to avoid acts that will make E harder to achieve. In other words, it consists (in part) in conduct that is guided by the end of realizing E. That establishes that they intend E. These and similar facts (e.g. that they have a sense of satisfaction at securing E) establish that they know that they intend E. It may be objected that that falls short of showing that these beings believe that they intend E. Possibly so, but if so then knowledge does not imply belief. We could keep an open mind on that controversial issue.

An open mind on that issue does not require doubting whether the duck can have any beliefs. What I observed may not warrant attributing to her the capacity for having beliefs whatever their content, for example she may not have the capacity to have self-referential beliefs. But it is entirely possible that she can have false beliefs (e.g. about ways of getting to the ledge), which would show that she is capable of having some beliefs. In conclusion, the three constitutive elements of intentions that we discussed imply that to have intentions one must be capable of having knowledge or beliefs that some acts would or may facilitate the realization of one's intentions, and therefore that one has those intentions. But one need not have belief in the value of one's intention or of its object, and therefore one need not have beliefs about the value of the facilitative steps.

Ducks can learn from experience. I was not assuming that my duck's successive attempts to get to the ledge were improved by the experience of her earlier failed attempts. Her learning may have involved correcting false beliefs.

[6] So far as I know any animal that can pursue an end can abandon the pursuit, the end unachieved. It does not follow that they can decide to do so. They may abandon intentions when their attention is diverted by something or other, etc.

But learning from experience need not depend on reflection on one's experience and changing one's beliefs as a result of such reflection. We are aware of ways in which people change their habits in light of their experience without even being aware of the change, let alone of its origins. Conditioning is one account of how such learning may occur, but we should not assume that either conditioning, or capacities due to some evolutionary advantage explain all learning. All we need acknowledge is that the possibility of learning does not require reflection about one's beliefs, and therefore it does not require belief in the value of the objects of one's intentions.

1.2 Human Intentions: How Do Value Beliefs Come in?

Does not that contradict my contention that human intentions (the intentions that humans have) involve belief in the value of their object? It does not. People (not all of them and my claim should have been qualified to apply only to people in full possession of their rational powers) do have rational powers that include the power to assess, affirm, or criticize the objects of all their intentions. It does not follow, and we need take no position on the matter, that people can abandon any intention they have, or that there are no intentions that they cannot avoid having, though if they exist these constraints would limit our ability to revise intentions. Nor does it follow that people assess the value, the point or worthwhileness, of everything that they are able to assess. Obviously, there are many matters about the value of which people have no view, even though they are able to have such a view.

But two points should be borne in mind: First, our rational powers are active and engaged throughout our waking life (though they are not always functioning at their best). We can decide to reflect on this matter or that. But we do not need to decide whether to reflect nor do we need an advance intention to reflect on a matter in order to do so. Our rational powers engage with matters which attract our attention. Certain phenomena, events, or happenings are salient, and they attract our attention and engage our rational powers willy nilly (though for how long and to what effect will then depend on the functioning of our rational powers). With time we develop habits and dispositions that make us take up for examination matters that, if those habits and dispositions are well judged, merit or require our rational attention.

Second, our intentions set us to act, they move us closer to the action in dispensing with certain controls over whether to act (as intended) or not. Adopting an intention is up to a point like adopting a purpose. It is subject to revision, and revisions do not require much to be justified, but so long as it is not revised it remains my purpose and I can pursue it in action without the need to reconsider it or re-adopt it. That happens when the action follows the intention right away (so that the opportunity for action is thought to be appropriate at the same time). 'Future-directed intentions' (as they are called) can be followed into action only upon judging that the opportunity for action is appropriate, but they set us to act intentionally in that we have already adopted the purpose that the intention constitutes.

Of course, saying that does not add to the explanation of how formation of an intention takes us closer to the intended action sketched above. And it reaffirms that intentions are forms of practical resolve. They are not beliefs. For human beings, however, having an intention means (a) that one has formed the view that the action is advisable, and (b) that means that one need not raise again the question of whether it is advisable to do so. That too manifests the way in which, for humans, forming an intention takes one closer to the action (to acting with an intention) than one was before.

But why? Perhaps we can agree that if for humans forming an intention to φ involves a belief (that is not an integral part of the intention) that it is advisable (right, or something like that) to φ then having a future-directed intention will make an intentional action (meaning here acting with that intention) possible without re-examining, re-confirming, that belief, and in that way it brings the agent closer to the action, an action that—being done with an intention—would otherwise involve forming such a belief at the time of action. But why does the formation of an intention involve such a belief at all?

The answer is in the two features just noted. Forming intentions is adopting purposes. A new purpose, even when it is a subordinate one, which is meant to facilitate or constitute the achievement of an already adopted purpose, is a step that can go wrong, and requires monitoring to make sure that it does not. That means that forming purposes is salient for assessment by our rational powers, powers that are always engaged and (more or less) alert to matters that should be examined. Risking circularity one would be inclined to say that we cannot act intentionally (meaning here acting with an intention to do what we do) without assenting to the action, without taking it to have a point. Hence, given that once we intend we waive the necessity for a further assessment, having an intention must involve having the view that its object (or the intention itself) is worthwhile.[7]

[7] For a more nuanced and detailed discussion, see J. Raz, *Engaging Reason* (Oxford: OUP, 2000) Chap. 2; Raz, *From Normativity to Responsibility*, Chap. 4).

But, one may object, none of this shows that we attend to and deliberate about the value of each one of our intentions. That is indeed true, but it is no objection to the thesis that human intentions involve belief in the value of their object. Having beliefs does not require attending to them. It does not require that the believer ever entertained the belief, or even was aware of it. I do not mean merely that people need not have their beliefs in mind, entertain them, etc. all the time. I mean that they can have beliefs that they never had in mind, beliefs that have never occurred in their deliberations or reflections. For example, until I thought it up now, to use as an example, the thought that 1300 + 1 = 1301 never occurred to me. Yet I had this belief for many years. This raises the question: if I never thought (i.e. it was never in my mind) that 1300 + 1 = 1301 what does my believing that consist in?

First, another question: Is it not the case that I know, and knew all along, that 1.3 + 1.7 = 3 rather than that I believed that to be the case? In this case, it is more natural to speak of my knowledge than about my belief. It does not follow that I did not have the belief as well. That I did have it becomes apparent when considering cases in which I do not have knowledge. Suppose I believe that no woman over 40 can bear children. I believe that because someone I trusted told me so. That is a belief that did occur to me, that I had in my mind at least once. It follows, that I also believe that women who had their 40th birthday 200 days ago cannot bear children. This is my belief even though I may never have had it in mind, and of course there is no question of knowledge here, since the belief is false. If I have the belief in such cases, there is a strong case for holding me to have it even when I not only believe but also know.

So, what makes it the case that I have a belief that I never had in my thoughts? It is common to take the content of each belief to be expressed or represented in a proposition. There is nothing wrong with that so long as it does not induce an over simplistic view of the conditions that determine what is the content of a belief one has and of the conditions that determine whether one has that belief.[8] The temptation to think that if one believes that p then the thought that p occurred to one, was in one's mind, at least at one time, is a result of such simplistic ways of thinking about beliefs. For one thing the thesis that if I have a belief that is not currently in my mind it must have been in my mind sometime before does not help much with the question 'in what does one's belief consist when it is not in one's mind?' Why would the fact that

[8] As will emerge, one mistaken simplification to avoid is the assumption that the two sets of conditions I just referred to are necessarily the same.

it was once in one's mind make a difference? After all we may forget, thus ceasing to have beliefs that we once had.

The answer that suggests itself is that we have a belief if and only if it comes readily to mind when the question arises (perhaps that thought can be fleshed out like this: when we have reason to ask ourselves whether p, we instantly affirm that p), and we do so even though there was no new source of information, or of putative information, that could establish that we have just acquired it, that it is a new belief deriving from that source. We should and could improve that test. For example, it is sufficient to show that we had the belief all along if affirmation of the proposition is instantaneous when our attention is not distracted, and our rational powers not dimmed (by tiredness, alcohol, etc.), and only if there is a plausible account of how we acquired it at some past time, or period (e.g. that we saw something that could have generated a perception-based belief, even though we were not aware of it at the time).

Possibly a test along these lines may provide a sufficient condition for possession of a belief, and one point in its favour is that it does not require that we ever were aware of having that particular belief. But unless enriched it does not distinguish having a belief from some cases in which we are merely disposed to form a belief, and form it, instantaneously, when prompted. Furthermore, even if it provides a sufficient condition for belief, the test does not suggest an explanation of why it is a correct test. What is it about beliefs that makes it a correct test? Moreover, the test does not show, is not meant to show, and it is not the case, that our beliefs affect us only through being recalled to mind. They are our beliefs, and they affect us and our life even if never called to mind, even if we never become aware of them or of having them, that is at least part of the difference between beliefs and dispositions to form beliefs—the latter do not shape our perspective on things while beliefs do. Explaining that is part of explaining what constitutes having a belief.

It is helpful here to recall one similarity between beliefs and intentions. They are both states in which one's orientation towards the world (including oneself) is set. With intentions, as we saw, one is set to act in a certain way, and that means that some of the steps leading to action with an intention have already taken place. Metaphorically speaking, one has waived the need for a certain additional control on whether to perform the action. Beliefs are less specific in the way they affect our orientation towards the world. We can only say that when we believe that p we are taking the world as being one where p is the case.[9] That affects what else we believe, what intentions we may have (assuming that there is some believed feasibility condition on the possibility of intentions), and which of the intentions that we may have it is sensible to have. It affects which emotions we can have, and which emotions are beyond criticism and which are not. It also affects the limits of our imaginative powers, and of the meaning and significance of various imaginings. In all these regards, beliefs differ from suppositions, hypotheses, desires, wishes, and many other psychological states that lack that 'being-settled' element, and obey different conditions for happy cohabitation with other desires, wishes, imaginings, daydreams, suppositions, etc.

And, as with intentions, the way beliefs are states in which one's attitude towards the world is set consists in waiving the need for some steps that mark one's control of oneself, of one's attitudes, so that even though beliefs are transient and revisable, one waived the need to take those steps. Once one came to believe that it will be warm tomorrow one could proceed, in thought, intention, and action, on that basis, without any need (though not without the possibility) of raising and answering the question: will it be warm tomorrow? So long as one has no view whether it will be warm tomorrow it is irresponsible, and sometimes irrational, to proceed in the same way. One has first to answer the question: will it be warm tomorrow? In forming the belief one has answered that question in advance (of later planning or deliberation on other matters, etc.).

Should it not be warranted beliefs rather than beliefs that entitle one to proceed without asking whether the belief is justified? By the same token, one could argue that it is not intentions but only justified intentions that bring one closer to the action. In making these observations about intentions and beliefs, we are not implying that the condition is good or justified in each individual case, regarding each intention and each belief. We are merely describing/analysing systemic aspects of the psychology of beings that have intentions and beliefs. Such beings necessarily have rational powers, as both beliefs and intentions are controlled and guided by one's rational powers. Hence, they are liable to be irrational, namely when the rational faculties malfunction, when the rational powers are lax, and these beings have beliefs or intentions that they should have avoided as unjustified, and they are

[9] Though belief can be imperfect, as well as a matter of degree, and that requires modifying the statement in the text above, as does of course the fact that we are sometimes irrational in not responding appropriately to our beliefs.

irrational, akratic, if they are aware that an intention or a belief is unjustified. The very possibility of having unjustified beliefs or intentions is a result of the fact that they set one's attitude to the world, take one closer to the action, in the way that justified ones do.

The grounds for attributing belief that there is some good in the object of one's intention are analogous to those for attributing to me belief that 3000 + 1 = 3001. Given what we believe and know (must believe or know to have intentions) and given that we have rational powers, we also have the attributed belief.

Six clarifications would help to establish that conclusion: First, some who would agree with the preceding would add a qualification to the possibility of people having beliefs that never occurred to them, namely that the people in question have the concepts used in expressing the content of the belief. If so then people who do not have the concept of value cannot believe that the objects of their intentions have some value. I think that this restriction is mistaken. Some restrictions along those lines apply, though I will not attempt to formulate any. However, as stated the restriction is not true of the concept of belief. Example: imagine a person who believes that there are some chairs in the room. It is true of him that he believes that the room contains some items of furniture, even if he does not have the concept of furniture. Another example: people who believe that the warmth of an object is affected by the warmth of its environment also believe that the temperature of an object is affected by the temperature of its environment, even if they do not have the (scientific) concept of temperature. More generally, in most contexts when people believe that some object falls under the concept G, and if it is true in virtue of the essential properties of G that any G is an F then they believe that that object is an F, even if they do not have the concept of F, unless they hold (on independent grounds) a belief that is inconsistent with 'all Gs are Fs'. And the same holds if G is an 'everyday' concept and F is a theoretical equivalent, the theoretical version of G. But for this it would have been difficult to develop any general account of any topic to do with people's beliefs.[10]

Second, does not the fact that some people believe that intentions do not involve belief in the value of their object show that at least those people's intentions do not involve such beliefs (that they fall within the exception mentioned above)? It does not, because the exception has to be qualified (or

[10] This clarification is sometimes made by saying that, special contexts apart, belief attribution is *de re* rather than *de dicto*. That statement, as well as my clarification, requires controversial qualifications that are avoided here.

understood to be sensitive to the following observation). People may have concepts and beliefs while being mistaken about some features of these concepts and beliefs. Our interest is in cases in which the mistakes are due to a theoretical misunderstanding of what those beliefs and intentions involve. They have the belief but they are unaware of the fact because they misdescribe or misunderstand it due to their theoretical mistakes. For example, if self-deception involves holding contrary beliefs then people who do not believe that self-deception involves such beliefs nevertheless can be self-deceived, in which case, contrary to their theoretical belief, they do have contrary beliefs.

Third, there is no cogent argument (analogous to the argument that intentions involve belief in the value of their object) that every belief involves another belief that it is true. Any belief is a belief that things are as it expresses them to be. No further belief is in play. Intentions, however, are not beliefs. But their formation assumes belief—as explained.

Fourth, many assume that there is some physical condition, for example some brain state, necessary for the existence of beliefs. Similarly, people may assume that there are psychological entities, beliefs, whose existence is necessary for any being to have a belief. Such suppositions are not discussed in this chapter. However, it is important that if some such suppositions are true, it does not follow that there is a distinct physical state, or a distinct psychological entity for each distinct belief. It would be more sensible to assume that there is one physical condition, say, underpinning the existence of any set of beliefs such that the person having them cannot have one of them without having all of them (for some kind of necessity, which I will not consider here). For example, for most people it is possible to believe that there are chrysalises in Victoria without believing that there are butterflies in Victoria, and vice versa. For such people having both beliefs may involve having two distinct physical conditions, each underpinning one of them. But as having simple arithmetical beliefs about real numbers requires a basic understanding of the arithmetic of real numbers, no one can believe that 3000 + 1 = 3001 without also believing that 3001 + 1 = 3002. Therefore, one physical condition may underpin both beliefs.

Fifth, allowing for everything argued for so far one may still doubt whether belief in the value either of the object of the intention or of the intention itself must accompany all our intentions. And that is a just observation. Given that the belief is not an essential feature of intentions, but rather a result of their nature and the possession of human rational powers, there are various ways, not all of which can be anticipated in informative detail, in which failure of our rational powers will make for intentions not accompanied by such a belief. Mostly irrationalities would lead not to intentions without value beliefs but to irrational beliefs in the value of the intention or its object; mostly, the intention will be abandoned, or the belief corrected once the conditions that degraded one's rational powers (intoxication, hypnosis, etc.) pass. But that would not always be so. Exceptions of that kind attach to most general truths about human psychology.

Habitual action is sometimes mentioned as intentional action undertaken out of habit and without any accompanying value belief. As a generalization about all actions out of habit this is mistaken as the habit may be accompanied by a belief that there is value in each and every one of its instances. Equally, some actions performed out of habit are not performed with an intention to do them, even though they are intentional actions. On most occasions when I leave home in a south-easterly direction, my destination requires me to cross Charing Cross Road. But often enough it does not, and quite commonly when I walk say to the National Gallery I will suddenly realize that I crossed Charing Cross Road, and will have to backtrack. When I cross it on such occasions my action is intentional, but it is not done with an intention to cross it, nor with any other intention. It is not my intention to walk to the National Gallery that made me cross it (as it would have done had I thought that it is east of Charing Cross Road). It is my momentary failure to be guided by my intention that causes my mistaken action.[11] In brief, there are too many kinds of habitual actions, but I doubt that any of them constitutes an exception to my general claim.[12]

Sixth, and final clarification: I mentioned at the outset that while normally the belief that accompanies intentions is about the value of the intended action it may also be a belief in the value of having the intention itself. The attempt by some philosophers to revive 'fitting attitude' accounts of value led to an extensive discussion of 'wrong kind of reasons' and many who hold no hope for 'fitting attitudes' accounts joined in. Some suggested that reasons that are state- rather than object- related are of a 'wrong kind'. Even if there is something to be said in favour of that claim regarding epistemic reasons, it has no application to reasons for actions, and none for reasons for intentions either. There are only two points to make about reasons for intentions that turn on the value of having the intentions rather than on the value of the intended action: first, for reasons explained above, they are not the normal

[11] Discourse regarding intentions and intentional actions is highly flexible, and allows for a variety of ways of explaining the phenomena I am describing. The text illustrates but one of them.

[12] For a contrary view, see D. Owens, 'Habitual Agency', *Philosophical Explanations* 20 (2017).

kind of reason for an intention. Second, some beliefs about the intended actions are a condition on having intentions to perform them. Some argue that they include beliefs about the possibility of that action, others that they include beliefs about the point of the action. If there is any truth in such views, then they limit the possibility of reasons for intentions depending on the value of the intention, for they limit the possibility of such intentions.

2. Value, Intention, and Motivation

For humans, and as all my discussion from here on will be confined to humans, I will not reiterate that restriction, acting for a reason involves being guided by what one believes is a reason, and that involves thinking that there is value in the action because it relates in an appropriate way to how things are. That, in turn, implies that one takes something about the action to confer value on it. It could be something that is bad and the action would help avoid (a fire) or a good opportunity that the action would help one to seize, etc. The schema is that the reason is a good in the action that is conferred on it by some feature of the situation that is either good or bad. When we act for that reason we act because we recognize it (as we see matters) as a reason for that action.

This schematic description is liable to strike many readers as altogether false to the realities of human motivation. The aim of this part is to dispel these doubts. First, I will discuss the role of the will and its relation to this account of intentional action. Second, I will consider a variety of human motivations and their function in leading to intentional actions.

2.1 The Will

The will may relate to the spirit with which we react to reasons: 'reluctantly I had to concede that he behaved decently' (meaning something like: I was reluctant to believe so, but the evidence made me come to that belief, even though I would have been happier had it not been so), 'I hate my tendency to be envious of my rivals, but against my will I do feel envy', 'I did not want to pay my debt, but I did so, however unwillingly'. In this regard, the will is an emotion, or similar to an emotion. We can be happy, or sad, delighted, relieved, surprised as well as welcoming a conclusion, or willing it to be true, etc. There is, however, a different aspect to the will, the will as resolve, as will power, manifesting itself in the ability to form intentions, to take decisions, and to persevere, to stick with them, to be firm in our resolve, etc. And of course, there are the opposite phenomena, of prevarication, indecisiveness, weakness of resolve, wavering, etc.

The will in the resolve sense applies only to actions, omissions, and activities, including mental acts. It does not apply to beliefs or emotions, except in special kinds of situations. I can intend to have ice cream tomorrow, decide to avoid smoking, or to run in the London Marathon. I cannot decide that the woman I am looking at in the street wears a hat, nor intend to believe that she does. Similarly, I cannot decide or intend to be angry, or resentful or joyful. I can of course decide to try to make myself less morose, or jealous, or to avoid my bias affecting my beliefs. And there are other specialized contexts in which the will as resolve can be manifested regarding beliefs and emotions. They call for explanation (such as that the will can protect beliefs from corrupting emotive influences, or aim at creating the circumstances in which we can have certain beliefs or emotions). But they do not undermine the general contrast between the ubiquitous presence of the will regarding actions and its limited and special possible effects on our beliefs and emotions.

This contrast raises a potential difficulty for a reason-based explanation of intentional actions, omissions, and activities. If recognition of epistemic reasons is sufficient to lead us to appropriate beliefs, without the intervention of intentions to believe or decisions to believe, why is not recognition of practical reasons sufficient to make us act appropriately without the intervention of intentions and decisions? Why is it the case that whenever we act for what we took to be a reason for that action it is true that (in some sense of 'want') we did what we wanted to do, whereas it is not true that when we believe what we take ourselves to have adequate reasons to believe we believe what we want to believe? And why are emotions genuine when it is not the case that we have them because we wanted to have them, and suspect when we have them because we wanted them, and beliefs that we have because we want to have them are irrational, whereas actions we perform because we want to perform them are suspected neither of inauthenticity nor of irrationality?

Of course, intentions and decisions, just like the actions they aim at, occur for reasons. That helps in explaining why that we acted as we intended does not cast doubt on the rationality of the action. But it does not help in explaining why intentions, decisions, and other manifestations of the will as resolve are needed at all. To explain that we need an account of differences between actions, omissions, and activities on the one side and beliefs and emotions on the other, an account that will show the need for the will on the one side and not on the other.

Three differences are relevant (and there may be others). First (a point that articulates aspects of the first constituent of intentions mentioned in the first section), we can in our mind determine what to do in the future, but not what to believe or feel in the future. We can hope to have or not to have certain emotions or beliefs in the future, but we cannot determine, mentally, to have or not to have them. We can determine what to do in the future. And such determinations require power of resolve. The ability to determine our future actions requires having will power. It is manifested by deciding and by forming intentions regarding future conduct. I can decide now to have an Indian meal tomorrow, but I cannot decide now to believe tomorrow that Indian meals are very tasty, nor can I decide now to be happy tomorrow at having an Indian meal.

The explanation is simple: if I know that a proposition will be true tomorrow, I now believe that the proposition will be true tomorrow, and if I know that tomorrow there will be adequate reason to believe that a proposition is true, I now have adequate reason to believe that the proposition is true. But if I now know that it will be good to do something tomorrow, I have no reason to do it now. If it will be good tomorrow, I have to do it tomorrow. There may be no reason for me to do anything about it now, or there may be reason to resolve, namely intend or decide, to do it tomorrow. As was observed above, intending moves us towards the action. It is a stage in moving to act. But that is as far as one can go. Hence the role of the will in action, a role that has no place regarding beliefs.

Decisions and intentions, just like actions, are taken for reasons, and, not exclusively but typically, these are the same reasons. Typically, when there are reasons to decide or intend, the reasons for an action are among the reasons for intending to, and for deciding to perform it.[13] The need for the involvement of the will as resolve is not in order to motivate. For all we know (and we will return to the point below) reasons or belief in reasons motivate both belief and action. But in action, unlike in belief, there are occasions when there is a case for forming a resolve to perform the action ahead of the appropriate time

[13] I say that they are among the reasons for forming the intention or taking the decision because, as Heuer (U. Heuer, 'Intentions and the Reasons for Which We Act', *Proceedings of the Aristotelian Society* 114/3 (2014) 291–315, and 'Reasons to Intend' in D. Star (ed.), *The Oxford Handbook of Reasons and Normativity* (Oxford: OUP, 2018)) has argued, reasons for an action are never sufficient to form a future-directed intention or decision to perform it. There needs to be something additional that gives point to forming the intention now.

for its performance. That is what the will—intentions and decisions—provides. We come to will as we come to act by coming to believe in a case for the intention or the action. The contribution of the will is to form and maintain our resolve till the time for action arrives.[14] Of course, intentions and decisions are revisable, but a tendency frequently to re-examine them shows lack of resolve, weakness of will, which may be justified. It may reflect residual doubts about the initial decision, suppressed or unarticulated concerns about it, and the like. I am not arguing for the correctness of any course, only about the role and function of the will, which is, to repeat, not to motivate but to form and maintain resolve.

The same lesson emerges from the second difference between actions and beliefs, their difference regarding the nature of conflicts of reasons for beliefs and for action. It too points to occasions for resolving to do something that do not arise regarding beliefs. Reasons for any particular belief are considerations that support the conclusion that it is true. Reasons for a belief may conflict with reasons against it, namely considerations that support the conclusion that it is not true. Given that if the belief is true, then it is false that it is not true, and vice versa, it follows that of conflicting reasons for belief at most one leads to a true conclusion, and at most one leads to a belief that is not flawed. Reasons for conduct (for actions, omissions, or activities) conflict when two or more independent reasons support the case for two modes of conduct such that if one is realized the other cannot be. Any conflict of practical reasons will involve reasons for an act or activity on the one hand and for its omission on the other. Inherent in conflicts of practical reasons is that both conflicting reasons point to something of value in the conduct they support. Whereas an epistemic reason is a clue to a truth beyond it, a practical reason is the fact that there is something valuable in the conduct it is a reason for. There may be stronger reasons for incompatible conduct. But any independent reason that is not conformed to marks a loss, something valuable that has been, rightly or wrongly, abandoned in favour of something else that is also valuable. Or, to present the point allowing that agents may have misconceptions about the reasons that apply, any time agents do not conform to what they take to be a reason for a conduct, even when, as they see matters, they do

[14] Some writers think that beliefs and/or intentions are commitments. Being committed differs from being resolved in many ways (and undertaking a commitment differs from becoming resolved in many more). To mention but two: commitments typically are towards someone else, and they are never subject to the will of the committed. Intentions may lapse with no fault when one turns away from them, without even noticing that one is abandoning them. Commitments cannot be shaken off by being ignored.

conform to another reason for incompatible conduct, the agents think that there is some real loss, namely the lost opportunity to realize the good pointed to by the reason they did not conform to. So, unlike epistemic conflicts, every practical conflict points to an unsatisfied reason(s), and is a possible occasion for a decision about ways of minimizing that loss. Even though such resolutions will not always be made, and will not always be appropriate, the prevalence of occasions for making them is an important aspect of our practical rationality, and—as explained above—it depends on the will, on the powers of resolve.

So far the account focuses on future-directed decisions and intentions where the role of strength of will and resolve is evident, lending—I hope—credence to the explanation that the will has to do with steadfastness rather than with motivation. The third difference between beliefs and actions complements the account by explaining the function of intentions during intentional conduct. Beliefs are psychological conditions, states, or dispositions or combinations of different conditions, which are relatively durable (though they can be forgotten, or fade away, and fail to resurface and affect judgement or decisions when needed, and of course one can come to reject them as mistaken). They are there, affecting one's thought, imagination, emotions, and actions in various ways, all as part of one's general mental condition. Intentional conduct is, typically, of limited duration and possessing a defined shape (apart from omissions it typically has a beginning and an end). Actions and activities are something we accomplish. That is why they require an executive power to oversee and guide their performance, and that is, as we saw in the first section, the task of the intentions with which the intentional actions are performed. So here again, the will is the power that keeps us on the track we chose, but it is not the motivation for choosing it.

This account can be developed a good deal further to explain, for example, how the will has a limited role in protecting our beliefs from the improper influence of wishful thinking and other emotions. For current purposes the important lesson is that recognition of reason motivates whereas the will does not. But saying that does little to explain human motivation and its relation to practical reasons.

2.2 Basic and Other Motivations

For there is no doubt that the capacity to respond to practical reasoning has a lot to do with human motives. The schematic observations that follow assume that, to a degree, explanation of conduct by practical reasons and its explanation by reference to human motivations are two complementary ways of referring to the same phenomena, first in terms of the reasons recognition of which leads to action and second in terms of the psychological dispositions to respond to those reasons. But the full account of the relations between responsiveness to reasons and motivations is much more complex. A simple view has it that directed motivation, that is motivation to realize some end, is triggered in some way that is explained non-normatively (hunger, hormones, conditioning, whatever) and that motivation sets the reasons we have. Normative reasons either OK or reject the motivation, providing reasons to allow it to move us, or to resist its promptings, and we have reasons to follow the steps that would lead to satisfying our motivations or to achieving their objectives. Examining human motivation even in only slight detail helps display the misunderstandings that breed variants of the simple view. The following observations aim to provide such a sketch. As it is based on lay observations much of it may be mistaken. But the burden of the argument is in the structure of the sketch, and it can survive many inaccuracies or outright mistakes in the details.

As the previous remarks show, I am using 'motivation' in a sense much wider than its meaning in English. I lean on its meaning as 'The (conscious or unconscious) stimulus for action towards a desired goal, esp. as resulting from psychological or social factors' (OED) but add to those stimuli for action stemming from biological factors (an extension that leads to dispensing with 'desired' in the OED definition). I am forced into this extension of the meaning of the term because I need a word with more general meaning than 'motivation' and do not know of any that would serve.

There are a number of apparently independent sources of native, untaught, motivations: the promptings of hunger are distinct in origin, in their phenomenological manifestations as well as in their objects and the means for their satisfaction, and they differ in all these respects from the promptings of sex, or from the motivation to escape exposure to extreme cold, etc. Second, the sources and manifestations of these motivations are largely species specific. For the most part, they are common to all members of the species, who differ in degree along all the dimensions in which any given source of motivation is manifested, but rarely do people lack any of them altogether, and even more rarely do they have types of motivations that are shared by only few members of the species. In making this observation, I do not mean either to commend or to denigrate any source of motivation, common or rare, or their absence. I am making the point because it is important for the emergence of cultures, of socially shared meanings, sensitivities, and practices. Indeed, it is among the culturally induced or enhanced motivations that we are likely to find a great divergence among people.

First, if only to put them aside we may notice a type of particularly elemental motivation, barely meriting this name, namely that which, when unimpeded, is manifested in reflex actions. Blinking at the approach of objects to the eye, recoiling from contact with hot objects, knee jerks, and many others are actions that are never intentional as they are never mediated by or guided by reasons. As our interest is in the interplay of reasons and motivations, we can ignore factors that trigger reflex actions.

There is a wide array of diverse motivations, namely urges or drives towards action that either are triggered from outside or arise through the operation of our bodies. Some of them are, like reflexes, 'hard wired' as it were towards a specific kind of action or activity. Others are not, but they cause discomfort, or worse, unless some action is taken, and the fact that these actions assuage the discomfort establishes them as the object of those motivations. Examples will help: our biology generates an urge to breathe, a very specific urge in its origin and its object. It leads us to breathe without an intervention of will or reason. But unlike sweating, and other bodily actions, it is our action because it can be suppressed and modified, at least to a degree, by forming an intention to suppress or modify it on occasion. And we can train ourselves to improve the degree to which we can intentionally control our breathing. Some actions arising out of bodily responses to some stimuli become important not, like breathing, for biological survival, but for social life. For example, smiling is often an involuntary, but controllable response vital for the ability to connect with others, and so are dispositions to emit various sounds (of joy or pain, etc.). Being hungry is my contrasting example. Yes, in a way it has a specific object: hunger motivates us to eat food. But for one thing we may be hungry for a while, feeling discomfort as a result, without realizing that we are hungry. Furthermore, hunger does not automatically produce action as the urge to breathe does. Rather it leads to intentional conduct to obtain, prepare, and consume food.

Both examples are of basic motivations; basic in not being mediated by reason, nor derived from any other motivation. There are of course considerable differences between the various basic motivations that affect us. But up to a point they share a common feature: they can drive us towards action on their own. Reasons, deliberation, and will come in later. They enable us to approve of the actions needed to satisfy these drives and urges (and in the second type of case I mentioned they then guide their performance), or they can lead us to intervene, repress, delay, or modify the actions we are driven towards. But this similarity uniting all the basic motivations may mislead. It is true of the narrowly focused motivations, the ones that can lead to action without intention or reflection, and it is true of some of our reactions to the second type. But they affect us in very different ways as well.

The drive to eat can again serve as an example. We learn that we need food from time to time, both to assuage hunger-sensations and for our health and for our capacity to function well—and these are only a few of the reasons for eating. I have not even mentioned the pleasures of eating. But just for a moment put aside all the reasons, other than avoidance of the discomfort that being hungry brings with it. We prepare food before we get hungry, and often we eat before we get hungry. Assume that we do so only to avoid the discomfort feeling hungry involves. Nevertheless, the drive to eat that hunger feelings produce does not operate when we prepare the food and often not when we eat either. In such cases, our actions are not triggered by our drives and urges. Typically, they are intentional actions taken because we believe that we have reason to take them. That is so even if the only reason is to avoid the discomfort of feeling hungry. So the basic motivation is in the picture, but not as initiating action that reason does not stop (as with breathing and the like). This is perhaps the most elemental way in which we acquire the capacity to form reason-led intentions, and to act for what we take to be reasons for those actions. What is the role of our basic motivation in a case like this? It is sometimes supposed that the appreciation of reasons for taking the means to some goal can lead to action only if and to the extent to which it channels some basic motivation to pursue that goal causing it to be attached to the means to that goal. When this image, derived from the behaviour of liquids, is taken seriously this statement is highly misleading. The kernel of truth that it contains amounts to little more than the assertion that the basic motivation to pursue the goal plays a role in leading us to form intentions and to act when we recognize the facilitative reason to do so (i.e. that the action will facilitate realization of a result of the kind we have a basic motivation to realize). What remains to be explained is how it does so.

The crucial point is that we take the facilitative actions because we see a reason to take them, that reason being that they will facilitate achieving a goal that is worth achieving. Our knowledge, even if implicit and inarticulate, of the experiences involved with the presence or absence of the goal makes us think that it is worth securing, and further, sometimes more complicated reasoning leads to an appreciation of the reasons to take the facilitative action. The process, even in the relatively simple example of securing food, depends on our evaluative attitude to the motivation for having food, and to the experiences that having it or avoiding it involve, or cause at a later time, as well as to the choice of means and ways of securing it.[15]

Derived motivations display additional aspects of the relations between value and motives. We can again use food as a source of our examples. Food, its preparation and consumption do, after all, play a major role in the economy, in shaping relations within families and structuring their life, in facilitating social interactions, in sex, in the arts, religion, and more. Obviously, social practices generate forms of activity that have at least the potential to respond to various basic motivations. However, habituation in the social practices that create and underpin activities such as working lunches, dinner parties, drinks, snacks, receptions, Sunday lunches, etc. generates a taste for, a motivation for some of them. These are new, derived, non-basic motivations. People develop a taste for some food-related occasions and not for others. Of course, sometimes one prefers one dinner party to another because one prefers the company of the diners in one of them, etc. However, I have in mind a different kind of response, a liking, say, for a drink and a quick dinner with colleagues and friends after work and a dislike of elaborate dinner parties with the same people. There are many diverse explanations for such tastes, depending on the circumstances of the people involved. Of interest for our purpose is the fact that a taste for a particular socially constituted form of activity may emerge and stabilize. It becomes a taste that cannot be explained or justified by the degree to which it satisfies basic motivation. It is acquired because the distinctive mix of the constituent activities and the attendant features of the activity are taken to be desirable, valuable. People who find it desirable acquire an independent, derived motivation to pursue it. The motivation is derived because it builds on some of their basic motivations. It is independent because—as can be seen when those people have to choose between options—its perceived desirability cannot be accounted for simply by reference to their basic motivations.

Experience, imagination, and judgement combine to breed motivations that are, as it were, 'value-bred', namely that are sustained by belief in the value of their objects. Needless to say, they are also responsible for mistaken beliefs about the value of options, and for the emergence of regrettable tastes sustained by such mistaken beliefs. This does not sustain any claim for the

[15] Perhaps in simple situations confronted by young children whose ability to adopt ends and secure them is not yet developed, and with other people who do not have it for various reasons, the process is of merely evaluating means in response to the promptings of basic motivations.

primacy of motivations for options over beliefs in their value in explaining intentional actions.

We are considering beings in whom rational powers and innate motivations combine in forming states of mind such as desires, hopes, aspirations, goals, beliefs, and intentions, in ways unknown to species with no rational powers. Our desires, hopes, aspirations, goals, just like our beliefs and intentions, are transformed by the injection of rational elements into the mix that goes into the making of those states of mind, which are complex states in all beings that have them. Normative responses are ones where a view of how things are, and what, if any, way of responding is appropriate, leads to an attempt, guided by that view, to realize that response.[16]

2.3 Does Motivation Survive Intention?

Let us accept that while motivations sometimes figure in non-normative explanations of actions, actions performed with an intention are explained normatively, that is as reactions to what the agents take to be reasons for them, reasons (or believed reasons) that either trigger and arouse motivations or that sanction and are supported by the motivations already active in the agents. Regarding intentions leading to action that begins right away this may explain how the role of intention is not to motivate but to keep the agent on course to the realization of the motivated intention. Both motivation and intention play a causal role in the explanation of the action, but they have different roles.

But think of future intentions: is it not the case that once formed the intentions themselves motivate the action? Do the beliefs that the actions are adequately supported by reasons and the motivations to perform them still have a role to play? Do they survive the formation of the intention, or rather would not the intention lead to the action even if they do not survive? Is it not the case that once we intend to do something we will do it because we intend to do it even though the belief that underpinned the formation of the intention has been abandoned and even though the motivation that led to it no longer moves us?

[16] Not all our beliefs about what actions are appropriate play a normative role in determining our responses to our situation. Self-deceived beliefs that some action is required, etc. usually play a non-normative causal role in masking the motivations that lead to our responses.

True, but that is irrelevant. The question is not whether we would act so long as we intend to act. Rather, it is whether we would intend to act even if we no longer have the belief that underpinned the formation of the intention and are no longer moved by the motivation that led to it. That is true too. We might still intend so to act, but that is still irrelevant, for it could be that the intention is now sustained by alternative beliefs about its point and by alternative motivations. This is analogous to the way belief survives the rejection of the evidence that led to it so long as one continues to believe that it is supported by some reasons. But unlike epistemic reasons, which are normally independent of the belief that they support, the reasons and motivations underlying intentions may be produced by or as a result of the formation of the intention. It may have changed one's frame of mind, arousing further, previously dormant motivations, and it may have led to changes in planning and in preparations that now make carrying out the intention a better option than abandoning it.

True, but these factors do not touch the way that intentions constitute a resolve but do not motivate: If their continued existence depends on the existence of appropriate beliefs and motivations, even though not necessarily those that originally led to the intentions, in what sense do the intentions constitute being resolved? What role is there for resolve given that the underpinning beliefs and motivations are there, doing all that is needed to make one perform the action?

These are good questions whose answer requires an explanation of a central aspect of being resolved. The matter has been explored by many, and my take on it is no more than a variant.[17] The central idea, as we saw at the beginning of the chapter, is that intentions constitute being set to act, in that they do not require revisiting the conditions that led to them (or, in case the intention is now held on different grounds, the conditions that replaced the original ones). Intending to do something in the future would lead one to doing so upon realization that the occasion for the action is now, without reconsidering the case for doing so. Being able to have intentions has advantages; relying on one's intentions on any particular occasion (i.e. without reconsidering the case for them) may be wise or foolish, etc. If one becomes convinced that

[17] See M. Bratman, *Intention, Plans and Practical Reason* (Cambridge, Mass.: Harvard UP, 1987), E. McClennen, *Rationality and Dynamic Choice* (Cambridge: CUP, 1990), and R. Holton, 'Intention as a Model for Belief', in Vargas and Yaffe (eds), *Rational and Social Agency: Essays on the Philosophy of Michael Bratman* (Oxford: OUP, 2014). They all take resolve to block revision, to be closer to commitments than I do. I do not deny that there are forms of strong, resistant to change, resolutions, see my discussion of decisions (J. Raz, *Practical Reason and Norms* (3rd edn, Oxford: OUP, 1999). Intentions, however, are more transient, less resistant to change than they suppose.

there is no longer a point to the intended action one would abandon the intention. Though sometimes one may, without fault, abandon it even if the case for it is unchanged—simply because one's heart is no longer in it. Can one believe that the point in having the intention disappeared and yet maintain it? One could if one could also, irrationally, believe that there still is a case for it—we are back with matters discussed earlier.

Given this understanding of intentions, especially future intentions, as being set to act, we can see that what motivate one to act are the background believed and motivating points the action is taken to have, while the intention is nonetheless also a causal factor leading to the action through the fact that it releases one from the need for further steps before performing the action.

2

Intention and Motivation

What is the role of intentions in the actions[1] intended? What do they contribute, and how do they contribute to the occurrence of the intended actions?[2]

This chapter will offer an account of acting with an intention and of having an intention to act. It will not offer an account of intentional action, merely suggesting that when intentional actions are not actions done with an intention, their explanation as intentional relates to that of actions with intentions, showing how like them and unlike them they are.

The first two sections locate actions with an intention in the wider category of actions, or doings, emphasizing both the importance of the kind of actions discussed in this chapter, and the range of other actions, including other intentional actions, which are beyond its scope. The third section suggests some features of motivation, mainly to distinguish its role in leading to action from the role played by intentions. Sections 4 to 6 offer an account of intentions. Sections 7 and 8 contest some rival accounts, while the last two sections conclude by explaining why 'future intentions' and 'intentions in action' are intentions in different contexts rather than two kinds of intentions. Section 9 explains the way intentions guide the intended conduct; and Section 10 is the conclusion.

1. Locating the Topic, and Its Significance

It would help in discussing our question(s) to bear in mind the broad significance in people's life of the actions to which they relate. To put it loosely, these actions are special in being the ways in which people can deliberately affect, or try to affect, how things are in the world, including in their own life. Needless to say, the success of a person's life, meaning here how good it is for

[1] Throughout the paper I will use 'actions' to include activities and omissions, as well as mental actions.

[2] The paper complements, develops, and slightly modifies some points made in Chapter 1 'Intention and Value'.

The Roots of Normativity. Joseph Raz, Edited with an Introduction by Ulrike Heuer, Oxford University Press.
 DOI: 10.1093/oso/9780192847003.003.0003

that person, depends on much else. It is affected by what he picks up about himself and the world without even noticing, just in virtue of being awake. It is affected by events affecting his body, by his bodily sensations, and by his perceptions, including those that are involuntary. It is coloured by his emotional reactions to what is happening to him without his involvement at all, or with involuntary participation on his part. But deliberately to affect how things are one needs to act, or, given that deliberately letting things happen is one way of deliberately affecting how things are, omit to act. Not all our actions and omissions do deliberately affect how things are. Many are, in one way or another, failures that happen in the course of attempting deliberately to affect how things are: we may aim to do one thing and by mistake do another. Or, in the course of doing or attempting an action we may accidentally (also) do another. Or, our action may just fail, or backfire and never affect things as we set out to do. There is also a second class of actions that never, as I shall say prejudicially, rise to the level of deliberately affecting or attempting to affect how things are. These divide into many subclasses. There are expressive actions, like shouting in surprise, or banging one's head in self-reproach, which express our attitudes and emotions, while not having any purpose, not even to express what they express. There are actions we do in complete indifference regarding their actual meaning or outcomes. There is what we do because we are living organisms, like breathe, or blush, smile, or tense up, mostly without even being aware that we have done them, but they are actions that we can, if we try, suppress or modify at least to a certain degree. There are other classes and subclasses. They are, some of them, of great significance for people's self-image, and for the ways people are perceived by others. Some people are accident-prone; others are transparent, as their body postures and facial expressions reveal their thoughts and feelings all too clearly. Some are pedantic and meticulously self-controlled, while others are relaxed, more happy-go-lucky. Actions of these classes contribute to making people what they are in these and related ways. It is worth remembering, as I am about to focus on actions taken deliberately to change or preserve how things are, that other actions, though in some ways perhaps less developed, are nonetheless of great importance in people's lives.

It is significant that many of the actions that do not constitute, and do not lead to any deliberate impact on how things are, are related to actions that do: some of them are failed attempts. Others are unintended consequences of actions deliberately aimed to affect things in certain ways. Others still are marginal cases of acts aimed at a specific effect (as when the agents are indifferent whether the intended impact is achieved or not). This is hardly surprising. We have an abiding interest in affecting how things are with ourselves and beyond, and we can only secure such effects at will by our actions (including activities and omissions).[3] Those actions of ours that aim to achieve such results are undertaken for a purpose, the purpose being that the act shall constitute or secure a result of a particular kind, which may be very specific (to bite an apple) or much more general and unspecific (to place us in a situation where advantageous options will come our way).

2. Some Basic Distinctions

The divide between actions for a purpose and other actions is one of two major divides among types of actions, considered in light of our actual or possible impact on the world. It is tempting to identify actions taken with a purpose or for a purpose with intentional actions, the intention being to achieve the purpose. However, there are quite a few kinds of intentional actions that are not done for a purpose. There are at least two radically different kinds of actions that are intentional but that are not done for a purpose. One kind, identified by Bentham in his account of responsibility, is the bringing about of foreseen but unintended results or consequences, which are performed while also doing something for a purpose.[4] The second class are actions that are independent of any action with a purpose, and that one could control, but as one does not do them to secure a purpose, they require, and typically enjoy, less attention from the agent. Similarly, there is no particular way in which they should be performed, and typically deviation from any pattern of performance does not indicate a flaw or a mistake in their performance. This does not mean, however, that their performance, or the ability to perform them, is unimportant, or that it is of mere marginal importance in the life of people.

[3] Using von Wright's distinction between results and consequences in G. von Wright, *Norm and Action* (London: Routledge & Kegan Paul, 1963).

[4] They are not always considered intentional. By and large the bringing about of those consequences is intentional if foreseen with certainty or close to certainty. Bentham writes that an act may be said to be obliquely or collaterally intentional regarding its consequence if 'the consequence was in contemplation, and appeared likely to ensue in case of the act being performed', but that was not part of what determined the agent to act (J. Bentham, *Introduction to the Principles of Morals and Legislation*, edited by J. H. Burns and H. L. A. Hart (London & New York: Methuen, 1970) 86). I suspect that while often what one 'intends obliquely' is not something that one intends to do; sometimes it would be appropriate to say that it is—much depends on the proximity of the unintended aspect of the action to its intended aspects, and on the point of the relevant discourse.

Which kinds of actions belong with the second kind is controversial. A relatively uncontroversial kind are expressive actions.[5] Arguably actions like doodling are also intentional, though they too do not have a purpose, and are often undertaken without fully noticing that one is performing them.[6] The expression 'actions taken for a purpose' is roughly co-referential with 'actions taken with an intention', and we may use them interchangeably.

So, 'X ϕ-ed intentionally' does not entail that X had an intention to ϕ. Having intentions means being set to act for a relatively specific purpose. Why not merely being set to perform a particular action? No reason; that is not what is excluded by the requirement. One's purpose can be to perform that (kind of) action. What is excluded is having no purpose in performing the (intentional) action, performing it without having in mind anything to achieve, not even to achieve its performance.

Is it that having an intention to ϕ without having a purpose for the sake of which one is set to ϕ is irrational? Or is it impossible? According to the account I will shortly develop it is impossible: if one acts with an intention (or if one has an intention to act) one acts for a purpose (or one has a purpose to be achieved by that action) the default being the purpose of performing that action. It is so in virtue of the nature of intentions. In saying this I am taking 'intention' and its cognates to refer to a psychological phenomenon, but I am not assuming that all utterances of the word do so, not even all linguistically acceptable utterances of the word, not even when they are used to refer (think, e.g., of the intention of parliament). This paper is not concerned with either language use or word meaning.

The second fundamental divide between kinds of actions (the first being between action with an intention and other actions) is between actions, or more broadly: things we do, that we can control, and those we cannot. Those we can control we can take or avoid for a purpose, even though on some occasions they are performed but not for a purpose. Those we cannot control we cannot take for a purpose.[7] Arguably, the kinds of action that we can control, whether or not any instance of the actions of these kinds is controlled, and that are therefore actions that it is possible to perform with an intention, are actions that are performed by us, whereas actions that we cannot control

[5] R. Hursthouse, 'Arational Actions', *Journal of Philosophy* 88 (1991) 57. See also J. Raz, 'Agency, Reason and the Good' in *Engaging Reason* (Oxford: OUP, 1999).

[6] Though typically actions of which the actor says something like 'I did it for no reason' are typically done for a reason, though perhaps an unremarkable one, or a reason to do something, where other kinds of action would have done as well.

[7] Both distinctions are matters of degree, and both admit of wide margins of indeterminacy.

are performed by our bodies or part of our bodies: I smile, sometimes involuntarily, sometimes purposefully, but my stomach digests.[8] If this is so it underlies the centrality of having intentions and acting with intentions to our understanding of human actions, and to the ways in which we are active rather than passive.

These divisions downplay the importance of the distinction between intentional actions and those that are not intentional. Merely intentional actions, that is actions that are intentional but are not performed for any purpose, share many characteristics of intentions, including possibly their motivations. They are, like actions done for a purpose, actions that we are responsible for, and thus they share the conditions of responsibility, though there may be assessments of actions that are unique to actions done for a purpose.

3. Motivation

The intentions people have are relevant to the explanation of why they act as they intend to act. Moreover, intentions are part of what produces the action, as we may awkwardly say, meaning that they feature in the explanation of actions as a cause (a causal factor) of the action. That much is clear from the fact that propositions of the kind 'X ϕ-ed because he intended to ϕ' can be straightforwardly true. That an act was intentional does not imply any significant information about why it was performed, or about what caused it. For example, the same expressive act, let us say banging the table, may be caused by anger or frustration or exasperation, etc. However, if an action is done with an intention the intention is relevant to its explanation in a more informative way: The intention is a causal factor of the action, and its content plays a role in the explanation of the act. So, of course, is also the motivation that led to the action.

Needless to say, not all causal factors that explain actions are part of their motivations. One may drop a glass because the heat makes one's hands slippery, or because one is anxious. But neither the sweat nor the heat nor the anxiety does motivate the action, nor do they motivate the person to act as he

[8] The boundary between what we do and what happens to us is, naturally, vague, and so is the degree of control we can exert over various happenings. That I stumble was not my doing (except when I stumble deliberately). Perhaps that I slipped on the way to the door was my doing, or perhaps it was not. It is possible that I would not have slipped had I paid more attention to what I was doing. So perhaps it is something I did, at least when that condition obtains.

did. These are causal factors regarding which the agent is passive. Neither do all factors regarding which agents are active belong with their motivation. For example, that the agent understands that the gun is loaded or that he falsely believes that it is loaded are causal factors, and are part of the explanation, for his removing the gun from children, but they do not motivate such actions.

Informally speaking, motivations are psychological states, dispositions, etc. that incline one to take an action of a particular kind, that prompt one to perform a particular kind of action. They can motivate a deliberate action with a purpose (inviting a friend to dinner) or an intentional expressive action, done with no purpose in mind (banging the table in frustration, touching one's hair in anxiety[9] about one's appearance).

Naturally, reasons to do something can motivate one to do it: that I will have a higher salary if I accept a new job offer may well motivate me to accept it. When an action is motivated by a reason for it the motivation would include other conditions, or—as we would also say—there are additional motivations, which explain what about the agent's psychology enables him to respond to, to be motivated by, a reason of that kind. For example, I might have been motivated by a love of luxury, or by being disposed to pursue luxury at the expense of stability. Or, I might have been motivated by fear of loss of respect from colleagues if I did not accept, what would commonly be regarded as, a superior offer. The motivations, we may say, constitute a chain: one specifying the other, and they may constitute several chains. Some of the chains may parallel chains of reasons: the pleasure of luxury leading in the instant case to the value of the higher income that will facilitate its attainment. But not all motivations need parallel chains of reasons.

It may occur to one that reasons are mere shadows of motivations. That thought may betray a mistake about the way motivations work. A motivation to perform an action may be the push factor featuring in an explanation of the action, if it were performed. But it can never constitute the whole explanation. It works, when it does, in combination with other causal factors, and they explain how the motivation succeeded in leading to the action. Other factors may explain how the motivation overcame fear, anxiety, laziness, or other such inhibitors and distractors. They explain how the agent identified that the circumstances make performance of that action possible, how conflicts between diverse and incompatible motivations were resolved and more.

[9] Note that here the anxiety has a different causal role than in the example above.

The fact that an action was done for a reason provides one kind of explanation for the effectiveness of the motivation for it. It means that the agent considered whether to perform the action and 'approved' (metaphorically speaking) its performance, though it does not specify the extent of the deliberation, which could have been elaborate consideration of the cases for and against the action but could also have been merely that the agent's rational powers were alert and alerted to the possibility of that action and did not stop it from going ahead. Nor does it indicate the strength of the 'approval'. I will explain this point below.

First note that there are two ways in which motivation can be related to reasons, and any number of combinations and variations on these two. In simple cases the agent, aware (or thinking that he is) that he is motivated to pursue some purpose (without that motivation being based on a belief in the value of being so motivated or the value of the purpose), deems its satisfaction to be good (either because it is good to satisfy the motivation and reduce its hold on him—while unsatisfied it may be distracting, paralysing, painful, etc.—or because the purpose it aims at is good) and acts on it. In the other kind of case, the agent, believing that there is some good in the action (or in intending or in trying to perform it) is motivated for that reason to perform it. To illustrate: I may hate Jeremy. My hatred may motivate me to be careless with his safety, when, let us say, I repair his car. In that case, while I repair the car intentionally, I negligently fail to observe all the safety checks required in this kind of repair. The hatred motivates my neglect, possibly unconsciously, but it does not involve any intention. The hatred may also make me refuse his request to look after his cat while he is away for the weekend. Here too I may be unaware of my hatred. I think that I am motivated by something else (my need to look after my baby perhaps) whereas in fact I am motivated by (or also by) the hatred. My reason, as I believe, for refusing the request is to make sure that I look after my baby.[10] But it could be different and my reason could be that my hatred is justified and should guide my action towards him. In that case, my reason is to treat him as he should be treated, being hateful as he is. Here the hatred, approved by my rational powers, becomes the reason that motivates my intention. Things are different when the recognition of the value of the action comes first: I learn of a stunningly beautiful and innovative theatrical event, and learn that there is reason to go to it. Given that that reason chimes in with my taste for the theatre (it would have been different

[10] For intentional actions in which the believed reason is a masking reason, masking the agent's motivation from him, see Chapter 6 'The Guise of the Bad'.

had I learned of a beautiful and innovative pop concert, given that I have no taste for pop) I intend to go to the event for the reason that it is so good (in those ways). The strength or stringency of many reasons depends on agents' tastes and/or their ability to appreciate and enjoy whatever is good in the action. Given that one's 'approval' of an action depends on one's view of the alternatives to it, the 'approval' may be qualified, at times conditional (conditioned by various factors), including the mood of the agents when the opportunity to act arises. Furthermore, often the 'approval' will be in light of an awareness that there are other options available to the agent that are no worse. In such cases, the formation of the intention is not dictated by the value of the choice. Some other process determines which motivation dominates, though all that is subject to the agent's 'approval' of the choice or its object, whichever way it may be reached.

4. Intentions: Preliminaries

Do intentions motivate? I intend to visit John next Saturday. What motivates me to do so? Perhaps that I miss him, or that I need to inform him of new developments in our company, etc. Those facts may also motivate my forming the intention to visit him, but that intention cannot motivate my visiting him. It comes too late, it is formed when I am already motivated, and because of that motivation. Nor does the intention become my motivation once I have it. The intention lapses if my motivation evaporates—I will return to this point later. True, as we noted, sometimes people correctly say that they did what they did because they intended to do so. Such statements point out that the act was done for a purpose, and therefore that the agent was motivated to pursue that purpose. But it does not tell one what the motivation was.

It would seem that on the one hand intending to perform an act is part of the causal factors that, if the act is performed with that intention, bring about its performance, but the role of intention in bringing about the performance is not in motivating it. That is not in itself surprising. We saw that acts that were done because the agents were motivated to do them are caused by the motivation alongside other factors. But what are intentions and what role in as it were the production of an action done with an intention do they play?

First, *what kind of thing are intentions?* Are they mental states, actions, events, dispositions, or what? I agree with those who reject all such possibilities, taking intentions to be *sui generis*. They are, one might say, a condition of the agents who have them. Nothing is gained by using the expression 'condition of the agent' rather than the common ones: 'I intend to...', 'I have the intention to...'. Of course, saying that intentions are *sui generis* implies that they are not susceptible of a reductive explanation. It does not imply that they are some sort of basic mental element. Intentions are manifested in and constituted by a myriad of other mental and physical conditions: they involve beliefs, imaginings, dispositions, alertness, and others, as is appropriate to the specific intention concerned and the conditions of the agents. We can provide illustrations of what constitutes having some intention in some circumstances, but we are far from having a general theory that would enable us to state generally what having intentions consists in. The explanation of intentions offered here consists of illustrations that are chosen to bring out the relations between intending to do something in the future and acting with an intention.

Second, *what are the objects of intentions?* This chapter considers actions, activities, and omissions as objects of intentions. But I can intend to be at home tonight, though being at home is neither an action nor an omission. And I can intend my son to graduate next year, or intend never to mix business with friendship (intend that my life will conform to this principle), or never to be in debt. Reflection on such cases shows that they entail an intention to do something to secure the condition intended. Such cases can be regarded as abbreviated statements that one intends the action that will secure that condition, when its nature is implied by the condition, given the context of the statement of the intention. They are particularly apt when the act intended is rather unspecific, perhaps merely to see to it that the condition obtains if I can help it. That is supported (and in turn supports) the explanation of intentions as involving being guided by a purpose, as will be seen below.

Third and final preliminary, *who can have intentions?* Obviously, agents and only agents, but not all agents. My heart pumps along, but with no intention to do so or anything else. Given that having a purpose is essential to having intentions, and that most of the other essential properties of intentions follow from it, we can safely say that only agents who can have purposes can have intentions.[11] The capacity to have a purpose involves a capacity to pursue a

[11] This chapter discusses intentions of animals that can have intentions. There are other agents capable of having purposes and intentions. Most notably, there can be group agents, e.g. people of Nicaragua, the inhabitants of London, the students of Oxford, and rule-constituted agents, e.g. corporations, states, universities, clubs. The account given here helps in understanding when and how they act with intentions, but it cannot apply to them without modification. Regarding non-human agents: see some observations in the previous chapter on 'Intention and Value'.

purpose, which is a complex capacity: (a) an ability to understand (at least to some degree) the nature of the purpose, (b) an ability to have some idea of how it can be pursued, and (c) enough ability to recognize one's environment to enable one to form a reasonably accurate judgement on whether it allows for the pursuit of the purpose and how, and (d) enough control of oneself and the environment to engage in such a pursuit such that its success, if it succeeds, may be due to the skills of the agent in doing whatever it is he was doing.

Some people would say that I forgot to include a capacity to adopt purposes, and a capacity to abandon them if they get one nowhere. There is a case for arguing that for some kinds of purposes, having the capacity to have them involves a capacity to abandon them when there is no point in pursuing them anymore. It is the concomitant of the ability to determine when to pursue and how. Though, perhaps the pursuit of some purposes would, given the nature of the purpose, run into the sand fairly quickly when unsuccessful, and the question of abandoning them never arises.

Analogously, given that some purposes cannot be pursued except through adopting and pursuing subsidiary purposes, the capacity to have such purposes involves a capacity to adopt appropriate sub-purposes. Some purposes are simple or direct enough not to require such a capacity. None of these considerations requires that all an agent's purposes will be adopted by it. A robot may have purposes implanted in it and it may develop intentions to pursue them. And so can living animals. They may be born with a disposition that once triggered causes them to have a purpose not of their own choosing, not one adopted by their own will. And the same is true of some of the purposes of human beings. The objection may be raised that unless people choose their purposes they are not really theirs, or they are not authentically theirs. But in these cases, as in others, the genuineness or authenticity of purposes is manifested in the attitude the agents have to them as demonstrated by the ways they are pursued and by attitudes independent of their actual pursuit.

5. From Purpose to Intention: Being Decided

Intentions involve having a purpose, and that implies that purposes affect one in a special way. One who has a purpose to perform an action or to see some other end realized, intends that action or intends to bring about or facilitate that end. Whoever intends to perform an action has a purpose in doing so, which can be just to do the action (or to intend to do it[12]) but it could also be to achieve some other end that that action (as he believes) will achieve or facilitate.

One who has a purpose is motivated to pursue it, and that motivation overcomes the inhibiting and distracting factors, and *pro tem* overcomes conflicting motivations. As we noted, the motivation and therefore the purpose it sustains, may cause one to do something accidentally, or be a causal factor in doing something accidentally. There are also the myriad ways in which a purpose may motivate or bias agents (epistemically and practically) subconsciously. Assuming, however, that there are no subconscious intentions,[13] this chapter is concerned only with the way purposes contribute to having intentions through these purposes being known, and consciously pursued.[14]

What makes the difference when we intend to pursue a purpose, what makes such cases cases of having an intention? Some people say that having an intention is the beginning of performing the intended action, that it is itself an activity.[15] In thinking about these matters bear in mind that while sometimes we come to have intentions by an action, by forming the intention, at other times we just come to have them, sometimes without even noticing. At a certain point we may realize that we have an intention. Or we may have had them for a long time without realizing that that is so. However, the crucial point is that even when we form them, having the intentions, once formed, is not an action or an activity.

The objection to the Thomson-Moran-Stone view is that it is factually false. We have intentions to do things in the future while we are not doing them or beginning to do them. The motivation for the view is not sensitivity to our experience, but a theoretical point that can be put by saying that in intending to ϕ we have already started moving towards ϕ-ing; we are already closer to

[12] See, for the explanation of this possibility, my discussion of the toxin puzzle in J. Raz, *From Normativity to Responsibility* (Oxford: OUP, 2011) 51–2.

[13] I am using 'subconscious' in a way that implies some psychological resistance to bringing what is subconscious to one's conscious awareness. Needless to say, as is the case with beliefs, assumptions, etc., one is not always aware of one's intentions, and one may come to have them or to abandon them without being aware of the fact at the time. The difficulty with the thought that intentions can be unconscious is that the repression involved appears inconsistent with agents' 'approving' of their intentions or of the pursuit of their object. I take no position on that issue.

[14] Having a purpose should not be confused with being attracted to something or believing that there is some point, value, in securing it. One can be attracted to something without it being one's purpose or goal to secure it, and one can believe that it has value without having such a purpose.

[15] These views are inspired by G. E. M. Anscombe, *Intention* (Oxford: Basil Blackwell, 1957) cf. 90ff; for subtle recent versions see M. Thompson, *Life and Action* (Cambridge, MA: Harvard UP, 2008); and R. Moran and M. Stone, 'Anscombe on Expression of Intention,' in C. Sandis (ed.), *New Essays on the Explanation of Action* (Basingstoke: Palgrave Macmillan, 2009) 132.

ϕ-ing than we were before we had the intention. That seems to me a cogent point and explaining it is the main difficulty in explaining an intention. The core of the explanation is simple: There is a step or a stage, call it what you will, in any action done for a purpose that occurs whenever one has the intention for that action, even if that intention is held prior to the action. That is, though this is only a rough first approximation, actions done for a purpose where the intention to perform them was conceived and held ahead of the time of the action (and I mean more than merely briefly before the action) are somewhat different from actions for a purpose performed with no prior intention—there is an element in the latter that is missing in the former because it has already taken place when the agent conceived the intention to perform it. What is the difference?

I will call it 'being decided', being decided to pursue that purpose, using the expression somewhat stipulatively to indicate a condition (of the agent) without any implication regarding the way one came to be in it. For example, without an implication that one is decided because one has reached a decision, normally after some deliberation. One may go to sleep undecided and wake up decided, and one may be unaware of the fact, having forgotten that the indecision was there. Being decided does, of course, imply that there is no need to decide. It does not mean that one cannot or should not decide, one can always revisit one's purposes; but as things are one is already decided. Nor does it mean that one will remain decided to pursue this purpose until one either acts or decides not to. We often slip in and out of that condition unnoticed; both acquiring and abandoning intentions can happen in such ways.

Where φ-ing is one's purpose one intends to φ if one is decided to φ. For example, if my purpose is to give a grand birthday party for a friend then to intend to do so is to be decided to do so. Many intentions are embedded in others: I intend to bake a cake for the party and baking the cake is part of giving the party. In many contexts it would be odd or misleading to say that, in such a situation, baking the cake is a purpose of mine. But that has to do with pragmatics of discourse only.

Can we describe the psychological features in which being decided manifests itself? Many are contingent on the individual concerned. The following three may be essential:

One continues to accept the acceptability of pursuing the purpose. This may involve belief, not necessarily expressed in these terms, that the case for pursuing the purpose is not defeated by contrary factors. Possibly, this condition may be weaker than a belief, consisting merely in the fact that one's acceptance of the pursuit of the purpose is close to one's awareness, is easily recalled to mind, etc., and that acceptance has not been reversed or rejected.

Second, one is alert to opportunities for performing the act that one is decided to perform, alert to the occurrence of circumstances in which its performance is possible (i.e. circumstances in which one is likely to do it if one tries) and in which the cost, the adverse consequences of doing it are relatively small.

Third, one is alert to the occurrence of changes, or the likely occurrence of changes, that will make performing the act less advantageous or that would facilitate its performance, that is, making it more likely when tried. And by the same token one is alert to changes that improve one's knowledge of whether existing conditions facilitate performance of the act or make it more or less advantageous.

Being alert means being primed to notice and react. It is a condition that can be dormant and inactive for a long time, but when something one is alert to occurs one becomes aware of it and can react as appropriate. What is appropriate depends on the circumstances and on the capacities of understanding and action of the agents concerned.[16]

Being decided does not include any emotional reactions—it may be accompanied by many and diverse ones, or none. It does not include any other preparations to perform the actions. Some may be undertaken, or none. They are not essential to having an intention. It includes a psychological orientation made to lead to the action, by alerting agents to an appropriate or right time to perform the action, and a system of alerts that may help to steer agents away from a course that would make acting with the intention impossible or more difficult or costlier, and alert agents to a course that would facilitate performing the action, or simply alert them that the pros and cons of maintaining the intention may change.

Two omissions may be alleged: first, I did not explain the way in which intentions are normative, and this includes failure to explain how they motivate the intended action. Second, I did not explain how we come to have intentions, only what they consist in once we have them. I'll take the second objection first.

[16] Jay Wallace suggested to me that motivations may involve the very same systems of alerts that I attribute to intentions. Other psychological conditions may well involve their own systems of alerts. But motivations do not involve the alert conditions I listed above. I may be motivated to pursue a goal that I know to be too unlikely ever to be realized (climbing Everest). In such a case it will, typically, not be accompanied by these alerts. The same is true when my motivation is believed by me to be unacceptable, or just decisively defeated by contrary reasons.

6. From Purpose to Intention: How Do We Become Decided?

The characterization of being decided has implications regarding conditions that must obtain for intentions to be formed. Most importantly for our purpose, agents can only intend to perform actions that they believe they know how to perform or how to attempt to perform.[17] Therefore, agents can only have intentions if they believe that they know something about the conditions in which the actions can be performed.

Incidentally, this condition does not apply to having a purpose. Agents who do not have any idea about the conditions in which an action can be performed can have the purpose of performing it. Having a purpose is closer to having a vague aspiration to perform the action, at some time, than to having an intention. Intentions require more knowledge about what is required for their fulfilment. Those who have a purpose have some related intentions, but they can be no more than the intention to find out what it would take to achieve it.

Back to the question how do agents come to have or to form intentions? How does an agent with various motivations, and therefore inclined towards various possible purposes, come to have the intention to pursue one of those purposes? There is no simple explanation that applies to all cases, and no single type of explanation. Explanations are likely to turn on the inter-relations among the agent's motivations, his capacities, and his circumstances. Perhaps one of the motivations (perhaps 'the lust of the blood') came to dominate his mental horizon to the exclusion of all else, 'forcing' his will to pursue it (forcing 'a permission of the will').[18] Or it could be the extreme opposite, and total boredom and the lack of any ability to focus on anything, led the agent to pick on some trivial purpose that just happened to be easy to pursue at the moment. The variety of possible explanations is enormous. To make progress we need to identify general capacities that prioritize, probably conditionally, some of our purposes over others, perhaps in the way that we feel that fear of immediate danger silences any other purpose and mobilizes the agent to flight or to fight. Though this is probably an extreme rather than a

[17] Is it enough if I know how to find out how to do it? In many contexts this would be enough, and would be part of knowing how to attempt to do it. In others, the distance to travel is too long, and one can only intend to find out how to do the action (flying to the moon).

[18] Shakespeare, *Othello* Act 1 Scene 3, Iago to Rodrigo: 'we have reason to cool our raging motions, our carnal stings, our unbitted lusts. Whereof I take this that you call love to be a sect or scion.... It is merely a lust of the blood and a permission of the will.'

typical case, and in any case real psychology should take over from folk psychology at this point.

We are familiar, however, with one capacity crucial in that matter: our rational faculties. Different agents, for example different animal species, have rational powers to various degrees. Our rational powers play a crucial role in coming to have intentions. During waking times our rational powers are always engaged, actively monitoring that changes in our beliefs, intentions, emotions are rationally OK. When the powers function properly they make sure that we form intentions when we have adequate reasons to do so, and we do not form intentions when there is no reason to do so. In these ways our rational powers contribute to the process of forming intentions, and in some cases they are decisive. But in many, probably most cases they are not. They screen out improper possible intentions, but they do not determine which of many possible purposes we should pursue: there is something to be said for each of them, and nothing to show that any is superior to the others. So, the rational powers are satisfied with any choice among such possible purposes. The choice itself, while influenced by our rational powers, is determined in other ways.

7. Do Intentions Involve Commitments?—Part I

Some people think that

(1) to intend to ϕ is or involves being committed to ϕ.

Others think that

(2) intending to ϕ involves having, and being committed to, a plan about how to ϕ, or a way of conducting oneself leading to or ending with ϕ-ing.

Needless to say, the truth of such views depends in part on the meaning of 'commitment' as used in expressing these views. I will be interested only in commitments in the sense of undertakings that can be broken, where breaking them is, *pro tanto*, a fault, something that should not have happened. In other words, commitments, understood in this sense, are reasons to act as one is committed to act. If intentions are commitments, or if in any other ways they are practical reasons, that is, if they are reasons to perform actions that possibly one had no reason independent of the intention to perform, then they are normative.

The normativity of intentions has been ably discussed by a number of authors. Quite a few take the view that intentions are normative.[19] Others deny that they are.[20]

Long ago, I suggested that some intentions or the way they are formed are reasons for the intended act. I will call them decision-based intentions, or decisions for short.[21] The distinction between decision-based intentions and intentions that are not reasons for the intended act is not linguistic. The use of 'decision' is a guide, not a test—though it is an unfailing guide where group decisions and decisions of agents constituted by normative rules (states, corporations, universities, clubs, etc.) are concerned. The difference can be established, for example by asking whether 'I have already decided to ϕ; it is wrong, or inappropriate, etc. to reopen the question' is ever a correct response to a request or attempt to revisit the decision. It is easiest to see the way decisions are normative when thinking of decisions of rule-constituted bodies. Take a mundane example: a social club provides a reading room with newspapers for its members. The list of newspapers provided has been decided yesterday by a vote of the club committee. One of its members is dissatisfied and proposes to drop two of the papers the committee decided to

[19] See for a variety of views of that kind the essays in B. Verbeek (ed.), *Reasons and Intentions* (London: Routledge & Kegan Paul, 2016). As with a number of the contributions to this volume, sometimes intentions themselves are taken to be reasons for the people who have them to perform the intended action, and sometimes they are such reasons only if some conditions obtain, or along with other facts. See also M. H. Robins, 'Is It Rational to Carry out Strategic Intentions?' *Philosophia* (Israel) 25/1–4 (1995) 191–221. Some writers focus on decisions in ways that suggest that the same is true of all intentions, e.g. C. Korsgaard, *Self-Constitution: Action, Identity and Integrity* (Oxford: OUP, 2009) see 77 and elsewhere. In this she resembles authors who took intentions to be similar to or kinds of self-addressed commands: see H.-N. Castañeda, *Thinking and Doing* (Dordrecht: D. Reidel, 1975), and A. J. P. Kenny, *Action, Emotion and the Will* (London: Routledge & Kegan Paul, 1973). Scanlon takes intentions to be tie-breaking reasons (T. M. Scanlon, 'Reasons: A Puzzling Duality', in R. J. Wallace, P. Pettit, S. Scheffler, and M. Smith (eds), *Reason and Value: Themes from the Moral Philosophy of Joseph Raz* (Oxford: Clarendon Press, 2004) 237).

[20] Or, use 'normative' in a different sense. Forming intentions involves one's rational powers, and that may motivate some people to regard intentions as normative. Besides, intentions affect the direction of one's attention (one is alert to some phenomena and not to others), and in doing so they affect which reasons one is attentive to (though not which reasons one should attend to). This too may induce people to think of intentions as normative. I use the term to indicate that what is normative is a reason or provides reasons. Finally, a person who 'forms an intention' and the next moment re-examines it, checks whether he really approves of the action, and does this again and again at short intervals, suffers from a neurotic anxiety that prevents him from forming intentions. When he is chronically reconsidering any intention he is not decided. Some people may think that if chronic indecision undermines one's ability to hold intentions then dropping an intention soon after one formed it is inconsistent with having it in the first place, and shows that having an intention is a reason for not abandoning it. But that is, of course, a non-sequitur.

[21] J. Raz, 'Reasons, Decisions and Norms', *Mind* 84 (1975) 481–99 and J. Raz, *Practical Reason and Norms* (3rd edn, Oxford: OUP, 1999).

provide. He is told: 'but we have just decided this matter yesterday'. 'True, he says, but that is not a reason for including the two papers I object to. Reasons for them have to relate to the merit of having them here. That we have decided yesterday shows no merit in having them.' 'Indeed', the Chair of the committee replies. 'But it is a reason for not reconsidering the matter. You cannot run an organization if its decisions can be challenged all the time.'

Whether one agrees with the Chair or not is immaterial. Everyone, I assume, will recognize that that is a common response, that such responses are accepted as adequate by organizations and that is sufficient to show that they are reasons, for those organizations, against reconsidering (without restriction) matters settled by their own decisions. Organizations take their decisions to be reasons against revising their decisions except where the rules and customs of the organization permit.

At the time when I explained the way decisions are normative I advanced the view that they are normative by being a certain combination of first- and second-order reasons. This may or may not have been a successful analysis of their normative character. The success of that analysis is immaterial here. What matters is that decisions, being reasons for constraining the occasions on which it would be proper to revise the intentions based on them, belong with a special kind of reasons, which—following H. L. A. Hart—I called content-independent reasons, for their rationale is not based on the quality of the content of those intentions.[22] Besides, the argument for decisions being such reasons does not depend on the value or utility of their being such reasons. The argument establishes that there is a coherent concept of decisions as normative, based on the coherent way in which many decisions are understood by those making and applying them. Whether or not any particular decision that is taken by those who make it to be a reason is indeed a valid reason, is a separate issue. Sometimes they are and sometimes, not. Some writers suggested that if intentions were not normative, planning and coordination, intra-personal or inter-personal, would have been impossible. I suspect that this is factually false. True, planning and coordination require some predictability of people's future conduct. But predictability is on safer grounds when it relies on people's dispositions and habits than on their commitments, even when they have commitments.

[22] See for the broader context J. Raz, *Between Authority and Interpretation* (Oxford: OUP, 2009) Chap. 8. They provide content-independent justification for action, which is non-transitive, i.e.: that A is a reason for B and B a reason for C does not entail that A is a reason for C.

8. Do Intentions Involve Commitments?—Part II

Not all intentions are decision-based in the sense explained. Many are formed in contexts in which those who form them take themselves to be choosing among several acceptable options.

> 'Red or White?', 'Red, please', I say as I form the intention to drink red wine with my food. But by the time the host returns with the wine, I have changed my mind, and ask for white. Not because of any new information or a new assessment of the reasons for and against them, but simply because I now feel more like having white wine.
>
> 'I thought you intended to find opportunities to spend time with him, in order to get to know him better, and now you seem rather lukewarm, and more inclined to avoid his company. What happened?' 'Nothing, really. I don't know why but I am no longer interested in getting to know him.'

These are unremarkable examples, suggesting that, other things being equal, intentions are not normative. People, or many people, may be disposed towards stability and be disinclined to change intentions once formed. But that does not mean that they have reason to do so. But perhaps this view overlooks something. It may be thought that the fact that forming intentions or deciding to change them are intentional actions, and therefore done for a reason, implies that changing or abandoning one's intentions is also done by a (mental) action, and therefore can only be done for a reason, or at least that when it is done rationally it is done for what the agent takes to be a reason. However, this argument does not apply to the many intentions that one comes to have or that one discards without reflection and without even being aware of the change, at least not at the time it happened. Therefore, it fails to show that intentions as such are normative.[23] On the contrary, the fact that there is generally nothing wrong in changing one's intentions raises doubt about their normativity.

Needless to say, there can be reasons for and against having certain intentions, whatever way they are formed. Nor is it surprising that in some circumstances the having of one intention may be a reason against having

[23] There is nothing surprising in our ability to do something deliberately that we sometimes do without deliberation. I can deliberately think about my mother, but thinking about her may be prompted without deliberation, simply because something reminds me of her, etc.

another (e.g. their combination may lead to adverse reactions from other people).[24]

One variant of the normativity of intentions thesis takes an intention to ϕ to be a reason to ϕ because if you intend to ϕ you are committed to maintain that intention, and therefore to act on it, unless there is reason to revise or abandon it. Bratman's 'bootstrapping' objection refutes a simple version of that view. If intentions were reasons for the action intended we would be able to manufacture reasons, for any actions, at will simply by forming intentions to perform them. This could not only provide, by the whim of agents, reasons to perform pointless actions, but will sometimes tip the balance, making an action there is conclusive reason not to perform into one that there is a conclusive reason to perform.[25]

There is something to this objection but not as much as Bratman and Broome assume. For one thing, we cannot form intentions, or sustain ones that we have, at will. We can only have them when, as we see things, there is a reason for us to perform the intended action.[26] For another, the thought that a mental state or condition that is aimed at an action cannot change the reasons for that action is itself implausible.[27] As mentioned above, decisions, or some decisions, are a special kind of reasons for action. Still the 'bootstrapping' argument shows that intentions that are not decisions are not reasons for the intended actions and those that are decisions are not ordinary reasons.

[24] Some people think that beliefs are normative because (and I will assume that to be true) we have reason not to believe anything unless it is true (one ought to believe that p only if p is true). That does not show that beliefs are commitments nor that they constitute reasons of any kind. It does not show that beliefs are normative if normative means 'constitutes or provides reasons'. Some people think that we ought not have contradictory beliefs. That is false (For a detailed argument see my *From Normativity to Responsibility*, Chap. 8: 'The myth of instrumental reason'), but even if it were true it would not show that, say, believing that p is a reason not to believe that not-p. It will merely show that the fact that the conjunction of p and not-p is false is reason not to believe that (p and not-p). I mention these points about beliefs as there are analogies, often exploited in the discussions of intentions, between them and beliefs. These analogies show that by their nature intentions, like beliefs, are subject to reasons. But that is not the issue explored here.

[25] See M. Bratman, *Intentions, Plans and Practical Reason* (Cambridge, MA: Harvard UP, 1987) 24–7 and following him J. Broome, 'Are Intentions Reasons?' in Arthur Ripstein and Christopher Morris (eds), *Practical Rationality and Preference: Essays for David Gauthier* (Cambridge: CUP, 2001). Their arguments are improved upon by J. Brunero, 'Are Intentions Reasons?' *Pacific Philosophical Quarterly* 88 (2007) 424. At 427–8 Brunero remarks how unlike ordinary reasons intentions would be were they reasons. He also warns against Broome's argument that if intentions are reasons they are self-justifying, noting that that is not the case if intentions to ϕ are reasons to ϕ rather than reasons to intend to ϕ. Of course, if they are reasons for the intended action they are also reasons to intend in cases where that would facilitate the action, i.e. would help its performance.

[26] See Chapter 1 'Intention and Value'; and *From Normativity to Responsibility*, Chap. 4.

[27] See R. Holton, *Willing, Wanting, Waiting* (Oxford: OUP, 2009) Chap. 7; N. MacLennan, *Rationality and Dynamic Choice* (Cambridge: CUP, 1990). In one form or another these considerations are recognized by Bratman.

The debate about the normativity of intentions is not settled by that objection. Intentions may be reasons for something other than the intended action (perhaps a reason for the agent to believe that he or she would perform it, or a reason to facilitate performance of the intended action), or the intention may be a reason only along with other facts, or conditional on other facts. So, the road to realizing the normative character of intentions may lie in the second view, that intending to ϕ involves having a plan to ϕ. That thesis, initiated by Bratman,[28] dominates much of the discussion in the area. At first blush it seems to be an exaggeration. The kernel of truth is that one can intend to ϕ only if one has some knowledge of what ϕ-ing is, and if, when ϕ-ing is not a basic action, one has some idea how to try to ϕ. Absent such knowledge one cannot be decided to ϕ. But remembering that one can intend to ϕ in the remote future, and that ϕ-ing can be a relatively unspecified action (I intend to protect the interests of my grandchild, born yesterday, once he grows up and becomes independent) it appears that no plan need be involved.

But this may be too hasty. A closer look suggests, or so it is argued, that intentions are normative in that an intention to ϕ, when combined with certain beliefs (e.g. that one would not ϕ unless one first ψs), is a reason to intend to ψ, because it would be irrational to intend to ϕ while holding those beliefs without intending to ψ. Given the irrationality of that combination of intentions (or their absence) and beliefs, it is argued, there is a reason to avoid such an irrational combination.[29] I have argued elsewhere that the fact that something is or would be irrational is not a reason to avoid it and that we have no general reason to avoid contradictory or conflicting beliefs and intentions,[30] and Bratman's and others' attempts to show that they are reason-giving in the case of intentions are not yet convincing.

But am I not missing the crucial point? Being decided would, if my rational faculty functions well, alert me to circumstances relevant to the success of my intention, but it would do nothing to advance the success of the intention or protect it from failure. I learn that unless I ψ now I will be unable to ϕ as intended. According to my account, it appears that that is it, so far as my

[28] See Bratman, *Intentions, Plans and Practical Reason*.

[29] See Broome, 'Are Intentions Reasons?', and Bratman's pragmatic argument in *Intentions, Plans and Practical Reason*, and his later argument from the conditions of self-governance in M. Bratman, 'Intention, Practical Rationality, and Self-Governance', *Ethics* 119 (2009) 411. That last argument is criticized by J. Brunero in 'Self-Governance, Means-Ends Coherence, and Unalterable Ends', *Ethics* 120 (April 2010) 579.

[30] See Raz, *From Normativity to Responsibility*, Chap. 8 on 'The Myth of Instrumental Rationality'. See also N. Kolodny, 'Why Be Rational?' *Mind* 114 (2005) 509; N. Kolodny, 'How Does Coherence MatterX', *Proceedings of the Aristotelian Society* 107 (2007) 229; N. Kolodny, 'The Myth of Practical Consistency', *European Journal of Philosophy* 16 (2008) 36.

intention goes. Of course, given that it is one of my purposes to ϕ, I may ψ. But that has nothing to do with my intention. So far as my intention goes I could just do nothing.

I agree that that is implausible, but it is not how things are according to my account. There are two ways to understand my account. First, intending to ϕ is being decided to ϕ, given that ϕ-ing is a purpose of the agent, and because of that. Having that purpose is not part of the intention, but it is a presupposition of having the intention. That is the account of intention as I presented it. It implies that if I know that ψ-ing is necessary to ϕ-ing and I do not ψ then, depending on a more complete specification of the circumstances, either I abandoned my purpose to ϕ or I am irrational. If I abandoned the purpose then I no longer intend to ϕ, and my intention is also abandoned. There is a second way to understand my account, according to which intending to ϕ consists in (a) having the purpose to ϕ, and (b) being decided to ϕ, (c) because one has that purpose. If one knows that ψ-ing is necessary to ϕ-ing and does not ψ the same follows: depending on further specification either one is irrational or one has abandoned one's purpose and intention. So, whichever way one takes the account it does not imply that it is possible for an agent to be indifferent to known or believed circumstances that affect the possibility of success or failure in acting as intended. It is merely indifferent as to whether the agent reacts by abandoning the intention or not.

Of course, most of the possibilities that being decided alerts one to are not all or nothing conditions, but circumstances that make ϕ-ing easier or more difficult, less or more costly, etc. The account, whichever way you take it, does not prescribe any reaction here either. It implies that once aware of such conditions the agent will react, depending on his judgement and motivation at the time. The agent's reaction may be wise or foolish, and that is not determined or required by his intention. His intention is not normative. That allows the account to permit great sensitivity to the circumstances, and maintains the basic insight that one may change one's intentions for any number of reasons or for no reason at all. One's heart may no longer be with that purpose.

The picture drawn here is simplified. It suggests that motivation and intention are seamlessly aligned, in that their motivations move agents towards their intended actions, while their intentions monitor that they are on course towards these actions so long as they are motivated to perform them. As one would expect the relations of motivation and intention are often more complex. Here are some examples: 1) Intentions to perform an action may persist while the motivation for the action changes. 2) There may be a time lapse between the fading motivation and abandoning the intention, partly because one may not be aware of the change in motivation, partly because motivations are of different strengths, whereas intentions are (by and large[31]) all or nothing, and partly because one may be mistaken about one's motivations (sometimes one thinks that one is motivated to ϕ because one wishes to be motivated to ϕ, etc.). 3) Belief, shared by some philosophers, that once one intends to ϕ one should not abandon the intention, or that one may abandon it only under restrictive conditions, may in itself motivate one to keep to the intention. Believed reasons can motivate even when mistaken, and even when irrational. 4) Motivation can be conditional (if I am offered a job in the city I will buy a house there) but if one believes that the condition will be met one may, rationally, form an unconditional intention to do what one would be motivated to do (given that I will be offered a job in the city, I intend to buy a house there). 5) Depending on one's character, having formed an intention to ϕ may strengthen or weaken one's motivation to ϕ (e.g. some people always doubt the wisdom of their own decisions). But there are some motivations generated by having intentions, at least in some types of cases. If the intention concerns something one cares about (I intend to get elected to the committee) then success in acting as intended may affect one's self-image (as competent, effective, in control, etc.) and that may add to one's motivation, and in some cases it may also give one new reasons to do as one intends because one so intends.[32]

Complications, mixed cases, etc. are to be expected in coming to understand our mental life. They do not change the basic view: intentions are neither normative nor are they plans. But if no plan is involved, what determines that the action when performed is done because one intended to perform it, that it is done in pursuit of that very intention? After all, that I intend to ϕ and I ϕ does not establish that I ϕ intentionally, let alone that I ϕ-ed with the intention that I had to ϕ before I did so. I may ϕ accidentally even when I intend to ϕ, and I may ϕ with the intention to ϕ, but not the same intention I

[31] There are, of course, half-hearted intentions, etc.

[32] Some other claims sometimes made about intentions show that their authors think of some subclasses of intentions. For example, it is sometimes said that forming an intention terminates deliberation on whether to perform the action. It may but need not do so. For one thing, intentions are not always preceded by deliberation, and when they are not there is nothing to terminate. For another, when forming an intention is preceded by deliberation, its formation indicates that the agent reached some conclusion in his deliberation (e.g. that he approves of the action), but he may continue deliberating about the case for the action: perhaps it is even stronger than he is currently thinking (which would not of course change the intention) or perhaps it is not. Forming an intention suggests that the agent feels that he need not deliberate further, not that he cannot usefully do so nor that he should not.

had last week. I may do so with an intention conceived at the time when I (begin to) ϕ. The question invites us to examine the relation between future intentions and intentions in action.

9. Guidance

Intending to ϕ is being decided to ϕ. One implication of being decided to ϕ is being guided to ϕ, or ϕ-ing guided by that intention. When we ϕ with the intention to do so the intention guides the action, which means that it keeps us on track towards successful completion of the action (though that is not always achieved; even after we started the action we may fail to do what we intended). In simple actions, such as opening a window, the guidance consists in a feedback process that monitors the movement of the arm and keeps it on target to reach the window handle, etc. In complex actions such as baking a cake it consists in monitoring the component acts, making sure of their success, that they are performed in the right order, etc.

How does being guided by an intention relate to being decided? As having an intention is being decided, it should be a manifestation of being decided. It is a process or activity that is the product of the two aspects of being decided: being alert to opportunities to perform the action and to likely changes that will make its performance easier or more difficult or costly. Remember that agents who have intentions are motivated to pursue a purpose that they are decided to pursue. What would make them perform the intended action is ultimately their motivation. They would let the intention fade away or abandon it outright once they lose their motivation to perform the action. While they are motivated, the intention keeps them on track, keeps them alert to opportunities to perform the action and to occasions where they may wish to take action to avoid making its performance more difficult, etc. The intention itself does not make them do any of those things. It just alerts them to the opportunities and the problems. Sometimes these alerts will invite re-examination of the intention, and may lead to abandoning or modifying it. Sometimes they will lead to the action being performed.

In this latter class of cases the agents, motivated as they are, start doing what they intended to do, or attempt to do it, and the intention, which is still with them, continues to function as before: alerting them to the fact that to complete the action they should move their arm to the left and avoid the obstacle on the right, etc. In short, there are not two kinds of intention: a future-directed intention and an intention in action. There is only one kind of intention and it functions both before the time for the action arrives, and during the performance of the action, both times in the same way, adapted to the specific conditions in which it functions.

Do these comments answer the question: does an agent who ϕ-s with an intention to ϕ, act for the same intention to ϕ that he had prior to the action? Yes and no. Insofar as the question has a definite answer it is answered by applying these comments: If the agent was decided to ϕ and remained so decided until he ϕ-ed being guided by the same alert conditions that constituted his intention all along then it was the same intention. But not infrequently there will not be a definite answer to the question. The continuity of the intention is not always easily established. Suppose one forgot one's intention to ϕ for a while, and during that period was not alerted to changes to which being decided would have alerted one. But then one again intended to ϕ, and, suppose that one never thought about the lapse in the middle, one was not, or not fully, aware of it. Did one's intention malfunction for a period but remain the same? Was it abandoned and then one came to have a new intention with (near-) identical content? There is often no answer and usually no importance in having an answer.

There are other sources of similar indeterminacies. I will mention only one, which is both common and interesting. Purposes evolve with time and intentions may evolve with them. My intention to protect the interests of my grandchild once he reaches maturity may morph into an intention to buy him a flat at that time. I intend to secure his interests by buying him a flat, and come to think that that would fully fulfil my original intention. When the time comes I buy him a flat with the intention of buying him a flat. Do I also in buying him a flat secure (to a degree) his interests with the intention to do so that I have had all along? Do I buy him a flat with that intention? Notice that once my intention morphed, and either implicitly or explicitly I came to the view that buying him a flat, and nothing else, is my way of securing his interests, my alerts change. I am no longer alerted to opportunities to secure his interests in other ways, nor to any changes that may facilitate or impede such other ways of securing his interests. Do I still have the original intention? Yes, because I do intend to buy him a flat in order to secure his interests. No, because I am no longer pursuing the open purpose of securing his interests. And this is a particularly simple case. Often intentions develop in much more complex ways. Often the result would be that while my intentions are reasonably clear, whether they are one or two, etc. has no answer, and normally that would not matter.

10. Conclusion

I offered an account of intentions, which hopefully fits the facts, and which explains the relative role of motivation and intention in leading to actions with intention. Both play a role in leading to the action, but whereas motivations so to speak propel the agent to act, intentions keep him on course. With rational beings like mature humans, motivations involve the adoption of a purpose for a reason, though the reasons alone often do no more than establish that the purpose is eligible, and other factors determine the agent to choose it among other eligible purposes. A purpose becomes an intention to perform actions that facilitate its realization or that constitute its realization when the agent is decided to pursue it. The reasons and motives to pursue a purpose do not always establish a case for intending to perform these actions well ahead of the time at which it would be appropriate to pursue them. But sometimes they do, and often it is rationally optional whether to form an advance intention or not, in which case the agents' personal characteristics will or will not lead them to form such advance intentions.

Advance intentions and intentions in action are one and the same kind of intention. They consist of being alert to opportunities to perform the intended action and in being alert to likely changes that bear on the desirability and ease of performing it. Such awareness guides the agent to adjust the intentions or, in the process of performing the action, to progress with its performance in a way leading to successful completion. Throughout the period in which one intends to perform the action, including the time it is being performed, the motivation to perform it is the propelling force. Intentions themselves, while contributing to the production of the action, do not motivate it, nor are they normative reasons to do it or anything else, except when contingent circumstances make them so.

3

Normativity

The Place of Reasoning

An important aspect of the explanation of normativity relates it to the way Reason (our rational powers), reasons (for beliefs, emotions, actions, etc.)[1] and reasoning, with all its varieties and domains, are inter-connected. The relation of reasoning to reasons is the topic of this chapter.[2] It presupposes that normativity has to do with the ability to respond to reasons using our rational powers.[3] The question is where does reasoning fit in?

I will compare two sketchy accounts. What I call the simple account takes reasoning to consist (roughly) in responsiveness to perceived reasons. It presupposes that intentions, attempts, or actions can be conclusions of reasoning. Those who affirm that possibility often regard reasoning that has such conclusions as practical reasoning. Hence much of the chapter will be about practical reasoning. I will illustrate some flaws in the simple account. The alternative sees reasoning as a search for a justified answer to a question, or for the justification of an answer, suggesting a different view of the place of reasoning in explaining normativity. I start by outlining this second account.

1. Reasoning Is an Activity: (a) Criterion of Success

Reasoning is something we do. It takes time. It has a beginning and an end. It is up to us whether to do it or not. Even though we sometimes drift into

[1] I discuss normative reasons and people thinking about normative reasons. Many are moved by normative considerations and reason about their implications without using or even having the concept of a reason. They use other concepts (duty, ought, what is virtuous, desirable, advantageous, prudent, moral, profitable, divinely commanded, etc.). These differ from 'reasons', but all imply that there is a reason, or even that the fact that they apply is a reason. When I say that a person relies on, believes in, or concludes that there is a reason I mean that they have a belief that entails that there is a reason.

[2] In such discussions we struggle to clarify our meaning, because the words we use or could use have more than one meaning. Unless otherwise indicated, I use 'reasons' to mean normative reasons, namely features of the world that, given their context, make certain responses appropriate for certain people. The reasoning I explore is neither system 1 nor system 2 thinking as explained by D. Kahneman, *Thinking, Fast and Slow* (New York: Farrar Straus Giroux, 2011) 20–9, probably overlapping system 2.

[3] See J. Raz, *From Normativity to Responsibility* (Oxford: OUP, 2011), especially Chap. 5.

The Roots of Normativity. Joseph Raz, Edited with an Introduction by Ulrike Heuer, Oxford University Press.
 DOI: 10.1093/oso/9780192847003.003.0004

reasoning, and sometimes find it difficult to stop, reasoning is an intentional activity. As with other intentional actions, while they can be intentional without being engaged in for a purpose, or undertaken for a reason, being intentional merely because their conduct is under our control, typically reasoning is an activity in which we engage for a reason. And typically the reason is to find an answer to a question. More accurately, *reasoning is essentially an activity aiming to establish the justification of, the case for, its conclusion, undertaken in order to establish whether the conclusion is a correct answer to its question.*[4]

The chapter will expose certain ambiguities in this formulation. But why take reasoning to be a search for an answer or a justification of an answer to a question? Why does it not simply establish that a conclusion follows from some premises? Some conclusion follows from anything one takes as a premise. Why reason from these premises rather than others? Given that it is an intentional activity the answer is that as the reasoner sees it there is reason to engage in it (reason for the reasoner to engage in it now), which is that these premises help with establishing something that the reasoner has reason to establish, which is more or less the same as saying that the reasoner has reason to find a justified answer to a question.[5] One condition for the success of the reasoning is that the question is well-formed, meaningful. Another is that its conclusion answers the question. A third is that the reasoning shows the answer to be correct. Relevance to justifying an answer to the question establishes which premises to rely on.

'Conclusion' is broadly speaking the end, termination of something. The ('real') conclusion of reasoning is its outcome; not necessarily its temporal conclusion. Often the reasoning continues after having reached the 'real' conclusion, when, for example, one re-examines its justification (without changing one's mind about anything at the end). Sometimes the 'real' conclusion is known, and the reasoning aims to confirm it. The 'real' conclusion is the answer to the question the reasoning is about. But answering a question need not involve reasoning. You ask me for my name or for the

[4] In part this view is shared (on different grounds) by P. Hieronymi, 'The Use of Reasons in Thought (and the Use of Earmarks in Arguments)', *Ethics* 124 (2013) 114; P. Hieronymi, 'Reflection and Responsibility', *Philosophy and Public Affairs* 42 (2014) 3.

[5] Cf. P. Boghossian, 'What Is Inference', *Philosophical Studies* 169 (2014) 1) who characterizes S infers from p to q as S judges q because S takes the (presumed) truth of p to provide support for q (4). But later he amplifies that inference is an activity with a purpose: 'it is something we do with an aim—that of figuring out what follows or is supported by other things one believes' (5). Most if not all reasoning has other aims. But he recognizes the basic point: it is an activity undertaken for a reason, though his 'taking' seems to be a feature of responding to reasons generally and is not confined to responding to reasons in reasoning.

way water came to be on Earth, and I know the answers and give them to you, without having to reason in any way at all. Similarly, one may know the proposition that is the answer to a question without knowing that it is the answer. One may know that there was a drought last year without knowing that that is the answer to the question: 'what caused the crop failure last year?' Reasoning involves looking for an answer, and for a justification of its being the answer.

A 'justification', in this context, is an argument, namely a statement of a reason or set of reasons given in support of an answer to the question the reasoning is about. The reasons are expressed in propositions, and most commonly when we report on our reasoning after it concluded we express the argument (or parts of it) that justifies its conclusion. If, as we see it, the reasoning ended in failure we commonly report on it by stating what question we tried to explore and for what kind of argument we were looking. So, the 'real' conclusion is a proposition that is taken by the reasoner to be an answer to the question. It is the *conclusion of the argument* that is taken by the reasoner to justify belief in it. Belief in the conclusion of the argument is the ('real') *conclusion of the reasoning*. The reasoning is abandoned and remains incomplete if the reasoner does not come to or reaffirm belief in the conclusion of its argument. For example, the reasoner may realize that his premises point to a certain conclusion, that P supports C, and yet stop short of believing that C. He has reached an interim conclusion, one that he believes, but has not yet answered his question (say, whether C?). Not endorsing/believing the conclusion of his argument, the reasoner has not yet reached the conclusion of his reasoning. He may continue it or abandon it.[6]

How much support must the argument lend to its conclusion to be valid (I use 'a valid argument' to designate that the support it gives its conclusion is adequate)? It must support it to a degree that would justify the conclusion of the reasoning, namely endorsement/belief in its conclusion, that is embracing the conclusion of the argument as an answer to the question the reasoning sought to answer. With this in hand we have the case for taking reasoning as aiming to establish the justification of an answer to a question. The question the reasoning is about is determined by the reasons for reasoning, and the question determines the strength of support the argument must provide for its conclusion, for the strength must be such as to justify endorsing it as the

[6] To avoid tedium I will often assume that the context makes clear whether 'conclusion' refers to the conclusion of the argument or of the reasoning. Similarly, 'argument' will be used to refer both to the reasons and to the propositions that state them.

answer to the question. In other words, the strength varies with the question and with the case for answering it.

'Justified in...' does not entail 'not justified not to...'. Is this consistent with the fact that to be valid an argument must establish that there is something amiss in believing/endorsing its premises without believing/endorsing its conclusion? It is, as I will illustrate in the case of justified belief, which I take to be an abbreviated way of saying that someone is justified in having that belief in the circumstances of the relevant time. There is a difference between justified action and justified belief. For a person at a point in time it may be justified to do or not to do any number of incompatible actions or activities. That is because any number of incompatible options may be supported by undefeated reasons. Each practical reason is a fact that establishes that there is some good in the action for which it is a reason.[7] So that when two incompatible actions are supported by undefeated reasons there is some good in each of them, and nothing to make a stronger case for one than for the other (this is what being undefeated entails). Epistemic reasons do not show that there is some good in the belief they are reasons for, rather, they show that there are some indications that it is true. If there are also equally strong indications that it is false there is no reason supporting either that belief or its negation. Therefore, for an argument to justify a belief (for a person at a time) it has to establish that the case for the belief is stronger than the case for its contradictory. That there is some case for that belief and some case for various contrary beliefs does not justify any of them.

Some epistemologists have taken to using concepts familiar from practical contexts, such as 'being entitled to believe that...' or 'being permitted to believe that...'. While these tendencies may speak of a growing interest in a general study of normativity, they overlook differences between normative domains. There is no sense in which a belief is permitted or prohibited (except by, sometimes obnoxious, laws or customs). Possibly, the ill-considered use of these concepts is encouraged by two considerations. First, the fact that the strength of the case required to justify the conclusion of the reasoning (the 'degree of proof' as lawyers say) is relative to what is at stake (criminal conviction or a private law remedy—to stay with the legal example). This appears to suggest that practical considerations are (sometimes) epistemic reasons. In fact it shows that they are among the considerations that determine the strength of the support the argument has to provide for its conclusion to

[7] This is a rough and misleading formulation. It has been modified and made more exact in Chapter 1, as well as Chapters 7 and 8.

be valid. In any case there is nothing here to suggest that the conclusion is 'merely' permitted. Second, in some domains, there is a vague range of strength of arguments where suspension of belief in the face of them is no fault, even though forming or sustaining the belief on their basis is justified. Whatever the explanation of this latitude the phenomena to be explained do not suggest that people have within the range of latitude a permission to believe or not to believe. That would mean that they can choose whether to believe. But in these as in the general case we do not choose what and when to believe. Rather, people's epistemic functioning differs regarding the strength of support that would lead them to have a belief, and within a certain range that functioning is rational.

In conclusion: We can of course assess an instance of reasoning by various criteria (was it efficient? elegant? etc.). The basic standard of success is (a) it was (at the start) reasonable to take the question to be well conceived; (b) the conclusion of the argument is an answer to the question (rather than being evasive, changing the question, etc.); (c) the argument associated with the reasoning is valid, it establishes that belief in its conclusion is justified; and (d) the reasoner concluded his reasoning by coming to believe, or confirming his belief in the answer to the question as a result of the reasoning.[8]

By this standard the success will be relative to the reasoner's other beliefs and to his rational capacities (was successful given that the reasoner was a high school student but would not have been had she been a research physicist). The standard relies on the semantics of questions and on the theory of valid arguments (deductive logic, non-monotonic logic, methods of experimental inquiry, etc., including the considerations that establish what can and what cannot be a reason for what) to determine the relevant parts of the tests for success. As indicated, I rely on only one aspect of the theory of valid arguments:[9] whatever kind of argument is concerned, it is common to all rules of valid arguments that believing or relying on the premises and rejecting or refusing the conclusion involves some defect, some imperfection. The right reaction, all things told, may be to believe in the premises and refuse the conclusion. But even so there is some epistemic imperfection in that condition. If one had more knowledge about the way things are, that outcome

[8] Two other conclusions to the argument bring it to a close: that the question cannot be answered, or that the answer cannot be known.

[9] Thus avoiding questions about the distinction between premises and rules of transformation or inference, the identification of tacit premises and presuppositions, the question of the validation of rules of inference, and much more.

would have been avoided; the rational outcome would have required revising some of the premises or believing the conclusion.[10]

2. Reasoning Is an Activity: (b) Its Scope

The criteria of success in reasoning allow that the reasons for reasoning may vary, relating to a case for finding an answer to the question, confirming or refuting an answer one has, finding an argument justifying the answer, or confirming or refuting an argument one has. But, as not all reasoning is successful, the criteria of success presuppose another criterion determining what is reasoning.

There are two broad cases in which people reason unsuccessfully. They may reach a conclusion on the basis of a defective/invalid argument, or they may not come to a conclusion, but abandon the reasoning incomplete. A distinct instance of reasoning is incomplete if it does not end with an answer (true or false) to its question. One can of course break off with a view to continuing it some other time. It can be cut short when one realizes that it may be dangerous, or otherwise undesirable, to have the answer or to continue with the inquiry, or for other causes.[11]

What makes unsuccessful reasoning (of either kind) reasoning is what makes successful reasoning reasoning. One distinct activity of reasoning is that of a person who takes it to be successful if, and because, it meets something like the criteria of basic success I outlined. These conditions of success are deliberately vague. They are meant to help us identify ordinary reasoning. Reasoning, being an intentional activity, cannot be successful accidentally (or rather what makes it reasoning is not that it is an activity that would have been accidentally successful reasoning had it been reasoning). And it can be reasoning even if unsuccessful. What makes the activity one of reasoning is the recognition by the reasoner that the activity is successful if it

[10] Perhaps the imperfection consists in not conforming to an epistemic reason, meaning that if the argument is valid then one has reason either to believe/endorse the premises and believe/endorse the conclusion or to revise at least one of the premises. That reason need not be conclusive. If it is overridden it should not be followed, but that would leave an epistemic reason that has not been conformed with. I am sceptical about this as the explanation of the imperfection. As noted, in general, overridden epistemic reasons—unlike overridden practical reasons—do not leave a remainder that makes the situation imperfect.

[11] Reasoning can also change course in midstream, abandon or suspend progress with the original question, and take on another.

is successful as reasoning.[12] But that cannot be a reference to an ideal or correct standard of success. People who have mistaken views about the standards of success for reasoning may still be reasoning, provided their understanding of these standards is not too remote from the correct ones. Therefore, and roughly speaking, reasoning is an activity attempting to be successful by those standards; or alternatively, an activity of a person who takes its success to be determined in that way. That 'taking' is manifested in accepting that deviation from relevance and from the other rules governing arguments is a mistake, being willing to correct such mistakes, and by realizing that one was mistaken if deviations from the rules come to one's attention after the reasoning is completed.

The above criterion identifies instances of reasoning by their core. It does not determine their outer contours: what does and what does not belong to a single complete instance of reasoning? When does it begin or finish? There is no point in pursuing these questions to the bitter end. Regarding many mental acts there will not be a fact of the matter whether they belong with the reasoning or not. But some broad criteria of the scope of a complete instance of reasoning are part of our understanding of what reasoning is.

The reason for reasoning determines its scope. There are two levels of reasons involved: the reasons for seeking either a justified answer to the relevant question, or a justification for the answer; and the reasons for conducting the reasoning in the way it is conducted (for pursuing subsidiary questions, for collecting and assessing certain data, etc.). The reasons for the way to conduct the inquiry are governed by the reasons for having it, but follow general principles regarding the conduct of inquiries about issues of the relevant kind. As we saw, given that the reasoning aims at a justification of a conclusion that is the reply to the investigated question, it is natural that in reporting on it one would produce the argument to the conclusion. But, of course, the stages in the presentation of an argument, proceeding in an orderly way from premises to interim conclusions to further premises, etc., to the conclusion, are rarely if ever in the temporal order of the stages of the actual reasoning. Some of the stages gone through in the reasoning directly reflect stages in the argument (call them the primary stages). They involve

[12] This way of identifying which activities are reasoning conforms to Boghossian's taking condition: 'Inferring necessarily involves the thinker taking his premises to support his conclusion and drawing his conclusion because of that fact' (P. Boghossian, 'What Is Inference', *Philosophical Studies* 169 (2014) 1) but interprets the 'taking' to include a reference to independently sound standards of success, and to be manifested in a myriad of beliefs and dispositions, which together constitute an intentional stance.

activities such as coming to view one of one's beliefs as a relevant premise in the argument, or postulating for the sake of the argument some assumption, or drawing an interim conclusion from some of the premises, etc. Others are connected to the primary stages, being ways of bringing them, or their content, to mind, focusing attention on them, being aids to seeing their relevance and interconnections. They involve free-floating ruminations, searches for ideas, vaguely coming to feel that some ideas are unlikely to work, and more. All these activities happen in the shadow of pursuing a justified answer to a question, the pursuit that in its totality is one's reasoning.

There is no reason to think that the loosely structured way in which we reason is disadvantageous, that we would have done better to regiment our reasoning and limit it to its organized primary stages. The best we can do in determining the stages of the reasoning is to say that broadly speaking one complete instance of reasoning consists of the various activities and attitudes that are part of the search for the answer to the investigated question and for its justification.

What makes them part of that search? We can reject the suggestion that mental activities or processes that causally contribute to the conclusion of the reasoning are part of the reasoning. Not all phases of the reasoning are causally productive, or contribute to its conclusion. I do not mean that some of them lead to dead ends, etc. Those can be constructive. I mean, for example, cases in which as the reasoning proceeds we forget what we did before and have to repeat our exploration. Furthermore, not all psychological processes that are causally productive towards the conclusion of the reasoning are part of it. One familiar and dramatic example is the sense people have that something happened during their sleep, or at a time when they put the problem aside and went swimming, something that suddenly opened the solution to their mental gaze. No doubt such things happen: psychological processes contribute to finding the argument and to leading to the conclusion, in ways that we are not aware of. But they are not part of the reasoning.

Mental activities and processes are part of the reasoning only if they include some conscious thoughts, and are governed in part by recognition that they strive towards an argument that would justify an answer to the relevant question. That recognition takes the shape of a feedback loop whereby steps that deviate from the goal are rejected. The feedback loop itself is not necessarily conscious, and the reasoner will often be unable to articulate its nature. But its operation constitutes the reasoner's control of the course of reasoning, a loose control that allows for many activities and processes not consciously controlled and not strictly governed by reasons to proceed this way or that, but none the less directed towards the goal of the reasoning. Concurrent attitudes and activities that are not related in the right way to the goal of the reasoning are not part of it.

It follows that not all the activities that are part of one's reasoning are strictly guided and organized by reasons. They are governed by the reason to look for a justification for an answer that led to the reasoning, and that means that the reasoner acknowledges that the process and its results are successful if they lead, reasonably efficiently, to a successful conclusion of the reasoning, that is, if the reasoner acknowledges that the activity he or she is engaged in is subject to criteria of success like the ones enumerated above.

3. An Objection and the Simple Account

If reasoning is a search for a justified answer to a question its conclusion can only be a belief or a proposition believed. Rhetorical metaphors aside, a killer asked what did he do (he killed Jones) cannot reply 'I answered the question what to do with Jones?' But there is a tradition going back to Aristotle taking actions, attempts, or intentions to be the conclusions of some instances of reasoning, often said to be practical reasoning. That cannot be shown to be wrong by taking one's starting point to be that reasoning is a search for an answer to a question. And the argument I gave for that starting point may not be sufficient to settle the issue.

Moreover, the account I offered, it can be objected, arbitrarily discriminates between reasons for belief and reasons for actions, intentions, or emotions. It takes reasons for belief to be followed by reasoning to the belief one has a warranted reason to have, but requires a different account for following reasons for actions, intentions, or emotions. Why is not reasoning the way to follow them as well?

The focus of an account of reasoning should be, the objection runs, on elucidating the relations of reasons to reasoning. This suggests a simple alternative account of reasoning. It may not have been defended in quite that way by anyone,[13] but it will be useful to examine the simple account (as I shall call it)

[13] In his 'account of the nature of practical reasoning' Dancy argues for a view similar to the simple account. He writes: 'when someone deliberates well and then acts accordingly, the action done is the one favoured by the considerations rehearsed in the deliberation, taken as a whole. It is a response to those considerations as together calling for or favouring it. And this is perfectly analogous to theoretical reasoning, when someone forms a belief as the belief most favoured by the considerations adduced as premises' (J. Dancy, 'From Thought to Action', in R. Shafer-Landau (ed.), *Oxford Studies in Metaethics* 9 (2014) 4). He further developed and clarified his view in J. Dancy, *Practical Shape: A Theory of Practical Reasoning* (Oxford: OUP, 2018). I criticized his account in J. Raz, 'On Dancy's Account of Practical Reasoning', *Philosophical Explorations* 23 (2020) 135.

as a way of bringing to light an important difference between two approaches to the understanding of reasoning.

The simple account consists of two propositions:

SA (P1): Successful reasoning is recognizing that something is a reason and responding to it, in the way it makes appropriate.

If, having realized that all told I should take this medicine, I take the medicine, then I reasoned from the premise that I have reason to take the medicine and other relevant premises to the conclusion that was the taking of the medicine. If realizing that today is Monday I come to believe that tomorrow is Tuesday then I reasoned from the premise that today is Monday and other relevant premises to the belief that tomorrow is Tuesday. Not all reasoning is successful. So the simple account contains a second part, which goes roughly as follows:

SA (P2): An activity that is taken by the agent to be successful if and because it is successful reasoning is reasoning.

The simple account offers an explanation of the relations between reasoning and normativity: reasoning is nothing but a way to respond to normative reasons. Generally speaking, so long as one has the belief or emotion or performs the action for which one has adequate reason one is free from fault.[14] But that may be due to luck or coincidence. Only when one's conformity to reason is due to reasoning, that is, recognizing and following the correct reasons, does one display the skills and attitudes that constitute rational responsiveness to reasons, as one also does when one reasons from perceived reasons that happen (not because of the malfunctioning of one's rational powers) to be mistaken.

4. Simple Objections

The simple account encounters difficulties. Suppose that you ask yourself whether the Conservative Party will win the next general election. As you are

[14] A reason to φ is an adequate reason to φ if it is neither defeated by any conflicting reason nor undercut or cancelled by anything. It may not defeat all the conflicting reasons. Having an adequate reason to φ implies that φ-ing is free from fault, and also that one has conclusive reason to conform to one of the undefeated conflicting reasons (whereas being permitted or being free from fault is no reason for anything). Some people think that adequate but not conclusive reasons are rare, some suggest that they are a failure in Reason, that it strives but fails to establish a conclusive reason. Some even think that that is my view (see Dancy). I see no case for these views.

deliberating a friend rings to ask you to meet him. You start preparing to go out. You were reasoning about the outcome of the election but did not come to any conclusion. Your reasoning was interrupted. Now suppose that you consider how to get to the airport the following morning. You conclude that you should leave at 6 a.m. to catch the 6:45 train. You fail to leave at 6.

You did not interrupt your reasoning without concluding it. Your reasoning was complete, and your conclusion was not a mere interim one. Failing to leave at 6 was not a failure to complete the reasoning. It is natural to think of your reasoning as a practical reasoning: you were deliberating about what to do. If so then some practical reasoning, in some sense of the word, does not have actions as its conclusion.

Suppose that you are walking to work. It occurs to you that you will not have time to lunch at the cafeteria. You wonder whether to cross the busy street to get a bun. Will this make you late for work? Would it matter if you are 10 minutes late? You conclude that all things considered it would be best to get the bun. You turn towards the traffic light when you stumble, knock your head, and are ferried to A&E. Did your reasoning whether to get the bun remain unfinished, being interrupted by your fall, just as your reasoning about the election remained unfinished, being interrupted by your friend's calling you? No. You concluded your reasoning, and your not acting on it came later. It was not an interruption of your reasoning.

Perhaps, actions are not the conclusions of practical reasoning; perhaps its conclusions are intentions? That view does not conflict with the preceding observations. And it is quite natural to say that I concluded my deliberations, forming the intention to φ. But then, it may be that the intention merely followed the conclusion of the reasoning rather than being its conclusion. For other indications suggest that it is not the conclusion. For example, knowing that you were not sure whether to apply for a certain job I ask you: 'Have you concluded what to do?' and you may say: 'I thought about it all day, and I know what I should do, but I am not sure what I will do', suggesting that you concluded your reasoning, but not by forming an intention. After all I cannot follow up by asking you: 'when will you finish your reasoning?'. It is clear that that is over. Only the problem of resolve remains. Or, when a friend who freely admits that he knows that he should give up smoking confesses that he cannot bring himself to decide to do so, I cannot reply with 'I did not realize that your reasoning powers are so poor'. His failure is one of resolve not of reasoning.

These observations do not amount to a conclusive argument. Some people would deny that they are objections at all. They simply beg the question, they will say. The so-called objections presupposed that neither intentions nor actions can be the conclusions of reasoning. They did not establish that this is the case. This is not quite right, however. True, the objections presupposed something. They presupposed that we are familiar with the concept of reasoning, and, barring difficult cases, we know what is reasoning when we see it, even while we are unable to provide an account of what it is. They take the cases to illustrate straightforward situations regarding which the simple account is mistaken.

If intentions and actions cannot be conclusions of reasoning a natural assumption is that all reasoning concludes with a belief or beliefs. There are additional candidates. Could not a supposition be the conclusion of reasoning? Or could not the acceptance of a proposition (e.g. accepting someone's innocence) be such a conclusion? I will not consider these possibilities. 'Accepting that…' is a mental act. If acts are not conclusions of reasoning neither is acceptance. Suppositions are different, being more like beliefs, but they seem to be subsidiary types of conclusions, mostly or always intermediate ones, and for present purposes can be left on one side.

Beliefs are the conclusions of at least some classes of reasoning. To remind ourselves: they need not be new beliefs. Reasoning can conclude in endorsing or reinforcing or weakening an existing belief. Reasoning to a belief (like many other ways of forming beliefs) is subject to the forms of interference familiar to anyone who considered the formation of intentions (and the processes leading to or frustrating the attempt to perform actions). Reasoning to a belief can be distorted by various forms of motivated irrationality (wishful thinking, rationalizations of desires for revenge, desires to please, etc.) or fall prey to other forms of distortion (anxieties, lack of resolve due to low self-confidence, low self-esteem, and others). They may lead to unsuccessful reasoning, and sometimes to incomplete reasoning. Whereas, on my account, reasoning that fails to lead to intentions or actions is not, in virtue of that fact, incomplete. That intentions are subject to akrasia and similar distortions does not establish that they cannot be conclusions of reasoning. But if they cannot, we must accept this asymmetry as a feature of reasoning.

The simple objections suggest that the simple account may be closer to the truth regarding reasons for beliefs than regarding other reasons. But such a restriction appears arbitrary and unmotivated. It is therefore not surprising that there are reasons to doubt it. The simple account, restricted or otherwise, purports to offer *a sufficient condition for reasoning*: given that reasoning has to do with rational reaction to reasons, that is the only part of it that is in doubt. But, if F is a reason for the agent to R, not all ways of coming to R when taking F to be a reason for it are cases of reasoning. For example, if I believe that John gave me a present for my last birthday because I remember his doing so, no reasoning need have been involved in forming the belief, even though that I remember him giving me the present is a reason to believe that he did. If sound this point refutes the simple account. The simple account does not provide a sufficient condition of reasoning to a belief, any more than of reasoning to an intention.[15] This, however, does not show that intentions or actions cannot be the conclusions of reasoning. We need to examine it further.

5. Practical Reasoning

We are trying to establish whether only beliefs can be the conclusions of reasoning in order to understand the role of reasoning in an account of normativity. One theoretical case for taking actions or intentions to be possible conclusions is that otherwise one cannot explain practical reasoning. If only beliefs can be conclusions what is practical about practical reasoning? This section will challenge this case.

One answer is that practical reasoning is reasoning in search of an answer to a practical question. 'What is to be done?' may stand as the prototype, though variations range wider than in time (what was to be done? etc.), modality (what is one permitted to do? Must do? etc.), relevant agent (what is the government to do?), or circumstances (what is to be done if things are so and so?). Reasoning aiming to answer some other questions may be classified together with the above. For example, reasoning about whether it would be cowardly or disloyal or mean or vain to act in a certain way, or to have certain feelings.

Making the classification of reasoning as 'practical reasoning' turn on the question explored, is in line with other classifications of reasoning, as economic, or educational and so on. Practical reasoning in that sense does not seem to be governed by special rules of inference. It is modal and defeasible (non-monotonic) but so is much ordinary reasoning. It deals with concepts, such as rights and duties, which have their own concept-specific transformation rules. It is common that any sphere of discourse or learning supplements the general rules of inference with concept-specific transformation rules. On this

[15] In the preceding section, when introducing the simple account, it was suggested in its favour that it avoids discriminating between epistemic and other reasons, the suggestion being that on my account we come to believe for reasons always through reasoning to that belief. It is now clear that that is not an implication of my account.

view, practical reasoning is ordinary reasoning regarding a particular range of questions.

Does that show that its conclusions are beliefs and not intentions, for example? It does not. The issue is not terminological. There is nothing inappropriate in using 'practical reasoning' as the name of the class of reasoning I characterized. But perhaps there are cases of reasoning (perhaps they are a subclass of practical reasoning as defined) whose conclusions are (the formation of) intentions. Call them P2 reasoning, and those that are practical according to the account I just gave, P1 reasoning. There are many cases of P1 reasoning that cannot end with the formation of an intention, that is, the premises that lead to their conclusion do not warrant forming an intention.[16] For example, I may reason now what to do now, and I may reason tomorrow about what I should have done now. Both episodes of reasoning may be identical in all respects (allowing for modulation of temporal reference) except that, if any reasoning can conclude with an intention, only my current reasoning can conclude with an intention to do something now.

Reasoning triggered by a 'what am I to do?' question can conclude with the belief that I have an adequate reason to φ. It will guide me in my subsequent thoughts and decisions. But neither it, nor the premises that led to it, require forming an intention to φ. For example, there may be quite a number of incompatible acts that I have adequate reason to perform, but it may well be irrational to form intentions to perform each action that I know to be supported by an adequate reason, and so far as my reasoning goes, nothing wrong in not forming an intention to φ.

In other cases, even though it may appear that an intention can be formed when the reasoning concludes with belief that one ought to φ, no intention need be formed. Suppose that I conclude that I ought to do something for my child when he reaches maturity (he is now three years old). My conclusion notwithstanding, I form no intention to do so, not because of any doubt, or weakness, but simply because it is not necessary. According to the definition proposed above I engaged in and concluded my practical reasoning on the issue (it is a P1 reasoning). According to the intention as conclusion view I engaged in theoretical reasoning only (it is not a P2 reasoning).

[16] One person's reasoning about what another person is to do is a P1 practical reasoning, but it cannot warrant as a conclusion the forming of an intention by the reasoner that what ought, let us say, to be done is that someone else should take a certain action. Some people see the use of the first-person pronoun in a reasoning as essential to its being practical. See A. Muller, 'Radical Subjectivity: Morality v. Utilitarianism', *Ratio* 19 (1977) 115, and J. M. Finnis, *Fundamentals of Ethics* (Oxford: OUP, 1983) 114. Hence my examples will all be of first-person reasoning.

I hesitated in introducing this example, for future intentions present more complex features than is often appreciated. Most relevant to our concern is that while future intentions can be formed without the agent as much as noticing the fact, when they are consciously and deliberately formed, forming them is an act that is justified when supported by adequate reason. As argued by Ulrike Heuer, the existence of a reason to perform an action at some time in the future is not a sufficient reason to form now an intention to do so.[17] Additional considerations are needed to establish a case for forming the intention. So, that I ought to or must φ in the future does not, without further premises, warrant forming now an intention to do so, and needless to say forming such an intention would not be a valid conclusion of the argument that concludes that I ought to φ in the future. Moreover, when the extra considerations are available, the conclusion will often be that forming an intention is permissible, rather than required. An intention to do something is not a valid conclusion of a reasoning that establishes no more than that forming or having the intention is permissible.

Such cases illustrate the range of types of reasoning often thought of as practical that do not warrant an intention as a conclusion, even if intentions can be conclusions of reasoning. The following cases illustrate a more far reaching point: They concern cases in which I ought to φ, but have no reason to form an intention to φ and have an adequate, perhaps conclusive reason *not* to intend to φ.

For example, suppose that I ought not to act disloyally, even when doing so would benefit the person to whom I would be disloyal. My reasoning led me to this conclusion. I never act disloyally in such circumstances, but I never form an intention not to do so. Why should I? After all I am not in the least tempted to act disloyally in that, or almost any other situation. The thought of doing so never enters my mind. Forming the intention not to be disloyal appears to me to be demeaning, to be saying to myself that I need to resolve not to be disloyal, otherwise there is a risk that I will be. According to the proposed classification I engaged in practical reasoning, and I live by it. If I were open to temptations of disloyalty I would have had a reason to form an intention not to be disloyal. But as I am not, I have no such reason, and have an unopposed reason not to form such an intention. My conduct is affected by the belief with which my P1 reasoning concluded. But I did not engage in P2 reasoning.

[17] See U. Heuer, 'Intentions and the Reasons For Which We Act', *Proceedings of the Aristotelian Society* 114 (2014) 291.

Nor are omissions the only cases of this kind. I may have a reason to perform an act that I will indeed perform, yet it may be demeaning or otherwise undesirable that I should form an intention to do it. It is said that Kant decided that a daily walk was what his health needed. So each day, come rain or shine, at precisely 3.30 p.m., he would emerge from his lodging, and walk up and down the street. Legend has it that so punctual and reliable was his walking routine, the neighbours used to set their clocks by him. Enabling the neighbours to set their clocks was, no doubt, a good thing, and Kant may well have become aware of the facts. Yet, I would understand someone in his position who sees no reason to, and does not form the intention to go out punctually at 3:30. He grants that he ought to go out at 3:30 (until he gives adequate notice that he will not). But given that he would turn out at 3:30 precisely, without intending to turn out at 3:30 precisely (his daily routine naturally leads him to do so), he may well reject the idea that he is a local clock.[18]

In such cases we have reasoning that rightly concludes that one ought to φ, and yet one has no reason to intend to φ and there are adequate reasons not to intend to φ. Both the reasoning to the conclusion that one ought to φ, and the reasoning to the conclusion that one may not, perhaps even should not, intend to φ are practical in the P1 sense, and guide the reasoner's conduct. But neither is P2, nor can they be turned into valid P2 reasoning. Yet it seems odd to conclude that there is no practical reasoning that applies to these cases. So, possibly even advocates of intentions as the conclusions of some practical reasoning would allow that not only reasoning concluding with an intention can be practical.

None of this argues that intentions cannot be the conclusions of some cases of reasoning. However, the examples undermine the thought that reasoning cannot be practical, or cannot guide people's conduct, unless its conclusions are intentions or actions. The loyalty case shows that if there are cases of reasoning concluding with an intention they are not more practical (namely

[18] Several of the points made in this chapter seem to challenge Broome's principle of enkrasia, which in its simple form suggests that one is irrational if, believing that one ought to φ and that one is able to φ only by intending to φ, one does not intend to φ (J. Broome, *Rationality Through Reasoning* (Chichester: Wiley-Blackwell, 2013) 170–3, 288–90). In fact, these points do not conflict with his principle so long as it is confined to cases in which one believes that one has a conclusive reason to φ that one can conform to, but only by intending to φ (and that one can so intend). What these observations do is illustrate how limited the application of the principle is, and that (partly as a result) it is not the key to the rational connection between belief and action and intention. Clearly, the argument of this chapter contradicts Broome's contention that practical reasoning has intentions as its conclusion. Part of the aim of the chapter is to distinguish between conditions of rationality and the rules governing reasoning.

have no greater influence on one's conduct) than at least some cases of reasoning ending with a belief about what one should do. An argument against intentions as conclusions of reasoning has to do more. It has to be grounded in an understanding of the nature of reasoning.

6. The Role of Reasoning in Our Normative Functioning

Just as successful reasoning to a belief establishes that there is something amiss, some imperfection, in retaining all the premises and not believing the conclusion, so to have an intention as its valid conclusion the reasoning has to establish that there is something amiss in retaining all the premises and not having the intention. Reasoning that an intention is permissible concludes with a belief to that effect. The permitted intention cannot be its conclusion. There is no blemish in not taking advantage of a permission. Therefore, for an intention to be a conclusion of reasoning, that reasoning must show that there is a conclusive reason to form or to have that intention. It follows, I will argue, that if an intention is the conclusion of a valid reasoning, the argument associated with the reasoning must include an interim conclusion that there is a conclusive reason to form or to have that intention. Borrowing Broome's style of presenting the argument that underpins reasoning that concludes with an intention, my contention is that a valid reasoning to an intention is supported by a valid argument a fragment of which has an intermediate conclusion (or premise) of the form:

(IC) There is a conclusive reason to intend to φ.

And whose conclusion has the form

(AC) I shall φ (this being an expression of an intention).

And people reason validly to the intention to φ when they form (or maintain) the intention because they take the argument to show that there is a conclusive reason for it.

This contention relies on two claims: (1) the argument that underpins the reasoning must include the interim conclusion (IC). (2) To reason validly to the intention, reasoners must believe or endorse (IC). Some people doubt one or both of these claims. They may not deny that one can reason to (IC) and from it to the intention. But if so, they deny that believing/endorsing the interim conclusion and reasoning from it are necessary steps in reasoning to an intention.

The argument from (IC) to (AC), if valid, is valid in virtue of an inference rule sanctioning that transition. Call it the Intention Derivation Rule (IDR). Those who deny my first claim, namely that in reasoning to an intention (IC) is a necessary step, cannot rely on IDR to validate the argument that they have in mind, the one lacking (IC). What alternative inference rule do they have in mind? It cannot be the inflationary rule saying something along the lines: 'given reasons for and against an intention form the intention'. What then is it? When we reason whether to intend or to act (the more common way of becoming aware of reasons to intend), the argument we come to rely on is normally complex. It identifies reasons for and against the intention, determines their relative stringency and strength by exploring some of their implications, on the basis of which it determines that there is a conclusive reason for the intention. We expect many rules of inference or other transition-sanctioning rules to be employed in the course of such arguments. It is unlikely that they can be lumped together into one, but even if they could that one would include as a phase in the argument the determination of a conclusive reason for the intention. That has already been established above. There is no rule or set of rules of inference that avoids IDR. Therefore it is impossible to avoid (IC) as a step in such an argument. That disposes of the objection to my first claim.

The objection to the second claim must therefore allow that (IC) is a necessary step in the argument, for it must allow that the move to an intention relies on IDR. Needless to say, it must also allow that the formation of an intention is the conclusion of reasoning only if one forms the intention because of a realization that the underpinning argument requires it. However, the objection proceeds, that realization need not take the form of a belief in (IC). One can rely on (IC) without believing it. How so? To reiterate, the intention can be a conclusion of reasoning only if it is formed because the reasoner takes the reasoning to have established a conclusive reason for the intention. Does that not mean that the reasoner came to believe that there is a conclusive reason? True, it may well be that the thought that there is a conclusive reason did not occur, that the reasoner did not consciously think: 'there is a conclusive reason…'.[19] But most of our beliefs never feature in our

[19] Something like this is Dancy's objection: 'I can adduce considerations, deliberate, and act accordingly without needing to form an intermediate conclusion that this or that course of action is the one I have most reason to pursue. The notion of a reason need not appear explicitly in my thought, because to respond to something as a reason is not, and does not require, believing it to be a reason' (Dancy, 'From Thought to Action', 11). He is right about the notion of a reason not having to appear explicitly, and about people responding to reasons without having the concept of a reason (see n. 2 above). But these observations do not constitute an objection to the view I express in the text above, and which I

thoughts. Determining when one has a belief is a difficult task, but given that the reasoner relies on there being a conclusive reason because his or her argument establishes that there is one, I see little doubt that he or she believes that there is such a reason.

The objections having failed, it turns out that any reasoning concluding with an intention divides into two stages: first, reasoning to a belief that there is a conclusive reason for an intention, followed by a second stage consisting of forming the intention on the basis of that belief.

The emerging picture appears to confirm the earlier surmise, namely that most of what we may have in mind when thinking of practical reasoning is reasoning about a specific domain, or domains, and like any other reasoning its conclusion is a belief. The conclusions of much, though by no means all, such reasoning may be properly followed by the reasoner forming an intention. That would be the case when the reasoning showed that there is an adequate reason for having or forming such an intention, and the reasoner chose to form that intention. Often, the reasoner will not form the intention, and there may be nothing amiss with that choice. Only in a proper subset of cases of such reasoning will the appropriate conclusion indicate that there is a conclusive reason for having or forming an intention.[20] In some of those cases the reasoner will not be able to form the intention, but normally forming it would not be impossible. Indeed, it will be what one should do after concluding the reasoning.

It seems clear by now that the simple account cannot be correct. Reasoning is not the way in which we intentionally respond to reasons. We had a counter example in Section 4 showing that not all beliefs formed for reasons are formed through reasoning, and the cases in which people form intentions because they have adequate reasons, but no conclusive reasons, to have them add counter examples. We still do not have an argument to establish that

defended also in *From Normativity to Responsibility* in the passages to which Dancy objects. To object one needs to claim that one's reasoning can validly conclude with an action without an intermediate conclusion that entails that one has a conclusive reason to perform the action. It need not be that belief. It can be a belief that one would be wrong not to perform the action, that one must perform it, or any belief that entails the existence of a conclusive reason.

[20] Some people maintain that as inevitably a reason for an action, even a conclusive one, is a reason for any action of a class of actions with some property, that alone shows that actions cannot be the conclusions of reasoning. I express no view on that issue. It is not to be confused with the general case in which the reasons for several incompatible options are undefeated. Dancy, misguidedly, suggests that reasons for belief are also reasons for a believing belonging to a class of possible believings (its content is determined, but the identity of the state, disposition, or attitude of believing is not). That is mistaken because an adequate reason to believe is a reason to believe from the time you should become aware of it. There is no doubt some leeway as to what that time is, but it is not indeterminate in the way that the particular identity of the act that you do when following a reason is underdetermined by the reason.

intentions cannot be the conclusions of reasoning. But we edged further in that direction. The last section removed or weakened the theoretical need to suppose that intentions can be conclusions of reasoning. The current section shows that there is an oddity in supposing that they are.

That is because successful P2 reasoning consists in nothing more than reasoning from 'there is a conclusive reason to intend to φ' to intending to φ. By now it may well appear that the step from that belief to the intention is not one of reasoning. Why not? It is not that reasoning requires greater complexity. I do not know of a measure of complexity that would establish this contention. Nor is it that there cannot be reasoning from a single premise. There are cases in which it is possible to believe the premise without believing the conclusion, and yet reflection on the premise, attending to the premise, may convince one of the conclusion. Furthermore, even if one believes in both premise and conclusion one may be unaware of the connection between them, but become aware of it when reflecting about, attending to, both side by side, as it were. In such cases one would be reasoning from the premise to the conclusion. Finally, if the transition from 'there is a conclusive reason to intend to φ' to intending to φ is not one of reasoning, that is not simply because the conclusion is not a belief.

The problem is not directly with the content of premises or conclusions. It has to lie with the kind of transition that constitutes reasoning, and identifying it is a central part of an account of the nature of reasoning. If certain alleged conclusions (e.g. actions), or combinations of premises and conclusions are ruled out that is because the reasoning-transition cannot obtain there. The remarks about reasoning from a single premise indicate the direction of travel: reasoning is an activity whose success depends on coming to realize that some items (premises) support others (conclusions). Not only the existence of the support relationship is essential to it, but the coming to realize that the relation obtains, not having been aware of it or certain of it before, and responding to it by adopting the conclusion. Reasoning is a special case of responding to reasons, responding by discovering, by realizing that C because of P, or that P supports C.[21]

Anticipating an objection: realizing is not the same as coming to believe. It refers to an experience: in extreme cases we refer to it as the Eureka moment. Reasoning is not a recitation of the argument that supports its conclusion. It is an activity that leads to a realization that the conclusion is a well-supported

[21] No intuitionistic element is smuggled in here, as the realization does not underwrite its own success.

answer to the question one is considering, and this is confirmed by our implicit knowledge of what reasoning is. Given that what one is led to when realizing something is a belief, it follows that the conclusion of reasoning is a belief.

Therefore, reasoning presupposes the possibility of believing the premises without believing the conclusion. If that possibility does not exist reasoning to that conclusion is not possible, and of course not necessary. And the possibility has to exist for me if I am to be able to reason from those premises to that conclusion. I cannot, for example, reason from the fact that my brother was named Ben to his then having that name. The existence of the required support relationship between items is not sufficient for the possibility of reasoning from one to the other. P&Q entails P, but I cannot reason from P&Q to P.

We had evidence, through generalizable examples, that actions are not conclusions of reasoning. Now we have an explanation and a general argument: when we reach the conclusion of reasoning the transition that takes us to the conclusion is in the nature of a realization. But there is none in the transition from a belief in an adequate or even conclusive reason for an action to its performance. We can come to realize that circumstances call for an action. But that means realizing that there is a case, perhaps a conclusive one, for the action. Not that the action is there. When we acted for a perceived reason, there was nothing we did not realize about the connection between that we ought to φ and φ-ing that led us to φ-ing. If we know that we ought to φ (or have a case to φ) then we know that φ-ing is what we ought to do (or have a case for doing). There is, of course, a relation between acting for a reason and believing that one has that reason. To take that to show that the action is a conclusion of reasoning is to reduce reasoning to responding to a perceived reason. It fails for not every action for a reason involves reasoning.

The same argument excludes the possibility of intentions as conclusions of reasoning. If the reasoning of some people established that there is an adequate or a conclusive reason for them to intend, it left nothing (relevant) for them to discover or realize. If they form that intention they do so for a reason, but no realization leads to that formation, only their prior knowledge that they have reason to intend.

So understood reasoning is an internal process in which our thoughts adjust our thoughts.[22] Reasoning relies on, but is distinct from processes or

[22] Mental acts, including the acts and activities that constitute reasoning, are not themselves the conclusions of reasoning either. They are guided by beliefs about, say, how the reasoning should continue.

activities in which our thoughts are formed by our interaction with the world, or which set us to interact with, to impact on, the world. For example, recognition and memory are not reasoning: seeing Martin in a crowd and recognizing him; recalling that I was at this restaurant where I am now yesterday; remembering that the alarm going off is a reminder that I should get up are examples of thoughts or beliefs formed by being impacted upon by the world. But while these beliefs may trigger reasoning, or just feature as a premise in some reasoning, they are not the conclusions of reasoning. Similarly doing something upon coming to the view that one should is a matter of setting oneself to affect the world or actually doing so, a reaction that may be justified by reasoning but is not itself part of that reasoning.

Intentions belong with actions and not with beliefs; both involve the will. Embedded intentions, for example the intention that makes my drinking a cup of coffee or running, intentional, are aspects of actions whose existence is inseparable from the actions they make intentional. If actions cannot be the conclusions of reasoning it would be surprising if embedded intentions could be. Independent, or future directed intentions, can exist when we do not perform the intended act, and the argument here offered relies on the explanations offered in Chapter 2 of the way they are close to actions.

Reasoning is the handmaiden of normativity. Inasmuch as features of the world make certain responses, emotional, cognitive or active, appropriate, where we have the capacity to respond to them through the use of rational powers, they belong to the normative domain. Reasoning is a reason-guided mental activity of finding out how we should orient ourselves towards the world. Practical reasoning consists of those reasoning activities that aim to determine how we or others should act in the world. The acting, including the intentions with which it is done, is not part of the reasoning, but is sometimes determined by it.

4
Can Basic Moral Principles Change?

Among the many, often conflicting, images and ideas about morality that nourish our thinking, permeating it even when they do not lead to specific conclusions, are thoughts about morality as dependent on human nature, and on the social conditions of human existence, and as meant for humans, having no existence without them, and as created, or invented, by humans, individually or collectively. These and other thoughts tend to make us think of morality as changeable and changing.[1] But no less pervasive are thoughts that morality is independent of us, facing us with demands whether we want them or not, thoughts that we are subject to morality willy-nilly, that sometimes, perhaps often, we are called upon to sacrifice the most cherished and desired things in our life in a moral cause. These and related ideas and images tend to make us see morality as unchanging, existing independently of us, so that we have to struggle to find out what it demands of us, and to struggle, sometimes against our nature, to comply with its demands, or to live up to its standards.

Ideas belonging to these two poles, or many versions of them, share important features. They all allow for a cognitivist view of morality, namely that there are morally correct and morally incorrect views. Even when they appear to conflict it is not obvious that they do, and theoretical attempts to reconcile them abound, the best known being Kant's idea of the moral law being both made by the self-legislation of rational agents, and binding on them in virtue of their rational nature, which leaves no room for choice as to which moral laws to make. This chapter is another attempt to explore the two apparently conflicting strands in reflections about morality prevalent in our culture, except that I will generalize and consider normative principles generally, taking moral principles to be among them. I will also simplify and discuss most of the time principles of duty only. The question will be can principles of duty change? The focus on them is not because they are more

[1] My interest is in the possibility of basic normative change, namely one which is not merely due to a change in non-normative facts yielding a change in the application of (independently existing) normative considerations. Much of the time I discuss the possibility of normative change generally, as a way of bringing out the problems involved with the possibility of basic change.

The Roots of Normativity. Joseph Raz, Edited with an Introduction by Ulrike Heuer, Oxford University Press.
 DOI: 10.1093/oso/9780192847003.003.0005

important or significant than other principles. I do not believe that they are. It is merely a simplifying device. The assumption is that if they can change so can other normative principles, and that by exploring the possibility of change and contingency in normative principles we will improve our understanding of the nature of normativity.

The difficulties in defending the possibility of change are considerable. That possibility runs contra to a common understanding of the nature of reality—roughly speaking affirmed by Hume—in the wake of the rise of modern physics, and the Galilean revolution. That understanding has been challenged by Kant and others, the most interesting under Kantian influence. Needless to say, this is not the occasion for an extensive discussion of these issues. But their presence in the background dictates the structure of the chapter. Its first part argues for the possibility of change by removing an objection to it, an objection that appears to be a compelling consequence of the nature of normativity. The second part of the chapter surveys and comments on difficulties of accommodating the possibility of change in normative principles with various common views about the nature of reality.

Part One: Removing an Objection to the Possibility of Change

1. The Arbitrariness Difficulty, and Its Background

A person's moral duties, rights, and other normative conditions may change from time to time. Often, we invoke a general proposition in order to explain the changes. It says that one has that duty only under certain conditions and they existed at one point in time, but no longer exist at a later point, and so on. But is it possible for the explaining propositions to be true under some conditions and not others? Most societies hold that one has a moral duty to bury one's dead kin. Let us assume that they are right and we have such a duty. Sophocles' Antigone died for keeping that duty. That proposition: one has a duty to bury one's dead kin, both explains and justifies her actions. But what if one's kin died of Ebola? During the recent outbreak, many people knowingly put their lives at risk, and fought nurses and police, to bury their loved ones. Did they have this duty in these, changed, circumstances? Possibly not; in which case the explanation invoked over many generations to justify the duty did not apply to them, and perhaps does not apply anymore at all. How are we to understand that change? One common reaction is to say that the principle invoked was incompletely stated, the case of deadly infection from contact with the dead was omitted because it is rare, and there is no need to mention it in most cases. Another reaction is to suggest that the duty to bury may be overridden by conflicting principles, as is the case in the Ebola example. One way or another these reactions suggest that there is always an unchanging explanation, and appearances to the contrary are due to incomplete statements of the explanation. People's normative conditions change, but the moral principles that explain their conditions cannot change.

Notice that confidence in that conclusion is often great, and is independent of actually having the complete explanation needed to establish the case. We are not deterred by ignorance of a complete explanation that is at least potentially unchanging. We feel confident that there is one even though we do not know what it is. Therefore, the way that we treat examples does not establish that moral principles cannot change. Rather it relies on that view. But why accept it in the first place?

I will continue to discuss the conclusion informally, but some clarification is required to avoid confusion: when referring to normative propositions I ignore propositions about people's actual or hypothetical or possible beliefs about the normative situation of this or that. I will also ignore propositions about whether or not, or to what degree people conform to, or enjoy, etc. their normative conditions. Rather, the propositions to be discussed here are general propositions that express the application, actual or conditional, of some normative property, such as having a duty, or its implications. Typically, these are propositions saying that x has a duty, or a right, etc. or has had it or will have it when C obtains, or they are propositions that entail some conditions for the application of a normative property. The conditions, C, can be non-normative or normative or a mix. Normally we say that such propositions apply when the conditions are met. My interest is in whether propositions that express principles are true, always or a-temporally, or not. We do not normally refer to all general propositions of this character as principles. I will use 'normative principles' informally to refer to true general normative propositions that have the power to explain or that non-trivially contribute to the explanation of the phenomena they are about. So, for example, that people should honour and care for their parents, truly states both how people should behave towards some people and that that those people are one's parents is part of the explanation why one should so behave. Or, schematically, that all humans have a duty to A is a principle if they have that duty because they are human. By way of contrast, that all males have a duty to A is not a principle, if they have the duty because they are human. The distinction is vague, but neither for our purpose nor for any other I know of, does the precise delineation of principles matter. When in doubt count it as a principle.

Note that principles are not rules or norms or standards, etc. These are made by people, individually or collectively. They may affect the duties, rights, privileges, etc. that we have, and there are principles that state when they do. Binding rules, like binding promises, come and go, and they give rise to rights and duties. There are principles that determine when a rule or standard or promise, etc. is binding.

The no change thesis says that normative principles cannot change. The challenge of arbitrariness may be the most powerful argument for the no change thesis. Consider the possibility that if people or their circumstances change, governments have duties that they do not have absent that change. Assume that governments do not have the right, let alone a duty, to place people in administrative detention; and that someone claims

C: if humans become subject to condition X governments have a duty to place those who have the condition in administrative detention.

We may well reserve judgement, because, we would say, it all depends on what that condition is. Compare the following:

(1) If humans become subject to deadly infectious diseases that manifest themselves only after long periods of undetectable incubation governments have a duty to place those who had contact with people who have the disease in administrative detention.

(2) If all people start losing the sight in their left eye during their 50th year governments have a duty to detain people on the day before their 50th birthday.

We are more likely to believe that (1) is correct than that (2) is. Why? Because we can imagine a normative principle that validates (1), for example:

(3) Governments have a duty to prevent the spread of deadly diseases,

but we find it hard to think of a normative principle that would establish that (2) is true. In the absence of a normative principle to explain and justify why the change makes a normative difference we reject the thought that it does. It renders the putative normative change resulting from the non-normative one arbitrary. And we do not believe that normative principles can be arbitrary.

But does the absence of a normative principle explaining it render the normative change stated in (2) arbitrary? Saying that it is arbitrary assumes that there ought to be an explanation of a certain kind and it does not exist. Without that assumption, the change is merely unexplained, not arbitrary. Why assume that there ought to be an explanation? And why assume, as I do, that there ought to be a normative explanation (i.e. an explanation where a semantically irreducible normative proposition is among the explanans)?

That second point is crucial, for obviously there can be other explanations. That the loss of sight in the left eye is due to a new mutation that has spread quickly and affects all humans may explain it, but it is not the kind of explanation that can explain the duty it is supposed to have generated. That if the government interns people before their 50th birthday there will be fewer people with limited eyesight at large is a consequence of observing the duty that (2) attributes to governments, but it can hardly be said to explain that duty. By way of contrast, that if governments observe the duty claimed in (1) the spread of deadly diseases will be halted, is a consequence of observing that duty, and it does seem to explain why governments have the duty. It explains that by connecting the duty asserted in (1) with the one asserted in (3), subsuming (1) under (3), and thus explaining (1) in the required way, it establishes that (1) provides a way of fulfilling the duty stated in (3).[2]

The example generalizes, and suggests that the availability of normative explanations is in the nature of the normative. Furthermore, their availability is a feature of the normative for reasons that do not concern 'our' problem of normative change. It is possible to explain the existence of any normative condition because it is in the nature of the normative that (a) it is intelligible to those to whom it applies (if it is a duty, it is intelligible to those subject to it, etc.), and (b) that intelligibility is communicable, in that normative conditions can be explained. Why?

2. The Normative Intelligibility Thesis

The first condition—intelligibility—first, beginning with what it is not: it should not be confused with intuitionism, at least not if intuiting that p is a transparent mental state (i.e. one of whose presence one cannot fail to be aware) whose presence makes it certain that p (or some variant of this condition). I will suggest that there is 'a feel' as part of finding something intelligible, but the same experience is part of mistakenly thinking that one

[2] I take a principle B to be subsumed under another principle A if either A entails B or following B makes it likely that A will be followed or that its goal will be realized.

finds it intelligible. Nor is the intelligibility of duty-related principles, or the intelligibility of having the duties that they relate to, a feature of or a condition of believing that the principles are true or correct, or believing in the existence of the duties. One may believe that one has a certain duty because one was so advised by a reliable expert, or because that is the common view and, in the circumstances, it is unlikely that the common view is mistaken, and yet find it unintelligible that one has that duty.

Perhaps we must, if we believe that we have a duty, believe that it can be intelligible to us even though it is not currently intelligible to us?[3] Not quite: there can be, and there are, views that take at least some domains of normative considerations, often a religious domain, to be beyond human understanding. We can know our duties because we were commanded what to do, but it is not for humans to comprehend the point of those commands, etc. Of course, people who have such beliefs are mistaken and by implication they have mistaken views of the nature of normativity. So, perhaps we could say of those who have a correct view of the nature of normativity that if they believe they have a duty they believe that it can be intelligible to them, even if it is not currently intelligible. This may be right, but does it apply to (presumably) the vast majority of people who have no explicit view about the nature of normativity?

What the intelligibility thesis says is that the existence of a duty can be intelligible to those subject to it. We may assume that generally (but not that universally) those who entertain normative thoughts implicitly believe that. That is why we assumed that they are more likely to believe the duty stated in (1) than in (2) above—it is more likely to be intelligible, and they believe, at least implicitly, that normative conditions are intelligible.

Does it mean that false beliefs about duties are not intelligible to those who would have the duty if the beliefs were true? The thesis is about the intelligibility of the fact that we are subject to duties, and to other normative conditions. If it is right that generally people would not believe in a duty-related principle that is not taken to be intelligible to those subject to it, then when they do believe in such a principle they implicitly believe that it is intelligible to its subjects. Those believing in the principle may believe (rightly or wrongly) that they themselves are subject to it. In that case they generally also implicitly believe that the principle, if it applies to them, is intelligible to them.

[3] Remember that the intelligibility thesis claims only that duties, and other normative conditions, are intelligible to those subject to them.

But what is intelligibility and why assume that the normative domain is intelligible? First, I have to disambiguate two ways in which I have been using the term without drawing attention to the ambiguity. In some contexts 'intelligibility' refers to (1) a property of a duty or principle. In others, it is (2) a relation between the person subject to the duty or principle and the duty to which he is subject. A duty is intelligible (1) when it can be intelligible (2) to the people to whom it applies. Hence, my duty may be intelligible to me, or I may find it unintelligible while knowing that it is intelligible, meaning that it may become intelligible to me. This is a natural way of referring to matters, though not when they are referred to in one and the same statement. Put it in other words: I may understand why I am subject to my duty, or I may not understand that, while knowing that I can come to understand it. (See on the relation of intelligibility to understanding in Section 3 below).

The normative domain is one in which we react, actively, using our rational powers, to situations in light of a (correct or mistaken) understanding of the proper way to react to them in thought, action, or emotion. These reactions, let me underline, are not knee jerks, nor cases of being propelled (by desire, fear, anger, etc.), having lost one's self-control. They are our active responses, ones that we take to be appropriate, and that means that we see their point or believe that they have a point. We react as we do because we think that that is the way to react—we understand (or think we do, for we may be prey to self-deception, rationalizations, etc.) that these are the ways to react. That means that normative considerations (the considerations we thus react to) are intelligible to us. We see their point, or believe that they have a point, and except in cases in which we succumb to self-hate, self-debasement, and other such psychological motives, we approve of how we react, we stand by it, as it were, or when convinced that we were mistaken, we regret our reactions.

Talk of intelligibility and of seeing the point of a duty may sound mysterious. Does it mean more than knowing or believing that one has a duty? I think that it does. Intelligibility includes a measure of understanding, which consists to a large degree in ability to place the knowledge or belief in context, seeing its place in relation to much else, and an ability to extrapolate, to derive more beliefs from it (all being a matter of degree). But intelligibility also comes with a certain feeling that accompanies or colours the belief or knowledge that there is a duty (or right or normative reason, etc.). It is indicated by the common choices of terminology: a feeling that acting as one has a duty to do is a fitting act in the circumstances, a fitting or appropriate response to the situation, and other similar expressions. We can understand something without realizing that we do, while continuing to feel puzzled by it.

This may be due, for example, to a misunderstanding of what understanding consists in, wishing for some miraculous answer which does not make sense. When a principle or the having of a duty is intelligible to us our understanding is coloured by that feeling that things are fitting, or something like that. When we explain why we have a duty it is this feeling that we explain by justifying it. We explain why we are justified to feel that acting as we have a duty to is fitting, and/or appropriate, and why our belief has that colour. But the feeling is there independently of our ability to explain it. Perhaps it is easiest to perceive it when our conviction is strong even though we find it difficult to explain. Many people firmly believe that incest is wrong, but are less sure about why. The feeling of fittingness or appropriateness accompanying the belief is there to see, often rising to indignation when their belief is challenged, or to discomfort when they sense a doubt in it. That kind of colour or feeling accompanies any securely held normative beliefs (whether right or mistaken), though it is possible to know that one has a duty without that feeling, without seeing its point.[4]

3. The Explainability Thesis

This does not entail that we can communicate, that is, explain, why our reactions make sense. We may see the point of having a duty without being able to explain it. For example, some versions of intuitionism have it that while the normative is intelligible it cannot always be explained. It can only be intuited. We 'see' why there is a duty in such circumstances, and the intuition can be shared, but those who do not have it cannot be rationally convinced that this is so by providing them with an explanation of why the duty is there. If an explanation does not compel (on pain of irrationality) acceptance, it is no explanation—they contend.

I will not try to argue that the normative can always be explained. But I want to offer some observations that may make it more plausible that it can be, by pointing out some of the things that even good explanations cannot, or at any rate need not, accomplish.

For example, the thesis that the normative can be explained is not at odds with intuitionism. Explanations convince people qua explanations only if they understand them and realize that they do. Understanding an explanation (and the point is general, not being confined to explanations of the normative)

[4] I am not suggesting that it is exclusive to normative beliefs.

presupposes having certain capacities, rational, perceptual, emotional, and certain experiences. Little can be explained to the very young. And that is not because of the limits on what can be explained, but because of the limits of their abilities and experiences that are required to understand the explanation. Given the required capacities and experiences, and the strength of mind to question beliefs that have been instilled in one, a good explanation, once it is understood, convinces. It convinces because one sees the point. It makes one see why there is a duty in such circumstances, and so on. In other words, explanations, to work, require the capacity to see how they explain, to realize that they explain, and that may be the power to intuit, or at least a power to intuit.

Second, the availability of explanations does not guarantee agreement, not even if everyone is given an explanation. Explanations can be based on false assumptions, and there can be disputes regarding which explanations are good ones. In any case, many mistaken beliefs about duties, etc. may be, up to a point, intelligible. We cannot expect that if there are explanations they will, if offered, eliminate disagreement, not even in the long run.

Even when people agree about the duties that they have, and even when they understand why they have them, they may disagree about the explanations of those duties. Given diversity in abilities and experiences different explanations may succeed with different people.

Perhaps this indicates that the practical importance of explanations is not as great as is sometimes supposed. All the same the theoretical question whether there are always explanations for the existence of normative conditions, such as that someone has some duty, is significant.

Perhaps we can make progress by comparing the explainability thesis with a view fast becoming very popular, according to which there is a special kind of relationship, the grounding relationship, such that every true normative proposition is true in virtue of there being a ground for the condition it expresses or describes. Call this the grounding thesis. It may be thought to vindicate the explainability of the normative: these explanations, it may be said, consist simply in pointing to the ground of the condition explained. If one has a duty then there is a ground in virtue of which one has that duty, and that ground explains the duty.

I remain neutral about the grounding thesis. Even if true it does not establish that explainability is true. In part this is because there are likely to be true normative propositions whose truth does not depend on a ground. For example, I doubt that there are grounds that can explain why propositions of the following forms are true:

(1) Necessarily, if x is of value then it is possible for there to be some circumstances in which x's value is a reason to protect x's existence or to bring it about that x.
(2) Necessarily, if there is a reason to φ then it is possible[5] to φ for that reason.

More to our point, however, is the fact that the grounding thesis does not establish that the grounds are either knowable or explainable. Moreover, one may know that G is the ground of some duty D, without understanding why D, and without understanding why or how G is its ground. Example: the ground of my duty to φ may be my having promised to φ. I may know that, and still not understand why when I promise I have a duty. Given that knowing the ground for a duty entails neither having an explanation of why the duty exists, nor that one understands why it exists, the grounding thesis does not guarantee explainability without the support of an additional thesis about the explainability of grounds.

The two theses have different intellectual sources, though the theses are compatible and may turn out to converge. The grounding thesis as commonly presented is based on the thought that whatever is normatively binding must be so in virtue of something. That *something* is, or is related to, the essence of the normative condition. This is an objective pull, drawing on the constraints or the appeal of metaphysical theorizing. It contrasts with the subjective pull drawing us to the explainability thesis, subjective because it draws on the way normative considerations function in the life of those capable of appreciating them. This is the kind of consideration that argued for the intelligibility thesis: The normative is the domain of considerations by which we guide ourselves, intentionally, because we see the point of those considerations, because we understand, or think we do or can do, their point. The case for the explainability thesis derives from the same source.

The explanations the thesis is about are, needless to say, good explanations. Explanations are good if the person to whom they are addressed can come to understand what they explain by considering the explanation and being minded to follow it if it is sound. In other words, explanations are good explanations if they succeed with a qualified and willing addressee.

Various arguments converge to show that what we can understand can be understood by others, provided they have the required capacities and

[5] Meaning: it is possible for there to be circumstances such that when they obtain it is possible to φ for that reason.

experiences. Given that explanation consists in bringing the other to understand, it is plausible to think that often Mary can explain to John why there is a duty (or whatever) by pointing out to him the features that made her understand why there is a duty (or whatever). Sometimes the differences between John and Mary will undermine that possibility. But then Mary could adjust her explanation to those differences, and point to features that would have made her understand had she been in John's position. She can explain this to John, provided he has the required capacities and experiences. The pointing that explanations consist in can be purely verbal. But it need not be verbal or exclusively verbal.

These reflections do not, of course, establish that everything normative can be explained. They even suggest that not everything can be explained to everyone, because people's capacities and experiences, including their potential to expand, may be limited. But given the intelligibility thesis, and the connection between intelligibility and explainability, it is plausible to think that an appropriately qualified explainability thesis is true.

This is not the occasion to try a relatively precise formulation of the thesis. But one aspect of it is important to our purpose. Our capacity to understand and communicate is enhanced and limited by the concepts, both normative and non-normative, that we master. There is no necessary sequence by which we acquire them and other concepts that we use to explain and to understand them. I mean that we acquire both normative and non-normative concepts at an early stage of growing up, and we explain concepts of one category with the help of concepts of the other. There is no priority, let alone independence, of one of those categories relative to the other.

4. Does Explainability Require Subsumption?

The arbitrariness argument against change is:

(1) The coming into being of a new normative principle constitutes an arbitrary change unless it can be explained.
(2) An explanation must include reference to a principle that is already in force, which, together with additional factors, explains the new principle.
(3) Such an explanation shows the new principle to be an application of the existing principle to some of the circumstances that fall under it. It explains the new principle by subsuming it.

Subsumptive explanation is a capacious form of explanation. It includes, of course, explanation by generalization as, for example, explaining why Americans have a duty not to kill by invoking the principle that all humans have that duty and Americans are humans. But it also includes constitutive explanations, namely explaining why A is valuable by the fact that A, which is a constituent part of B, contributes to the value of B, and since B is valuable, all its constituent parts that contribute to its value are valuable.

Accepting the first premise I will challenge the others. But before I do that, two important concessions:

The first is that there are forms of intuitionism that escape this argument, by allowing that the new principle is intelligible but cannot be explained. Its validity is simply intuited. I will not consider that possibility.

Secondly, given that by their nature normative considerations are capable of guiding and evaluating conduct, character, etc., and that therefore they are accessible to the people whose conduct, etc. they can guide and evaluate, it is reasonable to assume that no normative change can retrospectively reverse the standing of a person's actions, emotions, character, etc. For example, no change of normative principles happening today can make something I did yesterday wrong, if it was not wrong when I did it. In retrospect, it can turn out to have been an unfortunate thing to do, etc. But it cannot become wrong or dutiful or virtuous if it was not so at the time. This is consistent with changes to our understanding of our moral conduct, and indeed of moral and other normative principles, changes in their understanding that occur due to the emergence of new normative principles. The new principles may provide new explanations of the older principles, relocating them in a deeper context.[6]

Back to the argument against basic normative change: Its third premise was that normative explanations are subsumptive explanations. But not all of them are. I will mention only one other kind of explanation: explanation based on argument by analogy. I treat it as a distinctive kind of argument. Possibly it should be treated as a family of related arguments; that makes no difference to our purpose. I take analogical arguments to be defeasible (non-monotonic) arguments consisting of four types of premises or groups of premises.

(a) *The Target:* Some *a* has a feature F.
(b) *The Similarity*: both *a* and something else, *b*, have a feature G.

[6] See J. Raz, 'Moral Change and Social Relativism', in E. F. Paul, F. D. Miller, and J. Paul (eds.), *Cultural Pluralism and Moral Knowledge* (Cambridge: CUP, 1994).

(c) *The Relevance: a* and *b* having G is relevant to *b*'s having F: Roughly, given the background, that they both have G makes it likely that if *a* has F so does *b*.
(d) *The Closure:* There is no reason to think that the relevance is undermined in the instant case.

The conclusion is then drawn that *b* has F.

There are also negative analogies: given that *a* is F and that while *a* is G, *b* is not-G, *b* is not-F either. Their additional premises are inevitably different, but these differences do not affect our concerns and I will not discuss them further.

The key to the success of an argument by analogy is in the relevance premise: does it support the conclusion, and does it do so to the degree required given the nature of the conclusion, and the circumstances in which we draw it?[7] Naturally, there have been various attempts to formalize that premise, or at least to make it much more detailed,[8] and I have no doubt that various kinds of analogical arguments can be made precise, and some can be formalized to make them suitable for use by deterministic robots. But I doubt that analogical reasoning itself is amenable to these kinds of explanations.

We are familiar with the fact that people's knowledge, including their 'knowledge how', extends beyond their ability to articulate what they know, let alone to explain it. This ability to exceed one's power to articulate enables people to reason on the basis of deductive arguments. Many who rely in their reasoning on deductive arguments do not have explicit knowledge of what deduction is, nor what rules of inference they rely on. Probably the vast majority of people do not have explicit knowledge of all the rules of inference they rely on (not even all the rules of deductive inference) in virtue of which their reasoning is valid. The ability to reason well does not depend on an ability to articulate, let alone to defend, the (sound) rules of inference one relies on. It is sufficient that one relies on them, and that it was not by chance that one did.

Needless to say, the same is true of analogical arguments. Analogical reasoning may be special in that its rules of inference cannot be completely articulated and formalized. That is, it seems plausible that our knowledge

[7] See Chapter 3 'Normativity: The Place of Reasoning' for an elaboration.

[8] For a helpful survey and bibliography see P. Bartha, 'Analogy and Analogical Reasoning', in Edward N. Zalta (ed.), *Stanford Encyclopedia of Philosophy* (Fall 2013 Edition) http://plato.stanford.edu/archives/fall2013/entries/reasoning-analogy/.

extends beyond our ability to articulate it and that it always will. It is a necessary feature of knowledge that those who possess it cannot articulate everything that they know. And it may be a necessary feature of knowledge that regarding the knowledge possessed by any living organism, it is impossible to articulate it exhaustively.[9]

If that is so then it is plausible to assume that there is a form of argument, or a family of arguments, regarding which our mastery of them exceeds our ability to articulate in detail, let alone with robotic detail, their rules of inference. It is plausible that analogical arguments are of that kind, and therefore have special importance as a way of vindicating and explaining knowledge claims, including explaining normative knowledge claims. They are arguments our mastery of which exceeds the possibility of exhaustively articulating their rules. For it appears that, while implicit knowledge, as we can call knowledge that we have but cannot articulate, may be relied on whenever we employ other forms of arguments too, analogical arguments are particularly suited to reasoning that relies on implicit knowledge, that is, reasoning when our limited ability to articulate what we know does not enable us to describe in detail the inferences we rely on. Even though various special categories of analogical argument may yield their secrets and be formalized, there are others that will not. Our ability to employ analogical arguments will remain dependent on our implicit knowledge.

It also appears that we rely heavily on analogical arguments in political and ethical thought and discussion, and that makes them relevant to our concern here today. For analogical arguments do not 'work' by subsumption. The explanations they provide do not presuppose a more general existing principle. They explain not vertically but horizontally, metaphorically speaking. They thus remove the arbitrariness argument against the possibility of basic normative change.

5. The Possibility of Change (a First Go)

Removing this one objection to basic normative change does not establish that it occurs. Nor is it my aim to show that it does. Rather, mine is the more

[9] None of this implies that there is anything we know but cannot articulate. The claim is merely that we cannot articulate everything we know.

modest ambition: to illustrate that it can happen. Those who will be convinced of that will not, I predict, doubt that it has happened and will happen again.

The intelligibility and explainability theses point the way. We are comfortable with the thought that there are limits to our normative understanding and that changes in the world can change them. But, can changes in the world not only improve our normative understanding, but change the normative principles themselves? They can, seems to be the answer.

Suppose that research into dark matter reveals to us the existence of a condition we were unaware of, and indeed were unable to comprehend before the possible existence of dark matter could be thought of, and its mysteries cracked open by science. These scientific developments came along with mastery of new concepts. One of them, let's designate it 'akatem', refers to a condition that is dangerous to humans. So now we know that we should not expose people to akatem. This is new knowledge, but not a new principle. It is a simple application of the principle against endangerment. Morality did not change. Our understanding of what conforming to it involves has improved.

Now imagine that many things change in the dark matter age. Conditions of life, the economy, and technology change radically in unimaginable ways. Among other things a new form of human association, which they call 'demte', emerges, radically different from any form of friendship or other associations we can imagine today. It defies the distinction between public and private interactions, between a one-on-one relationship and group relations, etc. Demte-related reasons are, naturally, entirely new: when it is desirable to form demtes, when it is better to avoid them, how to conduct oneself towards demte associates and how to conduct oneself towards others, in matters that affect demte associates, and much else.

By hypothesis, demte is (at least potentially) a good form of association among people. And again, by hypothesis, the reasons or duties involved in it are no mere application of very general principles that we know, or can know. Rather, they constitute independent principles. Their emergence constitutes a basic moral change.

The considerations canvassed so far present no objection to the possibility of moral change of this kind. It can meet the conditions of intelligibility and explainability so long as its explanation is not by subsumption. And it can meet the condition that there should not be a retroactive change in the valence of actions and events, because it only applies to events and actions occurring since the arrival of the age of dark matter, for only then did demte associations become possible.

6. Does Explainability Require a Pre-existing Principle?

This concludes my outline of an argument for the possibility of basic moral change, based on rejecting the third premise of the argument from arbitrariness, the premise that took all normative explanations to be subsumptive explanations. As indicated above, there is another way to challenge the argument from arbitrariness: its second premise too is misguided. It stated that a normative explanation of a new principle must include reference to a principle that is already in force, or at any rate, one that is in force before that new principle becomes valid.

To establish that it is mistaken I will explore an objection to the preceding analogy-based argument. The objection fails, but it reveals the mistake underlying the second premise.

The objection is that I was wrong to assume, as the preceding argument does, that analogical arguments are an independent kind of argument. In fact, they are valid only in cases where both sides of the analogy are subsumed under a more general principle. Admittedly in one way analogical arguments can be independent of a subsumptive explanation. One can master them and reliably follow them without knowing the more general principle on which their validity depends. This makes them helpful and important. But *au fond*, analogical arguments are valid only if there are valid subsumptive arguments supporting the same conclusion. Therefore, their reach is no greater than that of subsumptive arguments, and therefore they cannot vindicate the possibility of basic normative change if subsumptive arguments cannot do so.

We can examine the objection by applying it to the case of demte. The previous argument assumed that demte-reasons are real, binding reasons for they are validated by analogy. Perhaps that analogy is cogent only if there is also an argument by subsumption validating demte-reasons. For example: If demte can be explained by analogy with other phenomena, let's say by partial analogy with C on the one hand complemented by partial analogy with E on the other hand, then there is a higher principle of which C, E, and demte are instances, and that vindicates the analogies. This higher principle explains demte by subsumption. Therefore, either the emergence of demte-related reasons is not a basic normative change, because the more general principle is valid prior to demte's emergence, or demte-related reasons are not valid. Possibly, the more general principle was not valid prior to the emergence of demte-related reasons, therefore we have no sufficient reason to think that they are valid.

Why doubt that the more general principle was valid prior to the emergence of demte-related reasons? On its face it is already valid, for it applies not only to demte-reasons (which have no instances yet) but also to C and to E conditions, and they can already obtain. However, it is possible, and the argument does not deny, that the more general principle can be known only to people who have concepts that do not yet exist, concepts that will emerge in the dark matter age.[10] In that case there is as yet no such valid principle; it will be a valid principle only once the concepts required to state and to understand it have come into being. That much is established by the intelligibility and explainability theses.[11] True, we are not subject to demte-reasons, but we are subject to reasons relating to C and to E, and the putative higher principle governs them too. Therefore, if valid now it applies to us now. But if it is not intelligible and explainable to us now then it does not apply to us now. Given that we do not know that it is intelligible to us now we are not warranted to conclude that it is valid now.

So far—the objection, or a version of the objection. What are we to make of it? Not much, I am afraid. It ignores the fact that while we debate and argue about the validity of various analogical arguments, we do not rely on ignorance of a subsumptive explanation to doubt them. Rather we use some analogies to undermine others, expressing our acceptance of them as an independent form of argument. We may of course be mistaken. But the inescapability of implicit knowledge and the intelligibility and explainability theses point to an unavoidable gap between what can be explained by subsumption, which relies on knowledge that can be explicit, and what can be explained by analogical arguments that rely on knowledge that is inescapably implicit.

The objection has to be rejected. But it draws attention to the possibility that as demte relations emerge so does a principle (which at that point is intelligible and explainable), which explains demte-reasons by subsumption. Suppose that people of the dark matter era do not have an analogical argument to explain demte-reasons, but they do have a subsumptive explanation of those reasons, though that explanation depends on a new principle, one that

[10] Even if the principle can be stated using concepts already available to us, possibly its validity cannot be explained at the moment for its explanation requires concepts that we do not and cannot have, concepts that will evolve only in the dark matter age.

[11] I am aware of course of a convention in some areas of philosophy to think of concepts as a-temporal, i.e. to deny that they have a history. This may be a useful fiction, or if you prefer, a useful stipulative concept, which is a close cousin of concepts, as we know them. There is no need to dispute the legitimacy of either concept of concepts.

employs new concepts. Can a new principle that does not refer back to prior principles be valid, and thus validate demte-reasons? We know that it must be explainable. But possibly its explanation can relate only to other new reasons and principles. It will have to be consistent with all other valid principles, including those previously valid (though it may conflict with them). To that extent its vindication relates to other principles, including those that are already valid. But must its vindication relate to all of them? Some people think so. In recent times, for example, Dworkin made that claim.[12] I know of no reason to believe that that is so. Absent such reasons we may be able to endorse a form of radical value pluralism, namely one that allows for the possibility of groups of valid normative principles that are intelligible and explainable and relatively independent of (some) other groups of principles. If that is right then the second premise may also have to be rejected.

Admittedly, even given radical value pluralism, the likelihood that there will be no explanation of the supposed new principle explaining demte-reasons that refers to existing principles or considerations is small. It is likely that it will enjoy supportive analogies with existing normative conditions. What is unlikely may still be possible.

7. Can the Possibility of Change Be Explained?

Radical normative change is possible. My illustration of its possibility derives from a specific, though very common and extremely important, social phenomenon that I will call 'normative social forms'. Some social actions, relationships, or conditions cannot exist without their participants having appropriate concepts to mark them. That is, people can perform those actions (give a gift) or be in those conditions (be married) only if they know what they are doing or what condition they are in. They need not have our concepts, but they must have some appropriate concepts. For example, 'gift' may be a very general concept that does not exist and is not available in all cultures. But people may have specific gift-related concepts and they give gifts only when they intend to perform an action that instantiates one of them (e.g. a thank-you gift, a wedding-gift). Typically, these concepts are normative in that by

[12] R. M. Dworkin, *Justice for Hedgehogs* (Cambridge, MA: Harvard UP, 2011). In J. Raz, 'A Hedgehog's Unity of Value', in W. Waluchow and S. Sciaraffa (eds.), *The Legacy of Ronald Dworkin* (Oxford: OUP, 2016) I explained how he failed to make good that claim.

their nature, their instances imply certain reasons towards their occurrence: gifts are appropriate or inappropriate, whereas chairs, watches, earthquakes, etc. do not essentially imply such reasons. Moreover, and that explains their normativity, these concepts are used to refer to, and to describe, aspects of cultural values, that is, values that are the products of culture, values whose existence is made possible by social practices that include actions done in the knowledge of the normative significance of those cultural practices (though not necessarily as practices). Marriages, friendships, money are examples. Some of these normative institutions (perhaps money) have only instrumental value. Others bring with them new values. There was no marriage before the social institution of marriage emerged. Without it the value of marriage could not be realized. Moreover, it is plausible that one could not know of or understand these new values before they came into being, that is, before instances of them became possible. Only once they are in existence could we think of them and realize either that they can be subsumed under a principle that explains them, or that they can be explained through analogies.

These social forms are normative, in that their existence generates new reasons for conduct for those who engage in them (and for everyone, regarding them and the people who engage in them). They are, when valid, intelligible and explainable in the usual way. Normally they will be explained either by subsumption or in some other way, for example by analogy, involving reference to already valid principles or other social forms.

The fact that so much of our life is embedded in the normative social forms, which evolve over time, often by transforming previously existing normative social forms, explains value pluralism and the emergence of new moral principles, with new moral rights, duties, and virtues that are intelligible as they can be explained by analogy, or by subsumption under new principles that emerge with the emergence of these social forms.

The emergence of new social forms out of earlier ones suggests that in some respects the mere applications of existing principles can resemble the emergence of completely new principles. Perhaps the distinction between mere application of the old and the emergence of the new is not all that important. The newness of some mere applications is as great and as significant as the emergence of a completely new principle, and the difficulty that people have in understanding it may be as great as the difficulty in understanding a new principle. And that is something worth learning, for it redirects our attention from wondering whether basic change is possible to trying to understand the significance of the emergence of principles, whether new or applications of existing ones, which could not have been known about or vindicated independently of the social changes that brought them about.

Part Two: Objections and Implications

The objections to be examined here are not so much objections to the arguments above as direct objections to the very possibility of basic normative change. But they are radically different from the objection of arbitrariness which was discussed in Part One. That objection arose out of reflection on the nature of normativity, which suggested that intelligibility and explainability seemingly imply that change, were it possible, would be arbitrary. The objections that follow are, if you like, external in origin. They aim to show that normative change is incompatible with fundamental features of reality or with well-established doctrines. I have no doubt that some will take this to make them particularly powerful objections. But the opposite view is also possible: they are weaker, because the argument can be reversed. One can take the possibility of normative change to constitute an objection to the views and doctrines that are incompatible with it. This role reversal was not available, at least not in simple form, in Part One. The possibility of role reversal sets a limit to the discussion of this part. It cannot be developed into a full-scale examination of the doctrine that leads to the objections. All the chapter can do is point to incompatibilities, where there are such, and hint at the implications of the possibility of normative change. It will have to remain a rough and informal discussion.

8. Propositions

To start with an objection to everything I have written here: I took normative principles to be true propositions with explanatory potential of the phenomena they are about. That makes it plausible to think of a radical change as a change in the truth value of a proposition that is a principle if true. But, the objection goes, propositions cannot change their truth value. They are a-temporal, or if one thinks of them as temporal then they exist and possess their truth value always.

It is convenient to take moral principles, and any other principles, if not to be propositions at any rate to be expressible in propositions, so that necessarily any principle is expressed by one proposition (or, to allow forms of vagueness: sets of propositions). The problem can be avoided, at least to some degree, if we understand principles to be true propositions that meet some additional conditions: I introduced one such condition explicitly: principles have explanatory relevance, and another condition implicitly: propositions can be known by those to whom they apply. Let's call putative principles, that is, ones presented as principles, but which are not necessarily principles, valid principles if they are true, explanatorily relevant and knowable by their subjects. A proposition can be a valid principle at one time and not at another if it has explanatory relevance and is knowable by its subjects at one time but not at another. I assume that it is true at both points in time. Its status as a (valid) principle varies, though its truth does not.

That may be part of the solution. But the considerations put forward above suggest that we should go further and deny that the truth value of propositions cannot change. True, some think that propositions are a-temporal, or that at any rate it is impossible for them to be true at one time and not true at another. That does not reflect the way propositions are commonly understood. We do understand the proposition that John was the best tennis player five years ago but is so no longer, as entailing that (the proposition that) John is the best tennis player is no longer true. It is best to avoid verbal disputes. The concept of a proposition whose truth can change, meaning that the truth of some types of propositions can change, as well as the concept of a proposition whose truth cannot change, have been explored in some detail, and there are accounts of the logical properties of each of them. Both have a reasonable claim to represent what one says when one asserts something, that is, to express the content of what can be asserted. After all, that notion, of what one asserts or can assert, is itself subject to the same ambiguities and indeterminacies as the notion of a proposition.

Some would be happy to allow that there is a concept of a proposition that admits that there are propositions whose truth value is neither a-temporal, nor unchangeable, that they may have a truth value at one point in time and not have it at another, but they claim that everything expressed in such propositions can also be expressed by propositions whose truth value is a-temporal or just necessarily unchangeable. For example, it can be argued that if there is a condition, C, on which the truth of a proposition, P, depends then there is a proposition: P only if C, that is, a-temporal or necessarily of an unchanging truth value. One way of understanding the thought that moral principles can change involves denying that all propositions with a changeable truth value can be expressed as, or are logically equivalent to, propositions with unchangeable truth value. So, if there is a case for thinking that normative principles can change there is a case for rejecting the thesis that all propositions can be expressed by a-temporal propositions.[13]

The temporal character of a proposition may manifest itself in being capable of being true at some times, and false or neither true nor false at other times. But the temporality of propositions may be due to other factors as well. One would be that the proposition does not exist at all times. If so then possibly its existence is time bound, though its truth need not be. Propositions that exist may be true (in a sense that is not time-relative) but that is relevant or assertible only when they do exist. Alternatively, and less problematically, the proposition is true whenever it exists, and when the proposition does not exist it has only conditional properties, properties it would have were it to exist. The fact that concepts have a history, and that propositions may have concepts among their essential constituents, shows that propositions have a temporal dimension, and that the content of temporal propositions cannot always be expressed by a-temporal propositions.[14]

9. Conditionalization

Some may be tempted to argue that we can have our cake and eat it: what attracts us to the thought that the basic moral principles can change is the supposition that (a) the content of moral principles depends on human nature, and (b) human nature is contingent and changeable. Hence, it may appear that moral principles are also changeable. But the conclusion is a non-sequitur. Suppose that one fundamental aspect of human nature is H1 and that the moral principles we have, call them P1, are valid only if H1. Suppose that human nature changes, and that H1 is replaced by H2, and therefore the moral principles that bind humans are now different, call them P2. It does

[13] We have discussed matters using 'proposition' in the sense that allows for the possibility that some propositions can change their truth value. Normative principles are (among other things) truths about the relations that they express. The principle that gratitude is a source of duty is a true proposition about the relations between gratitude and duty. That is, it is a principle if and only if and because the relationship holds. This leaves open the question what comes first, the principle or the relationship, or which is more fundamental, at least when that question is understood epistemically, or as a question about the order of understanding. E.g. if the only way to establish that the relationship exists is by *reductio* of the proposition that it does not, then the relationship comes epistemically first. Similarly, if the only way to explain, to make sense of the existence of the relationship, is through explaining the truth of the proposition then the principle comes first in the order of understanding.

[14] If normative principles can change then they are not necessarily true (or, if validity rather than truth makes them principles, not necessarily valid). But they can still be relatively necessary, e.g. relative to the laws of nature.

not follow that any proposition changed its truth value, nor that basic moral principles changed. Rather what follows is that the basic moral principles were (always, or a-temporally): If H1 then P1 and if H2 then P2. What changed is that previously when humans had an H1 nature P1 principles applied and now, with their H2 nature, they are subject to P2, but that is not due to a change of any principles, only that principles that were inapplicable before are applicable now and vice versa.

The difficulties with this approach can be brought to light by supposing that it is possible for humans to develop a sense perception they currently do not have, and indeed one that no animal currently has. We do not know what it will be, if it will be, and we cannot know what it will be, as it will be a new kind of sense. We lack a concept by which to refer to that sense, and can refer to it only by expressions such as 'the hitherto unknown sense', which tell us nothing about it other than that it is a perceptual sense. It is possible, though we do not know that for sure, that its emergence will make us subject to moral principles that we are not subject to at the moment. Needless to say, we have no clue, and can have no clue, about their content.

The question is whether given this situation there is something we are ignorant about, something we do not know. It is not something that can be known, but so are many truths. It may be impossible now to know whether there was a speck of dust on top of my desk lamp five minutes ago. Principles, however, are not like specks of dust. They are essentially knowable. They are guides to thought and action, and while they may be unknown, which leads us to look for them, it seems odd to think that they can be unknowable. In what way are they guides for thoughts and action if unknowable?

Perhaps, however, principles can be temporarily unknowable. Or, they can be unknowable under some conditions provided that they are knowable under others. If we turn our attention from the future to the past, we can entertain the thought that there were principles that applied to people who lived in very different circumstances and do not apply to us. Such principles may be unknowable to us. Perhaps they can be unknowable for the very same reasons we are considering: perhaps some people in some remote circumstances possessed mental capacities, perceptual or other, that we do not, and we have no idea what they were, or what they could have been, as they are not some variant of capacities we are familiar with in our or other species, but are entirely unlike anything we know of and in ways that we have no idea about. We cannot deny that there were such principles, after all they applied to the people who had those capacities.

And we have no reason to think that these principles do not exist anymore. They do not apply anymore and cannot be known anymore, but that is, given our assumptions, possible.

However, there is, and not only in this case, an asymmetry between past and future. One way of thinking about it is to focus on the concepts involved. The arrival of a new sense will bring with it a new concept, related to that sense as the concept of eyesight is to the sense of sight. Concepts exists once their instantiation is possible. They may apply to nothing anymore, but that does not mean that we ceased to have the concept. If it becomes unknowable this is contingent on loss of evidence that would enable us to understand it. However, a possible but not yet existing concept is necessarily unknowable, until it comes into existence, if it does.

10. Normative Autonomy

I am not assuming a unity of explanations. That is, I am not assuming that all the sound explanations there are can be thought of as parts of one comprehensive explanation, using the same methodological principles, of everything that can be explained. I see no objection to the view that there are radically and irreducibly different forms of explanation, such that there is no explanation of how they all relate to one another, other than by pointing to what they are and are not. We can call this the assumption of radical explanatory pluralism. I assume that the truth or falsehood of that assumption can be known.

I am also assuming what I will call the autonomy of the normative. That is, the chapter proceeds on the assumption that we have ways of referring to normative properties that make possible knowledge of the conditions under which they apply, and explanations of why they apply or fail to apply and of the normative consequences of their application, which essentially and non-redundantly employ normative concepts that refer to or apply to normative properties and are not reducible to any non-normative propositions or explanations.[15]

[15] Normative autonomy is consistent with some forms of so-called ontological reduction of normative properties. I will not consider such possibilities in this chapter. Furthermore, the 'normative concepts' I refer to should not be identified with so-called thick concepts or terms, a heterogeneous category, only some of which refer to normative properties.

The autonomy thesis, if correct, both falls short of and reaches beyond what may be called epistemic autonomy. It falls short of it because it leaves open the possibility of knowledge of the conditions for the instantiation of normative properties based on non-normative evidence. It even allows for knowledge of normative propositions by beings who are incapable of understanding some or all normative properties, except possibly in partial and limited ways. Such people may acquire normative knowledge by imitation—possibly the way most young humans acquire some normative knowledge well before they reach any understanding, and the way some people with depleted mental capacities retain moral knowledge even after losing the ability to understand it.

The autonomy thesis reaches beyond epistemic concerns. It is about explanations of the normative presupposing normative properties and deploying normative concepts expressing them. In this respect, some would regard it as having ontological implications. But here objections are possible. Why assume that explanations of the normative relate to normative properties? Take a familiar example:

- [Conclusion] John has a strong reason to jump out of the window!
- Why?
- [Premise 1] Because he will die by fire, if he does not.

This appears to be a good explanation. The autonomy thesis implies that it is incompletely stated; that anyone who takes it to be adequate implicitly includes in it an unstated reference to a normative property, unstated because it is obvious and needs no explicit mention. Perhaps something like:

- [Premise 2] It would be better for him to stay alive.

However, the objection goes, Premise 2 is not really an invocation of a normative property. It is tantamount to affirming that the explanation is complete, that the specified facts are indeed a reason for the indicated reaction, etc. In other words, some version of a buck-passing (or, perhaps, of an appropriate attitude) account of value would be invoked here. So, perhaps Premise 2 can be rephrased as something like:

- [Premise 2'] There are no other facts bearing on what he should do.

A familiar reply is that the fact that an action has some value properties not only indicates that certain reasons follow, it explains why they follow.

Buck-passers are inclined to say that 'This action is good'[16] is too thin a remark to have any explanatory power. It merely states that the action has some (non-normative) feature that is a reason to perform it. On this view, not only is it always true that if one has reason to perform an action then there is some good in the action, it is also true that whenever one has reason to perform an action that is because there is some good in the action. But the second claim is false to our understanding of such claims. The fact that there is a reason to perform some action establishes that there is some value in that action, making the first claim true. The question is, however, in virtue of what is there such a reason (and therefore, what makes this action good)?[17] It may be because the action is good in itself (and not merely because there is reason to perform it) or a constituent element in something good (e.g. a movement in a beautiful dance) or that it will produce something good. In such cases it is plausible to say that saying that the action is good is saying that it has some features (say, some consequences) that are reasons to perform it. But not all reasons are of this kind: that I promised to do something is a reason to do it, and that is consistent with the fact that giving the promise was bad and regrettable, and that the act of keeping it has no other merit than being the keeping of that promise. In this kind of case it would be wrong or misleading to say that one has a reason to perform the act because it is good. It follows that saying that one has a reason to ϕ because ϕ-ing is good is informative in a way that buck-passing does not allow: it tells us something about the character of the explanation of the reason we have, it has a character that not all fact-producing reasons have.

However, the most important failure of buck-passing accounts is in dealing with other value properties. Suppose the reason for some action, for example, refusing to answer a question whether John was in Knox Street on the first of May, is that answering the question would be disloyal to a friend. That entails that there is some good in the action (the refusal). It does so by specifying what good that is: the good of loyalty to friends. If buck-passers take this to mean that my telling whether John was in Knox Street is bad they are missing the gist of the matter, and ignore the explanatory power of the value statement. They cannot retreat to saying that they mean that answering the question is bad in the special way in which telling about a friend is bad. To say that is to give up on being a buck-passer. It admits that there are different values which

[16] Where it means 'this has some value', and not all occurrences of 'good' do mean that, not all are normative.

[17] Note that 'action' refers to what is sometime called action-type, i.e. generally one can perform an action more than once, and others can perform the same action one does.

differ in ways other than that they are reasons for action. Worse than that, this way of understanding my situation (a) employs irreducible value concepts, namely that of telling and of friendship, and (b) still does not get to the value that actually motivates me: loyalty, as not all telling on friends constitutes disloyalty, and there are other ways of being disloyal than telling.

These reflections do not prove the autonomy thesis, but they lend it some support.

11. Queer Properties

I have been defending normative autonomy in this chapter because the chapter presented an explanation of normative change in terms of changing normative properties in a way that implies normative autonomy, or at any rate a way that would encounter additional difficulties if there is no normative autonomy. However, the implied realism about the existence of normative properties encounters the charge that they are peculiar properties, the charge whose current form originates with John Mackie. There are various ways in which the charge can be understood and developed, and I will present my own understanding of it. The gist of it is that normative properties are not connected to reality because (1) their instances do not interact causally with the rest of reality; (2) their existence cannot be explained in the way that we explain other aspects of the reality; (3) if they are properties of objects or events it would be a mystery how they can move people to act as they are supposed to do; (4) they give the impression of real properties because within groups with shared culture there are conventions that govern discourse about them, and members of those groups by and large observe those conventions, with the result that it appears as if discourse purporting to refer to these properties can be true or false, whereas in fact it is merely conforming to the conventions or failing to do so.

Briefly, and admittedly inconclusively, a few comments addressing these points in reverse order. (4): As this chapter argues for the possibility that normative principles can change, and illustrates such changes by appeal to cultural changes, the allegation that if normative properties exist they depend on social conventions is not exactly an objection. True, they are not, for the most part, the product of conventions[18], but—and this is the whole point—they are dependent on social practices. Is there any objection to the possibility

[18] Though see A. Marmor, *Social Conventions: From Language to Law* (Princeton: Princeton UP, 2009) Chap. 3, on deep conventions.

of properties whose existence and instantiation depend on social practices, properties without which we would not have institutions and their products such as money, intellectual property, novels, or poetry?

(3): As an objection this point (it is a mystery how they move people to act) is out of place. It amounts to no more than denial of the existence of normative properties. That they provide normative reasons is the essential feature of normative properties. And normative reasons are essentially capable of moving people to action, thought, emotions, or imaginings. So, we should take the point not as an objection but as a question: normative properties are peculiar and call for explanation. The explanation, or explanations, come in many parts. Some explain the relations between reasons and actions or beliefs or emotions or imaginings, others explain the specific character of each normative property.

(2): The second part of the peculiar properties objection is, at first blush, not an objection. Why should these properties be explained in the same way, using the same patterns of explanations, etc. as others? If we assume that all explanations have the same character we are of course in trouble. It turns out that non-normative properties are peculiar because they cannot be explained in the way that normative properties are explained. So, the objection must be taken to be more radical: there are no possible explanations of normative properties. The issues raised are too numerous to be even mentioned here. But just to indicate the direction of travel let me divide them into two types: disputes regarding specific purported normative properties, and disputes about the more general possibility of there being any normative properties. The two feed into each other. Think of the explanation of specific properties first: Of course, not all purported normative properties exist. Some are illusory. The question is whether any can exist, and be intelligible. One possible argument proceeds by (a) criticizing all the explanations of all normative properties that have been so far offered, and (b) showing that their failure is not that they are incomplete, but that they are in principle no good, and (c) that their failure of principle is of the same kind in all cases. That, perhaps with one or two additions, would constitute an inductive argument to the conclusion that no explanation of any purported normative property can succeed. I detect nothing that gives one hope in the success of such an argument.

A more common alternative is to argue: (a) True, we know that (in certain contexts) people use arguments about some normative properties that carry conviction even though, needless to say, not always with their intended audiences. This may be thought to point to a tendency for views to converge when those who hold them are well informed. More importantly, a larger degree of convergence exists regarding an understanding of what constitutes a good argument. However, these contexts are ones where speaker and audience share a common culture and are simply relying on unexamined common assumptions and conventions. (b) Beyond such islands bound by local conventions there is no sign of agreement or of a tendency to converge on a common understanding of what constitutes good argument. That means, the objection goes, that there are no objective standards of judgement regarding the existence or character of normative properties, and no possibility of such standards. Hence, they do not exist.

In assessing this and related arguments it is important to trace the causes of disagreement. For example, it seems to me that many of them derive from non-normative disagreements, especially from disagreements about matters derived from, or being part of, religious outlooks, but which are not themselves normative. Belief in miracles, and the use to which such belief has often been put, is an example. Non-normative beliefs that are not necessarily involved with any religious outlook are also at the root of some normative disagreements. Racist and homophobic views are often nourished by ignorance, entrenched by deep psychological disinclination to correct mistaken beliefs about these matters. When this is the source of normative disagreements it may be taken to cast doubt about the possibility of non-normative properties. More plausibly these sources of persistent disagreements show that the significance of disagreements may have been exaggerated.[19] Another common source of disagreement is of interest here. Many disagreements are sustained by mistaken theoretical views about the nature of normative facts. For example, I have long argued that indeterminacy and incommensurability are very common within the normative domain. Many people think that that is necessarily false. This view inclines people who see reason to believe that their own way of life is legitimate to believe that ways of life that are incompatible with theirs are not legitimate, because they reject as necessarily false the correct view that both are legitimate.

One ought, and it is possible, to explore in detail these sources of disagreement, and others like them—like them in that their explanation refutes the argument from disagreement by showing that its sources are not due to there being no normative properties, and do not cast doubt on their existence.[20]

[19] I am assuming that the claim that regarding objective matters there is a convergence towards agreement at the end of inquiry, either as a mark of objectivity or in any other way, has been effectively criticized, mostly as empty, and need not be considered in this context.

[20] Arguably, if people, perhaps the people of some society, share fundamental theoretical mistakes then we are in error theory terrain, for a shared understanding of the basic characteristics of normative claims at least partially determines their meaning. Be that as it may, the crucial point is that that does not mean that one is free to 'invent' a new meaning. The correct theoretical understanding is not

Remembering that various doubts about normative properties ignore the possibility that the existence and instantiation of normative properties are the product of social practices, the preceding comments soften the force of many arguments against the possibility of such properties. But they leave the core doubts (as I understand them) untouched. Doubts about the ability to explain normative properties, if they are real non-naturalistic properties, may derive from the claim that they are not connected with the rest of reality in a way that would enable us to refer to them, to come to know them, or, therefore, to explain them.

12. The Connectedness of Normative Properties

At first blush the charge that normative properties are peculiar because they are unlike anything about the world that we understand, and that the explanations that enable us to understand the world around us, namely scientific explanations, do not apply and cannot be used for explaining normative properties, is appealing to contemporaries who came to see the natural sciences as the only source of knowledge and understanding. As a matter of fact, few people understand the natural sciences beyond a rudimentary level and few people understand aspects of the world surrounding them through the natural sciences. Instead people trust (quite sensibly) that other people do know science and that the natural sciences explain aspects of reality to the satisfaction of those who understand them. On the other hand, all those people whose knowledge of the sciences is poor know and understand much of the world around them in ways that are independent of the sciences, and that the natural sciences do not explain, and this includes their understanding of themselves and other living beings, and of social practices and institutions, and the culture and economic opportunities, or lack of them, that those social practices and institutions sustain.

This is not to cast doubt on the importance of the natural sciences, nor to deny that psychological and social and economic phenomena benefit greatly from specialist expertise, even though it is not widely shared in the population. I am only denying that they are the sole sources of knowledge and understanding for human beings.

invented. It is determined by the same considerations that determine the theoretical underpinning of any area of common discourse. There are issues here of the possibility of providing a correct account of the theoretical underpinning of a range of phenomena when many people hold mistaken views on their character.

Nor is knowledge and understanding of normative phenomena unconnected to our knowledge and understanding of other phenomena. We have a fair grasp of the way normative phenomena depend on the existence of certain physical, psychological, social, and economic conditions, even though there is much more that remains to be discovered about these dependencies. Normative explanations of the conditions for the application of normative properties typically rely on a mix of normative and non-normative phenomena. And the normative properties of how things are in the world have a considerable impact on the way matters develop in the world, even if this impact depends on people realizing how things are normatively speaking.[21]

Throughout this chapter I have been relying on the assumption that there may well be distinct types of explanation and argumentation in different domains.

There is much that, so far as I can see, we do not understand. We do not know how far the explanatory methods we rely upon in various sciences and other domains can reach. We know that they have changed and were transformed in the past, and expect that they will further develop in the future. But we do not know how far they can extend, and therefore we do not know whether their future development will lead towards greater integration of the different types of explanations known to us today, or towards their absorption in more comprehensive methods of explanation. That means that we are ignorant of the reasons for the existence of different types of explanation, and their inter-relations. As a result, we are also in the dark as to the possibility and nature of conflicts between types of explanations. Various scientists are quick to declare that they have explained what was unexplained before about human conduct and more, and that their explanations replace the common, non-scientific explanations we rely on. Often enough such claims are exaggerated, and while the new scientific knowledge is valuable, it does not conflict with nor make redundant the types of explanations we had relied on before. There is much still to discover about these matters, and until we do, many of our views, including those expressed in this chapter, remain tentative and conjectural.

[21] And, to repeat: the impact of the way things are normatively is not the impact of how people are brought up, socialized, etc. Needless to say, people can understand normative principles, just as they can understand physics, only if they are brought up and socialized in certain ways. But as most values are cultural products, this increases the reliability of people's views of normative matters, rather than undermining it.

PART II
REASONS AND VALUES

5

Value and the Weight of Practical Reasons

Assuming that the value of options (actions, activities, or omissions) constitutes the proximate reason for pursuing them, I will advance some considerations that encourage doubts whether we have reason to promote or to maximize value. A proper argument would require establishing a negative: that there is no reason to promote value, or something like that. Raising doubts is less demanding: it consists in explaining some aspects of the relation between values and reasons that enable us to dispense with the doubtful thesis by illustrating alternative relations between values and reasons. Theses such as that value should be promoted bring with them a way of determining the strength of reasons (of two reasons the stronger is the one that promotes more value, etc.). Abandoning the thesis reopens the question of how to determine the strength of reasons. For the most part I will leave this task to another occasion. Starting by outlining briefly some of the assumptions and terminology I rely on and use,[1] I indicate the theoretical doubt about promotion of value, and proceed to outline a novel argument to show that the disagreement is not merely terminological. The argument establishes that even though the value of things and of activities is a reason to engage with them, there is a range of cases in which there is not always a reason to choose the best. The concluding section touches both on the limits of the argument and on its importance.

1. Background

We get to normativity and to reasons through an attempt to understand intentional actions. A central class of intentional actions, those that can be said to be actions done for a purpose, is marked by being explained in a special way, namely by reference to the agents' (normative) reasons for performing them, as they take them to be. Reasons in general are factors that

[1] I am relying on the account of these matters in J. Raz, *From Normativity to Responsibility* (Oxford: OUP, 2011). Among other things, it distinguishes various senses that can be given to the promotion of value thesis. Here I identify it informally only enough to identify the basic idea behind it.

The Roots of Normativity. Joseph Raz, Edited with an Introduction by Ulrike Heuer, Oxford University Press.
 DOI: 10.1093/oso/9780192847003.003.0006

explain (or that can be used to explain), or that are central parts of explanations.[2] 'Last year's severe cold was the reason for the poor crop this spring.' 'The reason he stammered was a sudden drop in his blood pressure.' Normative reasons are distinctive in that they can explain people's (and some other animals') reactions to certain factors in ways that depend on their awareness of these factors, and on taking those reactions to be appropriate because of these factors.[3] Normative reasons are marked by three features. First, the reactions they lead to can be assessed as successful or unsuccessful along a number of dimensions, one of which being that they can be rational or irrational. Second, when the reaction is successful, in that the factor that explains it really does make it apt, we can specify both the awareness of the factor and the content of that awareness as reasons that explain the reaction, only the second being a normative reason, whereas if the reaction is unsuccessful, if the factor does not exist or does not render the reaction appropriate, only belief in its existence is the reason for the reaction. And it is a reason in the explanatory sense only, though the explanation includes belief in a normative reason. Third, factors that render certain reactions appropriate are reasons for those reactions even if the agents are not guided by them (and possibly not even aware of them), provided that in principle they could be guided by them. Factors that meet this last condition are reasons, whether or not they explain any human reactions. They are normative reasons.

The formal, uninformative, answer to the question of what makes an action an appropriate reaction in a certain situation, is that in that situation there is a point to it, a value in taking it, some good done by taking it. Those who, as I do, take the value of things to constitute or provide reasons for action, allow themselves to stretch the way the term is understood in non-philosophical English. It is a natural stretch. Aspiring, as philosophers do, to very broad generalizations, we often have to use words beyond the context in which they are comfortable, for natural languages are resistant to words suitable for these very general and relatively context-independent uses.

It is also natural to use 'good' and 'better' interchangeably with 'valuable' and 'of greater value'. But here extra caution is needed. Not everything that is good has value, nor does what makes something good always make it valuable. Possibly, there is no value in good amoebas and what makes them good (presumably that they are good—i.e. free from defects—specimens of

[2] Not every factor that can be used to predict or retrodict is a reason, for not every such factor contributes to an explanation of what is predicted or retrodicted—e.g. epidemiological evidence can be a good predictor without explaining what it predicts.

[3] I will assume that reasons can belong to different ontic categories: facts, events, states, etc.

amoebas) does not makes them valuable.[4] Furthermore, generally, though not without exception, anything that is good is good because it is good of its kind. This hammer is a good tool because it is a good hammer, meaning that it excels as a hammer. I will return to the genre-dependence of goods later. The caution here is that there is great freedom in devising species or genres with their own autonomous, and possibly arbitrary or nonsensical, excellences. One may win a competition for the best green paint drinking. One does so if one is the best green-paint-drinker on the day. Is this really something of value? Possibly not. When I refer to what is good I will be referring to goods that are valuable. What is the difference between those that are and those that are not? There is no general operational test telling them apart. But they can be told apart because value is intelligible, so that what is of value and why can be explained.

Part of the explanation has to do with the fact that where the good of something is a value in it, it, that which is good can be good for a being whose good matters, is of value. A good car can be good for people, and a good banana can be good for a baboon, and these goods indicate something of value because the good of people and baboons matters, because the life of people and baboons is of value. Note that for something to be good for a being it need not be that its absence is bad for that being. Possibly that being would not exist, or would not be alive without the good we are talking about. If so, then the absence of the good is neither good nor bad for him. But its presence is good for him if it is one of the factors that makes, let us say, his life a good life for him to have, a life that is good for him.

Note that something may be good, of value, and indeed may be good for a being (whose good matters) and yet there may be no reason for that being to engage with it, or to protect it, etc. I will assume that the lives of both people and blackbirds are valuable, but that people do and blackbirds do not have rational powers. Certain conditions are good for blackbirds; others are good for people. It is possible to explain what they are and why they are good, including explaining why the life of these beings matters, is of value (if it is). And we can reflect on the ways natural processes, ones that do not involve blackbirds or people realizing that some conditions are good for them, tend to secure these good conditions. We regard these conditions as reason-giving

[4] Nor are they in any interesting ways conditionally valuable. True, for the purpose of some experiments, let us say, good amoebas are valuable. But then for the purpose of some other experiments bad, i.e. defective, amoebas, or green amoebas, etc. are valuable. Another context in which 'good' is stretched beyond its meaning is in taking it that ϕ-ing is good if it is what one was commanded to do by a legitimate authority, or what one committed to do, etc.

when we think of them in relation to beings that have rational powers. So, the good of blackbirds may provide reasons for people (though not for blackbirds, who do not have rational powers). The good for blackbirds provides reasons for people when it can[5] guide (and thereby explain) their conduct. Generally speaking, it is good for agents to engage with the good. Hence, if something is good and someone can engage with it, that person has a reason to engage with it, and engaging with it is good for him or her in some respect (even if not overall).[6]

So at the core of reflection on normativity is an attempt to understand aspects of the life of persons, particularly their purposeful conduct, including actions, activities, and omissions. Purposeful conduct is conduct guided by what the agents take to be appropriate to their situation in the world. That is the thought expressed by the familiar saying that action aims at the good.

2. Weight of Reasons—Preliminaries

Let us turn now to the relative strength of normative reasons. Our rational powers, we said, enable us to recognize how things are and what conduct is appropriate. Using them, we guide our reactions, our conduct, in light of those believed reasons. It is natural to suppose that an inherent part of forming the view that a certain fact constitutes a reason for an action is forming a view as to how strong that reason is. Comparing the strength of the reasons for all available options, we conclude which options are supported by adequate, namely undefeated, reasons.

But this description distorts the way we reason about what to do. We can form the view that a certain fact is a reason for a certain option, without any view about its strength, or about the strength of reasons of that kind (life-saving reasons, etc.). We may even be able to determine which of our options is supported by a conclusive reason without any view of the strength of the reasons involved. This is clearly the case in the event (unlikely but perhaps possible) that we have several options, all but one of which serve no reason, and only one reason applies to the remaining option. We should take the

[5] Can in principle, meaning that opportunities to follow that consideration can exist.

[6] The last few sentences alert us to another complexity that I will generally ignore in this chapter: that an action is good in some respect is a reason to perform it. That one performed (or will perform) an action that one has an adequate reason to perform is good (in some respect) and that may provide a further reason, e.g. to the friends of that person, to encourage him, etc. I will generally write as if the value of an action is independent of the fact that it is one that one has a reason to perform.

option that is supported by a reason rather than any of those that serve no reason. Or, consider situations in which two reasons partially conflict: the agents have two options such that in taking one of them they would conform to one reason but not the other, whereas in taking the second option they would conform to both. Assuming no other reason bears on the situation, the agents have conclusive reason to take the second option, a conclusion not supported by any premise about the strength of the reasons.

The first example shows that so long as only one reason applies to a situation its weight is immaterial to its bearing on the situation.[7] The second example shows that even when several reasons apply, their weight is immaterial so long as they do not conflict. The examples also show that the determination of which reasons are conclusive depends on additional premises that are not themselves propositions stating reasons, for example that no other reason affects the matter, and that one completely conforms to reason by conforming to all the reasons that apply to one.

The examples illustrate another point: that a reason is conclusive (when it is) is not an inherent feature. It is relative to a situation, so that the same reason may be conclusive in one situation but not in another, and in each situation that depends on its relations with other reasons that apply in that situation.[8] A situation consists of an agent and options open to him or her at a given time. One feature of many situations is that with any single option there are several reasons for and several against it. We do colloquially sometimes refer to all the reasons for an option taken together as the reason for it, and to all the reasons against it, taken together, as the reason against it. It is convenient to do so in theoretical writings as well. The reason for an option is conclusive if the reasons for it have more weight, are better, more stringent, or stronger (and I will use all these terms and others interchangeably) than the reasons against it (where the loss of opportunities involved in taking that option is among the reasons against it). A reason for an option is undefeated if none of the available options is supported by a stronger, weightier, or better reason.[9]

[7] Jonathan Dancy has suggested that there are reasons that can be ignored for no reason. They are enticing reasons, but there is nothing amiss in just ignoring them (see J. Dancy, 'Enticing Reasons' in R. J. Wallace, P. Pettit, S. Scheffler, M. Smith (eds), *Reason and Value* (Oxford: OUP, 2004) 91). I have cast doubt on the possibility of such reasons (J. Raz, *Engaging Reason* (Oxford: OUP, 1999) 101–2), and on the difference between them and reasons that are defeated by all others, and are incommensurate among themselves.

[8] I avoid various difficult questions, such as the duration of the time that defines a situation, and what is the likelihood that an act, activity, or omission would take place if tried, which would make it an available option.

[9] As is evident from these terminological stipulations, often no single reason is undefeated or conclusive, because in the given situation the undefeated or the conclusive reason is all the reasons for an option taken together.

One important principle lies behind these remarks: compliance with many reasons allows for degrees (simplest example: I owe the bank $100—repaying any sum below that would be partial compliance with the duty to pay $100). Any reason is also a reason for partial compliance (if I have only $50 I cannot refuse to pay on the ground that I do not have a reason to pay that, I have only a reason to pay the full debt). And of course, we should comply with all the reasons that apply to us, we should come as close as possible to complete compliance with the reasons that apply to us (call it the principle of complete compliance).[10] Where there are several independent reasons of equal strength and I cannot comply with all of them, I have to comply with as many as I can. Some rescue examples considered in philosophical discussion are like that: Assume that the only reasons that apply to me are the ones detailed in the following story. Several people will drown if I do not save them. I have reasons to save each one of them, and they are all of equal strength. I should save as many as I can. That is the only way I come as close to complete conformity with reason as possible. Needless to say in many cases different reasons will vary in strength. That is when the weight of reasons determines what comes closer to complete compliance.

Doesn't that explanation make me care about the number of reasons I conform to rather than about the drowning people? That would be doubly to misunderstand the situation. First, I take practical reasons to be reasons for a particular mode of conduct: an act, activity, or omission. They are satisfied when that conduct occurs. Unless the conduct they are reasons for includes an intention or a motive—for example, reason to volunteer out of love of country—they are satisfied when the conduct occurs, whatever the agent's motivation that brought it about may be—for example, I have reason not to turn on the light even once it gets dark, and I do not because I am asleep—I have conformed with the reason. But what matters is not that there is yet another reason I conformed to, but that my conduct should be appropriate to how things are in some respect, and my conduct is appropriate to how they are in that respect. That is stated by saying that I conformed to a reason that applied to me, but the statement does not express a fetishism of compliance with as many reasons as possible, but concern about how things are and how my conduct is related to the way they are. The second distortion is to think of a person concerned to behave as he should, one who follows the reason that applies to him and is not merely conforming to it, as someone who has this

[10] Here and throughout when referring to reasons (in the plural) I assume that they are independent reasons.

fetishism about clocking up as many reasons he conforms to as possible. Perhaps such attitudes are possible. But they are neither typical of those concerned to follow reasons that apply to them, nor are they rational. That one has, let us say, a conclusive reason to ϕ tells one that one would do well to ϕ, that one would conform with reason to ϕ. But it does not tell one why one should ϕ, meaning what good one would do by ϕ-ing. This is not a point about the appropriateness of using this expression or that. There is no linguistic impropriety in saying that one does know the answer to the question 'Why should one ϕ?', namely that there is a conclusive reason to ϕ. But that is not an informative answer. People who are responsible about their conduct are moved by considerations that constitute reasons—the plight of the poor, the delightful quality of the wine—and respond to them.

3. Promoting Value: A Theoretical Doubt

Advocates of the thesis that we should always promote value are led, regarding rescue cases like those mentioned here, to the very same conclusions to which the considerations explained above led. My aim was to show that no assumption about promoting value is needed to reach these conclusions. They follow from the fact that if we have reason to rescue one person then we have reason (of the same kind) to rescue each of the people who need rescuing in that situation, and from the implications of that fact. That shows that, at least in cases of this kind, rejecting the promotion of value thesis does not lead to absurd results.

But why doubt the thesis? After all, one may say, saving the life of one person does some good and saving the life of several people does more good. I should do as much good as I can. Therefore, I should save as many people as I can, and in doing so I am promoting value. The doubt may be subtle, but it is important. Of course there is a sense in which if I save two people I do more good than if I save one: I do the same good to two people, rather than just to one. But it does not follow that in doing so I increase the amount of good in the world, or that I promote value (and therefore, it does not follow that I have a reason to increase the amount of good in the world).

The doubts I am airing here are well known: As I mentioned, any good is or can be good for someone who matters, someone whose good matters, namely is of value. This is not a claim about the priority of 'good for' over 'good *simpliciter*'.[11]

[11] And of course it is not an observation about the meaning of any term.

Good novels and good food are good *simpliciter*. But they are good only if they can be good for people, or for other beings that matter.[12] Which beings matter is, of course, a normative question. Possibly a family (a group) or a university (an institution) matters in itself. There clearly are things that are good for the family or the university, making them a better family or a better university (or making their history better) independently of whether or not they are good for any member of the family or of the university. Possibly there is value in those goods, independently of their value to any individual person. I am not assuming that only individual people or animals of some other species matter in themselves.

Whether or not families or universities are valuable in themselves, what raises the question, what makes them candidates for being 'beings that matter' is that they are agents with psychological and normative properties (such as intentions, determination, indecision, bigotry, generosity) that are not reduced to those of any individuals, even though they may have them only in virtue of activities or properties of individuals. If these are preconditions for being beings that matter then the world is not such a being. Whatever value there is in it or in its existence is simply due to its ('instrumental') value in facilitating the existence of beings that matter. There are additional issues that cannot be considered here.[13] The rest of the chapter aims to illustrate one complexity in the relations between value and reasons, which illustrates how thinking of reasons as based on or reflecting the principle of the promotion of value obscures the ways the value of options affects the weight of reasons.

4. On Not Having Reason to Choose the Best: Examples

Consider a range of activities that can be good for beings who matter: a good dance, a good holiday, giving or attending a good party, a good climb to the top of the mountain, a good lecture, and so on. And consider also a range of

[12] What makes novels good is their insight, humour, etc. and they are good for people to read because they are good novels. But they would not be good novels if people could not read them in the right spirit.

[13] For my views on the value of people see J. Raz, *Value, Respect, and Attachment* (Cambridge: CUP, 2001), and on the relation of value and well-being, see, e.g., J. Raz, 'The Role of Well-Being' *Philosophical Perspectives* 18 *Ethics* (2004). I argued that people do not have their own well-being as one of their ends, and that there is no reason for them to pursue it. I also allowed for the rationality of adopting various aspirations regarding the shape and manner of one's life, e.g. some people may aspire to have a well-rounded life, with a wide range of experiences of radically different kinds. Others may not care for that at all. Some people may be risk seekers, others not. Such optional aspirations could explain why some people seek the best in this context or that. My argument here is merely that there is no general reason to do so if one does not have the relevant aspirations.

objects that can be good: a good film, or novel, or poem, or painting, and so on.[14] Engagement with, involvement with all of them can be good for the people involved. I will assume that participating in the activity or attending to the object in ways that are sensitive to their good features is good for the participants or those so involved.[15] I do not mean good overall, but good in some respect. So dancing rhythmically, being attentive to one's partner, etc. is good for the dancer, as is reading a novel with understanding, and so on. In this section I will rely on examples. The next section will explain them. Only in the final section will I demarcate the range of cases to which the examples belong.

What I doubt is that one has more reason to engage with a better object or activity than with one that is good but not as good, that is, while what is a good about an action (or activity or omission) is a reason for it, I doubt that the fact that it will either engage with a better object or will be a better act—that is, belong to a better kind of action, activity, or omission—is essentially a better reason to perform it, or to omit it. Perhaps there are some kinds of objects or activities such that one has more reason to engage with the better one of the kind. I doubt that that is generally the case. I will illustrate the doubt by a few examples that stand for many others. Imagine a person writing a novel, and suppose that he is as talented a novelist, as talented in writing novels, as anyone is ever likely to be. I am assuming that we could say of such a person that he can write a novel that is better than any so far written, and that it is not certain that he will succeed if he tries. He has the ability, but not in a sense that, barring bad luck, trying assures one of success (which is what is implied by my ability to cross the street). I am also assuming that regarding the best novel, the best painting, the best holiday, etc., best is best *pro tem*, and there is nothing that is the best possible. Probably my reflections on the subject do not depend on that assumption, but it seems true.

My novelist may have reason to write (or to try to write) the best novel. He may have taken a bet that he will, or his mother will die happy if he does. My question is whether he has a reason to try to write the best novel in the absence of such contingent factors, to do so just because that would be the best novel. I do not think that he does. Furthermore, the very ambition seems inappropriate for a serious novelist. A person whose sole reason for writing a

[14] My examples do not assume that all items of the kinds discussed can be ranked by their values—there may be a large degree of indeterminacy and of incommensurability among them. Furthermore, they are neutral as to the determinants of degree of value: the examples allow for relativities to taste, etc. as well as to changes over time.

[15] And that applies to what are sometimes called 'other-regarding' goods, like attending to the sick.

novel is to write the best novel, and whose decisions about characters, narrative style, tone of voice, trajectory of development, and anything else are taken just in order make it the best, is score keeping, and cares not at all about any of the goods that novels can realize. But suppose that the writer's reason is different: to bring to life and preserve the glory and the tragedy of the culture of X, or to give voice and rid himself of the inner pressure to do so, to describe the agonies he suffered in adolescence, or to expose the ridiculous pretensions of this or that group, or to chance his ability to express in literary form the vagaries of communication and how our fortunes, good or ill, depend on the failures and fragilities of communication, in totally unpredictable absurdist ways, and so on and so forth. Whatever his ambition he will want to realize it successfully, namely to produce a good novel, though not necessarily by the standards currently known as the standards of good novels. He may even aim for ridicule or to display another form of dissociation from some existing novel that is a foil for his. But there is no reason for novelists to aim to write the best novel. Similarly, a writer whose reason is, say, to portray the life of a neglected community, does not have a stronger, weightier reason to do so, namely to portray that community in a novel that will be the best novel. To aspire to do so is in many circumstances to be moved by an unworthy competitive urge, exposing the hollowness of one's ambition. The same does not apply to a hope that the novel will be the best. That is consistent with having a serious aim in writing it, and a hope, not necessarily endearing but otherwise unobjectionable, that in doing so one would also produce not only a good novel, but one better than any other.

Let me take a more concrete example. Suppose one is a Florentine sculptor living in the 1470s, not long after Donatello. Would it be an unworthy ambition to make a St. John that will be better than Donatello's? Not necessarily. One may wish to do so because one sees the Baptist differently from Donatello and wants to show that different vision, artistic or theological, or because one wants to test oneself, or to establish one's reputation, to gain recognition or acceptability, etc. When we deal with more concrete ambitions of this kind, one can imagine some artists having reasons to better this or that work or other artist, perhaps not as their only reason for a work, but as one of them. What these examples do not show is that every artist has reason to aspire to be the best, or the best at the time, or to surpass the most admired work of the time, and so on. Nor do they show that creating the best would be, other things being equal, a better experience, or a better activity for its creator than creating a good work that is not the best (or more generally that, other things being equal, it would be a better activity or experience to create a better work than a good work that excels in other ways even though it is not as good overall). The existence of a valid reason of that kind will depend on contingent factors.

Similar conclusions apply to other objects and activities (organizing a wedding reception, a piano competition, and so on). But what about consuming or enjoying the creations of others? Isn't it the case that of two novels the stronger reason is to read the better one? Of two paintings the stronger reason is to attend to the better painting, or of two concerts the better reason is to go to the better concert and so on? Not necessarily.

Let me start with ordinary reasons for choosing a novel to read: I am tired and want something soothing to take my mind off the day's troubles. A detective story will hold my attention and keep me off my daily worries. That book brings to life the experience of Bangladeshi women who migrated to Britain, and will open up to me the experience of a troubled and fascinating community. This book develops new and fascinating narrative techniques. It is both challenging and rewarding in its control of narrative forms. She (the novelist) has a unique insight into the difficulties of relationships. I always respond to her work. It is a novel about loyalty and its ambiguities, a topic that always fascinates me. And so on.

Let such reasons be conceded. But, one may ask, is it not the case that, other things being equal, the stronger reason is to read the better book, either because its being better is an independent reason or because it increases the weight of the reasons for reading it?

The language I used in discussing the examples in the previous section implied the claim that being better than..., or better than some, or better than all, while providing information on how good the object or activity is, or how good it is of its kind, does not establish that that is something agents have reason to pursue, and it does not establish that that is something that is good for them. In some circumstances engaging with what is best or better is good for some agents, and they have reason to do so. These can be instrumental reasons or a result of a promise or of a valuable personal goal of the agents. Many people would be curious about what is happening in literature these days. One of their aims is to be knowledgeable about what is best on the literary scene. In other words, people's personal projects will provide many with reasons, sometimes strong reasons, to keep up with the best books, or the best holiday resorts, and the like. Such cases do not establish that just being the best, or among the best, constitutes a reason. After all, personal projects may provide reasons to read Armenian literature of the early nineteenth century, without thereby establishing that being an Armenian writing of that period constitutes a reason.

While my examples aim to illustrate theoretical truths, they presuppose a substantive view of the value of this or that case and of the reasons the values do or do not provide. The hope is that those who do not share these beliefs about the cases illustrated would, nevertheless, be helped by them to find other cases that, given their substantive beliefs, do illustrate the theoretical points. Others may realize that they do not disagree after all; that they were misled into thinking that they do by overlooking the role of personal goals, and the like. But we need a general explanation of that view, an explanation that will tend to substantiate it.

5. On Not Having Reason to Choose the Best: Exploration

So, again: is there no reason for everyone to prefer the better book? I am not sure. I am inclined to think that we have an epistemic reason to believe that, other things being equal, we are more likely to find something responding to reasons we have in a better book than in a good but less good one. It is a weak epistemic reason, but when all else is equal it has some force. What I do not see is how it is a practical reason for reading the better book. More accurately, that the book is good, has some valuable features, is a reason to read it. My doubt is about the claim that as between two good books, the features that make one the better book or the fact that they make it the better of the two provide a reason to read it rather than the other good book, or that in the given circumstances they enhance the strength of the reason to read it.

Before proceeding to explain why this is so I wish to put aside one objection to the claim that it is so. It may be thought that my examples point to a mistaken conclusion because they assume that all goods that are goods of a kind must be ranked, if at all, relative to a stable, agent-independent kind. The novel that I have best reason to read tonight may not be the best novel, but it is the best instance of the kind 'novel I have reason to read tonight', or if we assume that the novel I should read tonight is the most entertaining of those within easy reach that I have not read before, then I have most reason to read the best novel of the kind 'entertaining novel within easy reach tonight that I have not read before'.

So far as I can see there is nothing wrong in speaking of such a kind, and the linguistic awkwardness or inelegance of doing so does not matter. Many such ephemeral kinds will be of little consequence, but perhaps they may be relied upon to sustain the theoretical claim that one always has best reason to choose the best option of those available. Except that in order to do so the kind must be a normatively significant one, and the grounds for ranking the relative value of the options of that kind needs to be independent of the reason for pursuing them. That is, it must be the case that one has reason to do the best of the kind because it is the best, and not that it is the best because there is best reason to do it. These conditions are not met in the illustrations of the objection: the only reason why the kind mentioned has any normative significance is because it reflects the strength of reasons that the agent has in the situation postulated in the example. That is why the objection fails.

In the previous section I suggested that some common motives for pursuing ambitions such as to write the best novel are unworthy. In a way they are analogous to the ambition to conform to as many reasons that apply to one as possible, an ambition I discussed in Section 3. There I distinguished caring about the substance of the reason and caring about it as being a reason. Analogously, we should distinguish caring about writing the best novel from caring about writing a novel that has features that would make it best. Does one not have reason to write such a novel? One does. My claim is that that reason does not necessarily have greater weight than reasons to write a novel that has other valuable features, even though they do not establish it as the best. In other words, that the good features make it the best novel does not establish that the reason to write a novel with these features is the best reason (among reasons to write a novel). This is the claim that needs explaining.

We need to return to the dependence of cultural goods on genre. We need to understand how, even though the features that make a cultural good good are features that provide reasons for engaging with it, the fact that they make it better than other members of the genre it belongs to does not make those reasons stronger or more stringent reasons. Cultural goods, and all my examples are of cultural goods, and most intrinsic goods are cultural goods, belong to genres. We understand them by understanding the genres to which they belong: is it a novel or a poem or a history book or an autobiography? Without an answer we cannot understand the object we are reading, nor can we evaluate it. Cultural goods, namely literary genres, artistic genres, types of social activities and relationships, are constituted by standards, and some of them are among the standards that determine criteria for excellence within the genre. Thereby they determine the criteria that vindicate (or contribute to the vindication of) this or that as the best novel or painting, etc. Alternatively, if one rejects, for all or for some cultural goods, the possibility that anything is best, these standards determine the criteria by which works of the genre, or relationships or activities that belong to it, are compared regarding their relative excellence.

The best novel is best because of, first, certain of its features (its mastery of language, of narrative style, its imaginative sweep, its understanding of social complexities, its psychological insight, its sense of the absurd, its playfulness, its variability of tone and texture, its ingenious plotting, etc.) and second, the way they are mixed together, the ways they interact: Each one of the features that contribute to its excellence provides a reason to read it. Similarly, various of the ways in which the elements of the novel are related to one another contribute to its excellence and provide reasons for reading it (or enhance the weight of the other reasons for reading it; the distinction will often be artificial, and therefore immaterial). But why should my or your response to them or interest in them correspond in inclusivity and degree of interest or appeal to the ranking that determines their position as best or better?

My interest and yours should be guided by good-making features of the work, its valuable components and their interrelations, when those are valuable. But if by the standards of the genre certain features in a certain mix make the work better than others, then the reason to produce or engage with such a work is stronger, weightier, than the reasons to engage with the others, and other things being equal I am at fault (and if aware of the facts and in control of my faculties and actions, I am irrational) in not pursuing that option, the one that the standards determine to be best, rather than the less good one. While my interest should be guided by good-making features, why need it be guided by the relative excellence of works, etc. in the different genres? I do not know of any reason why it should.

It is quite typical that different people should be drawn to the same novel, or the same painting, or the same holiday resort, or want the same person to be a friend, for different reasons, and they may all be valid reasons. Moreover, there can be valid yet conflicting reasons (naturally in different objects): some may be attracted to irreverence, others to an instinctive manifest respectfulness, and so on. So long as they all derive from genuinely good-making features of the object, we must acknowledge that they are all valid. That is compatible with it being OK for us personally to prefer some of them, while having no taste for some others. However, most of our tastes are acquired tastes (even though they may have roots in some of our hard-wired tastes), and their acquisition should be guided by the good features of their objects, and of the activities and experiences of engaging with them. Once we acknowledge that there is a stronger reason for one, our liking must follow that reason. We now have a reason to like one object better than the others, and it is a failing in us if we do not, even if we cannot. As already avowed, I do not see any reason why we must adjust our liking in that way, because I cannot see why we have a better reason to engage with the better object.

This view is reinforced by the nature of genres. Far from being immutable, they are constantly in flux. Part of the way they, and the standards of excellence that define them, function is by providing not only models to emulate, or to immerse oneself in, but also ways of defining oneself, and one's aspirations and hopes in life, against them—there are wonderful activities that (without denying their excellence) are not part of one's life, and possibly one does not wish them to be. Or, one may wish to engage in the goods of the genre in ways that reveal new or neglected aspects of it, thus subtly positioning oneself both within the common standard, and also somewhat outside it. As when one throws parties that are recognizably like the best that others do, but also show one's own twist on that pattern. And there are many other variations from the established standards of excellence, including their rejection in favour of alternatives, alternatives that do not make sense except in reaction to the existing norm. Perhaps the emergence of Brechtian theatre is an example of both imitation of and reaction against the theatre of his time. I am not suggesting that every time I choose to go to a lesser play I am changing the standards of excellence for drama. I do not, and may have no such wish. Sometimes my choice itself is an acknowledgement of the excellence of the experience that I am rejecting or postponing—now, I say to myself, is not the right time for it. I have adduced the different ways in which standards of excellence for a genre function in the life of the genre and of people familiar with it to suggest that while reaction to them should acknowledge their value, it need not give preference to the better instances of the genre over the less good ones. The observations about the way genres, and their defining standards, function also help to meet the main challenge to my argument.

Is not the thought that one novel is better than another inconsistent with the thought that I have no better reason to read it than to read the other? The assumption that they are inconsistent is precisely what I am challenging. My suggestion is that the standards that govern genres develop in ways that while determining what are degrees of excellence of that kind, do not automatically translate into what one has better reasons to engage with, not even *pro tanto* reasons. This suggestion would be challenged if the view I am taking would, if shared, undermine the existence of genres and of the standards that constitute them. This is not a totally fanciful possibility. These genres, and the standards defining them, constitute cultural goods. They exist and persist because they are sustained by social practices, at least in some places and for some times. If the view I am advocating would undermine the ability to participate in the practice, or to value and respect such practices engaged in by others, then this view would, if shared, make the continued existence of cultural goods impossible.

But in fact my suggestion is not inconsistent with interest in and admiration for cultural goods, though it is—and should be—at odds with taking them to be immutable. As we saw the standards that constitute these goods fulfil a vital role in their development. They are essential both for understanding and for the appreciation and valuation of works of the genre, and vital for their development. But they do not fulfil these functions by inspiring veneration and acceptance. On the contrary, both the creation of new works and new types of valuable activities and relationships, and their understanding and interpretation, strive against the limits that those standards establish, and acquire their meaning through the way they modify, reaffirm, or challenge the standards. Acknowledging the crucial roles of genres and their constitutive standards does not require, and does not justify, taking them to determine the strength of reasons to engage with these works or activities. Thus, a proper understanding of the way genre-constituting standards function in the life of a genre undermines the thought that we should be guided by them in the sense of taking the objects or activities that they designate as better or best to be supported by stronger reasons.

Furthermore, the view I suggested does not deny that the degree of excellence of paintings, buildings, and other cultural goods affects the strength of some practical reasons. Values provide two kinds of reasons: reasons to respect what is of value and reasons to engage with it.[16] The reasons I have been discussing so far are reasons to engage with cultural goods: to organize parties or participate in them, to write novels or read them, and so on. But we have other reasons regarding cultural goods, reasons to respect them that include reasons to preserve and protect them. These reasons are sensitive to degrees of excellence of individual works. Other things being equal, the reasons to save or to protect the better work are stronger than the reasons to save or protect lesser works of the same genre. These reasons, to preserve and protect, are reasons to respect the value of those objects and therefore they are sensitive to their relative value.

[16] See my *Value, Respect, and Attachment*, Chap. 4.

6. Value, Good for and Reasons

I have argued that regarding some cultural goods, while the features that make them valuable provide reasons for engaging with them, the fact that one of them is better than another does not in itself establish that the reason to engage with it is weightier, better, than the reason to engage with the other. It establishes that the good satisfies the criteria of excellence of the genre to which it belongs to a higher degree. But that is not in itself a reason to engage with it, nor a factor that affects the weight of reasons to engage with it, special conditions apart.

Am I not confusing the value of a good (a novel or a party) with the value of the option to engage with it? An option is an action that is available to the agent at the time, one that he or she can choose. The proximate reason for an action (or activity or omission), that is, for the option of performing it, is its value. Its value may be due to the fact that it is an aspect or a constituent of a larger whole, or because it facilitates something worthwhile. Naturally, when the value of the action is derived from the value of what it is a part of or of what it facilitates, its value may differ from the value of what it derives from. The argument of the last section is, however, still relevant. The argument applies directly to cases in which the good in question is the activity that constitutes the option—for example, a solo rock-climb, or singing with no audience. But it is also relevant to cases in which the option is engaging with some cultural good, thus deriving its value from that good. In such cases one would expect that, other things being equal, the better the cultural good, the better the option. That expectation turns out to be unfounded regarding cultural goods to which my argument applies. That is one lesson of the argument of the last section.

Am I not confusing what is good with what is good for the agent? No, for as explained it is good for agents to engage with what is valuable, provided they can do so in the right way (with understanding, with the appropriate attitudes, etc.). Of course, engaging with one valuable thing may not be as good as engaging with another. My claim is that the fact that one cultural good is better than another does not establish that, other things being equal, engaging with it is better for an agent than engaging with the other.

Here, in considering how the value of different options makes them good for an agent, we encounter considerable complexity, and we also realize the limited range of cases to which my argument applies. First of all, the argument does not apply without much modification and qualification to the facilitative, instrumental, value of options.

It has other limits as well. Think of a choice of career (and careers, occupations, and professions are almost always cultural goods): Should one not always choose the best career? To the extent that careers can be ranked in quality (and I am more sceptical about this than most people) the answer is: No, because the best career may not be best for that person. But should I not choose the career that is best for me? And to the extent that my conduct affects someone else's choice of career, should my conduct not be directed to get them to have the career that is best for them? Here the answers are Yes and No. Considering the No will take us beyond the scope of this chapter and into an examination of the moral constraints on the ways we may affect other people, with the intention to do so.

The Yes is simpler. I argued, in effect, that it is a mistake to think that necessarily what is better is, other things being equal, better for agents.[17] In this discussion what is good for people should not be equated with what they have adequate reason to choose. We are looking for an asymmetric relation: they have adequate reason to choose because it is good for them, but not the other way round. One view has it that what is good for people is what serves their well-being. I will rely on that view in discussing careers. The claim is that analogous arguments would apply to these, if not to other examples, whatever view of what is good for people turns out to be correct. Careers belong with a different class of cases than my previous examples. The careers people pursue affect the quality of their lives in a variety of ways. Occasional activities, like the novel they read this week or the party they attend, do not except contingently (at the party they may fall for the person who then becomes their partner, etc.). My examples belong with cultural goods that bear on the quality of one's life only if they are part of one's long-term pursuits or relationships.[18] Careers are themselves long-term pursuits, and therefore have properties that bear on the quality of one's life. Hence deliberation about choice of career is bound to be different from deliberation about occasional engagement with cultural goods. But that does not undermine the argument of the chapter, which applies at least to cases where the action does not bear on the quality of the agent's life.

The upshot is that the fact that normative values constitute reasons, and that some valuable objects or activities are better than others, does not establish that other things being equal the better (or weightier) reason is to

[17] And the argument assumes that the agents can appreciate and benefit from engaging in activities, and with objects of value of the kinds we deal with.

[18] For a discussion of these matters, see my *The Morality of Freedom* (Oxford: OUP, 1986) 289–320, and 'The Role of Well-Being'.

pursue the better or more valuable good. What we have undefeated or conclusive reason to do depends in part on the principle of complete compliance. It also depends on the values options serve. But it does that in complex ways that remain to be explored. The argument of this chapter highlighted the difference between the way the value of options affects the weight of reasons to engage with cultural values, and reasons to respect cultural values.[19]

[19] I am grateful to Barry Maguire for helpful comments on a draft of the chapter.

6

The Guise of the Bad

My remarks will focus primarily on the connection between what I shall call the Thesis, meaning the thesis of the Guise of the Good, and actions under the Guise of the Bad. I will argue that to the extent that action under the Guise of the Bad is possible it does not contradict the Thesis.[1]

1. The Two Versions: Reason and Motive

The discussion will proceed on the assumption that actions (and I use the term to refer to actions, activities, and omissions) can be bad in some regards, as well as bad all things told. Furthermore, the discussion assumes that the fact that an action is bad, or bad in some regard, is not a reason to perform it. So, what would constitute an action under the Guise of the Bad?

The expression 'the Guise of the Bad' is a stipulative one, whose meaning is not well-entrenched in the philosophical lexicon. Various theses can reasonably claim the name. But its meaning cannot be so wide as to include action taken for a reason that is believed to be defeated, meaning taken to be weaker than conflicting reasons that apply in the circumstances.[2] Ordinary

[1] This paper was written for a conference on 'Acting under the "Guise of the Bad"?' (Vienna, May 2014) and I am grateful to Professors Herlinde Pauer-Studer and Hans Bernhard Schmid for inviting me. It was written to be intelligible on its own, but obviously it grew out of and presupposes claims I made elsewhere. The Guise of the Good Thesis is discussed, refined, and defended in J. Raz, *From Normativity to Responsibility* (Oxford: OUP, 2011) Chap. 4. Both there and in my *Engaging Reason* (Oxford: OUP, 1999) Chap. 2, I discuss what I call 'anomic reasons', showing how many of the examples discussed in recent writings can be accommodated with the Thesis, defending it against M. Stocker, 'Desiring the Bad—An Essay in Moral Psychology', *Journal of Philosophy* 76/12 (1979) 738–53 and 'Raz on the Intelligibility of Bad Acts' in R. J. Wallace, P. Pettit, S. Scheffler, and M. Smith (eds), *Reason and Value: Themes from the Moral Philosophy of Joseph Raz* (Oxford: OUP, 2004) 303–32; D. Velleman, 'The Guise of the Good', in D. Velleman, *The Possibility of Practical Reason* (New York: OUP, 2002) 170–99; and K. Setiya, *Reasons Without Rationalism* (Princeton: Princeton UP, 2007) 59. My discussion allows for exceptions due to psychological contrariness. D. Sussman, 'For Badness' Sake', *Journal of Philosophy* 106/11 (2009) 613–28 argues that relying on contrariness is insufficient, and I agree. Contrariness can lead to various kinds of normative responses. Much of this paper deals with one kind, the explanation of its intelligibility as well as of its failure.

[2] I will follow the custom of often referring to all the reasons supporting one option as a single reason, and to all the reasons conflicting with them as one reason, relying on context to disambiguate the meaning.

The Roots of Normativity. Joseph Raz, Edited with an Introduction by Ulrike Heuer, Oxford University Press.
 DOI: 10.1093/oso/9780192847003.003.0007

akratic action falls under that description. It involves action done for what the agent believes to be a defeated reason, defeated by considerations that establish that the action should not be done, but it is done, and it is done for what the agent believes to be a reason that shows that it has some merit, that there is something good about doing it. The view that I will examine says that it is possible to perform an action that one believes to be bad (to have bad-making features) and for the reason that it is, as the agent believes, bad.[3] I will call that version of the Guise of the Bad Thesis the 'normative version'.

As is obvious, by 'reason' I refer to a normative reason. Reasons generally are facts that explain. Normative reasons are somewhat different. They may explain nothing. There may be a reason for an agent to perform an action (that is not also a reason for any other action, nor for any belief, emotion, intention, etc.) and because that action is never performed the reason for it does not explain anything.[4] Normative reasons, however, can explain (or be central parts of explanations of), for example, actions that are taken for those reasons.

Normative reasons can explain various objects: beliefs, emotions, intentions, or actions. Given our topic, I will ignore reasons other than reasons for action. The view that we examine is not about whether bad properties can in themselves provide or constitute a reason for an action, but about the possibility of actions taken in the belief that they are bad and that that is a reason to take them. One way of expressing the difference is that it is not about whether the badness of actions can be a reason for them (I proceed on the assumption that it cannot), but about whether it is possible to believe that the bad features of an action are reasons to take it. And that is close to asking whether actions taken in the belief that they are bad are susceptible to normative explanations. This oracular statement itself requires clarification.

Explanations are of various types. For example, Aristotle famously distinguished four types of causes and four types of (causal) explanations depending on which kind of cause features in them. Whether an explanation is a good or successful one often does not affect the type it belongs to. If it fails because it asserts the existence of facts that do not exist, it nevertheless belongs to the same type of explanation it would have belonged to had they obtained. Similarly, if it claims that certain facts explain in a certain way (e.g. are an efficient cause of the explanandum) while in fact they do not explain in

[3] The discussion to come will clarify one ambiguity in this formulation of the thesis.

[4] However, the reason can figure in the explanation of its normative and logical implications—in that sense everything is a reason, i.e. figures in the explanation of what it entails.

that way, it nevertheless belongs to the kind it would have belonged to had its claim been true (i.e. efficient cause explanations in my example). To give an example, an epidemiological explanation is an epidemiological explanation even if the statistical connection it relies on does not obtain or the theory of statistical explanation it relies on is mistaken, with the result that the explanation fails.

Matters are a little more complex with what I will call reason explanations. Successful reason explanations are explanations whose core is expressed in statements commonly made using sentences of the form: 'X (an agent) φed because of F', where 'because of F' means because F shows the action to be worth doing. For example: Jane ate the apple because it was tasty, watched *Away from Her* (a film) because it is insightful about the way advancing dementia affects couples, etc. In other words, reason explanations connect a reaction of the person (in the cases we are examining—actions) to features of the world that make the reaction appropriate, when that is why the agent reacts as he does.

But of course people may act because they are mistaken about how things are, or about what is an appropriate reaction to the way things are. In such cases, the action taken is not an appropriate response to the facts that prompt it either because those facts are not a reason for the action or because the belief that they exist is false. The agent is not connected to the world in the way he thinks he is. But in acting as he did he attempted to react as one does to normative reasons. That is why the explanation of such actions is similar to successful reason explanations. Of course, it is not a successful reason explanation because there is no reason that can explain the response. It is a failed reason explanation. But there is a successful explanation nearby. It contains a segment of a successful reason explanation: it explains the action by the agent's attempt to conduct himself in a way that is appropriate to how things are. Agents, we may say, take themselves to be normatively guided, guided by a reason, and that is what led them to act as they did. And even though they are not guided by a reason, they tried to be. The explanation, the successful explanation, of their action is therefore an explanation (of at least one kind of case) of attempting to be guided by a reason. Therefore, it is an explanation of normative guidance. As a terminological abbreviation (which roughly conforms to the way the terms are often used[5]) let me call explanations

[5] I have not distinguished in this way between the two kinds of explanations before, nor do I know of anyone who has. The distinction relates to the familiar difference between action for a reason and action for a believed reason.

of conduct in which agents attempt (successfully or not) to be guided by reasons 'normative explanations'. Successful reason explanations, because they embed in them normative explanations, can also be said to be normative explanations.

So far I have been explaining the normative version of the Guise of the Bad. It says that there can be normative explanations of people's actions in which they take the badness of some actions to be reasons for their performance. Another version, which I will call the 'motive version',[6] concerns the possibility of acting out of bad motives. That version asserts that *an agent can, without having any relevant false beliefs, perform actions motivated by the badness of those actions—namely by features of the actions that make them bad.*

The condition that the agent is free of relevant false beliefs excludes from the scope of the Thesis those cases in which the agent believes that the features that motivate him are good, are features that make the action good in some respect. The condition may be too strong, as it excludes from the scope of the Thesis cases in which the agent is ambivalent or self-deceived, cases in which he knows that the features are bad but deceives himself into believing that they are good, and other more complex psychological ambivalences. Later, other kinds of motive explanations are tacitly introduced.

Motive explanations are productive explanations. They explain what brought about the performance of actions. (As is the custom, I will sometimes refer to them as causal explanations, not meaning by that more than that they explain what produced or brought about the explanandum.) So do normative explanations, but, unlike the latter, motive explanations do not imply that the agents knew, or believed, that they had any particular motive, let alone that they knew or believed that they acted out of the motives that explain their actions. Motives can be guided or triggered by reasons and they can bring people to act for certain (believed) reasons, but they can also bring people to act without reason, as when they induce an accidental act, or a false and masking belief about one's reasons.

[6] This chapter, like much work in this area, strives to explain some psychological phenomena by clarifying common concepts and explanations. As a result, it sometimes relies on the reader's understanding of these concepts while striving to clarify other concepts; others still are stipulatively introduced to facilitate these explanations (e.g. 'Guise of the Bad'). I use 'motive' non-technically, relying on readers' knowledge of the concept, and its context-sensitive use. Given that the term is used somewhat technically or stipulatively by other writers, it is helpful not to assume that I rely on their use of it. Anyone interested in philosophical discussions of the concept as we have it could consult G. Ryle, *The Concept of Mind* (London: Hutchinson, 1949) Chap. 4; and A. Kenny, *Action, Emotion and The Will* (London: Routledge & Kegan Paul, 1963) Chap. 4, and A. Kenny, *The Metaphysics of Mind* (Oxford: Clarendon Press, 1989) 58–63. I say more on the relations between motive explanations and explanation by reasons in Chapter 2.

Let me explain: first, accidental actions, for example accidentally knocking over and breaking a wine glass, are not done for a reason (though they may happen in the performance of an intentional action that is taken for a reason, as when we break the glass while passing the salt, as requested). Needless to say, such accidental actions are caused, and the agent's motives can be among the causes of the accident, often—perhaps normally—without the agent being aware of the fact.

More complex are cases in which a motive causes what I call a false masking belief. In these cases, agents deceive themselves into a belief. Such beliefs are motivated, for example by wishful thinking, or by anxieties and fears about facing what they know to be the case, etc. They think that they act because of their beliefs, but in fact their actions are explained by their motives and not their beliefs, whose role is limited to masking from the agents the true nature of their actions. I will return to masking beliefs shortly.

All this is to show that acting for a bad or worthless motive is a distinctive phenomenon, different from taking the fact that an act is bad or worthless to be a reason to perform it. We thus have at least two different phenomena that could reasonably be taken to be action under the Guise of the Bad, a normative version and a motive version. I remarked earlier that in some respects the motive version as I defined it is too strong. Some would say that in another respect it is too weak. It does not require that the agents either know or believe that their motive or its object is bad. There is of course no objection to additional versions of the Guise of the Bad. I will not consider this stronger view for two reasons. First, insofar as judgements of people (rather than their actions) go, people are bad if significant actions of theirs are motivated by bad motives, regardless of whether they believed them or their objects to be bad. But that of course is a topic for another occasion. Second, to the extent that the stronger version is philosophically problematic in ways that the weaker version is not, the difficulty or problem is with the possibility of believing that a feature that makes an action bad is a reason for it because it makes it bad. That problem will be examined when considering the normative version, which is the main focus of this paper.

2. The Theoretical Case for the Guise of the Good

One difficulty in explaining the possibility of acting for the reason that the action would be bad arises out of the case for the Guise of the Good Thesis. Here, too, there are diverse versions of the Thesis. The version closest to the truth (simplified to avoid various qualifications and complexities) is that when people act with an independent intention or for a purpose, their action is done in, and because of, a belief that the action has some feature that makes it good, at least in some respect.[7] Not all intentional actions are done with independent intentions. However, to abbreviate and avoid awkward formulations, and as we will not be concerned with other kinds of intentional action, I will use 'intentional action' to refer to actions done with an independent intention.

Why accept the Thesis? Because intentional human actions are performed by agents who identify them, and take them to have, among other features, some that constitute a reason for doing them that makes them worth doing (at least in some respect). And the features of actions that are reasons for performing these actions are those that make the actions good. That is what makes them worth doing.[8]

This not only assumes that agents believe the action they are about to take will have some feature that appeals to them but also assumes that the agent is aware of the feature and its appeal.[9] That assumption reflects the fact that people who act intentionally recognize that they may be mistaken, that it is possible that the action does not possess the feature they think it does or that they are wrong to think that the feature makes the action worth doing. That kind of mistake is different from dissatisfaction or disappointment with the action once it is performed because it is not as enjoyable or is not as admired by others, etc. as one wishes that it were. That disappointment can be

[7] For the more complete statement and defence of the thesis, see Raz, *From Normativity to Responsibility*.

[8] If one chooses an option, and, not being able to identify it, succeeds by luck in performing it rather than some alternative, then the action, while intentional, is not performed with the intention that motivated it. To be done with that intention, the intention must guide the action, including identifying what one is doing as that action. The point is important to an understanding of intentional action. As argued by Frankfurt, and further explained by Setiya and Sussman, the fact that intentional actions are not merely initiated but guided by the agents' believed reasons solves Davidson's problem of deviant causation. Therefore, the point is central to establishing the relations between intentional action and action for reasons, sometimes exaggerated into a claim that all intentional actions are actions for a reason. In itself this is not sufficient to establish the Guise of the Good Thesis. As is underlined by Setiya, and recognized by, e.g., Sussman and Gregory, a further step is required, connecting reasons with the good, a step whose cogency they doubt. See H. Frankfurt, 'The Problem of Action', in *The Importance of What We Care About* (Cambridge: CUP, 1988) 69, 72; Setiya, *Reasons Without Rationalism*, 31–2; Sussman, 'For Badness' Sake'; A. Gregory, 'The Guise of Reasons', *American Philosophical Quarterly* 50/1 (2013) 63.

[9] This could be that it is more important to act quickly than to do what would otherwise be the best action to perform. In that case the chosen action is one that satisfies that condition: it can be chosen and performed quickly. The feature can also be one that is believed to be manifested by several actions among which the agent thinks that there is nothing to choose.

experienced without the thought that one made a mistake, and agents can tell the difference between these two reactions.

I should underline that this view of human intentional action does not derive from the nature of intentions or of choice. There are animal species incapable of judgements of that kind yet capable of intentional action. There are humans of whom that is true. However, *Homo sapiens* is among the species whose members can possess rational powers of a kind that enables not only choice of action but also recognition of the value of things, and these powers once possessed are automatically used (unless disabled by sleep, drugs, etc.). Hence, human choices and intentional actions depend on beliefs that humans have and are able to reassess. The point relevant to our purpose is that those beliefs attribute to one or more of the options that agents take to be available to them, features in virtue of which the option merits choosing. That is what the Thesis asserts. And if that is true, then how can one act for the bad, that is, how can one choose an action for the reason that, as the agent believes, it is bad?

3. Clarifications

Some possible misunderstandings of the Thesis can be easily clarified. Others pose greater difficulties.[10]

(a) It does not maintain that agents always have a view as to which feature of the action makes it worthwhile, only that they believe that it has some such feature.
(b) It does not assume that agents have adequate competence to identify verbally the features that lead them to think that the action is worthwhile. Their knowledge may be implicit and exceed their ability to articulate it.
(c) In taking features that make an action worth performing as properties that make the action good, at least in some respect, 'good' is stipulatively assigned a wider meaning than it has in English. English is

[10] A most important clarification, only lightly touched upon in the remarks that follow, concerns the implication for the Thesis of the fact that mastery of concepts comes in degrees. I have discussed some aspects of the problem in my *Between Authority and Interpretation* (Oxford: OUP, 2009) Chap. 2, and in 'Intention and Value'. A helpful discussion of some aspects of the issue is offered by J. Hawkins, 'Desiring the Bad under the Guise of the Good', *Philosophical Quarterly* 58/231(2008) 244–64. She endorses psychological views that may be controversial, but her description of the psychological phenomena is instructive and points in the right direction.

naturally more specific: 'moral', 'attractive', 'enjoyable', 'rewarding', 'helpful', and many others are the sort of concepts used and, while it is always true that an action is good because it is moral or because it is attractive, etc., it would often be awkward or misleading just to describe the action as good. Moreover, many features are contextually good: being funny is good at the right place and the right time, and can be anything but good otherwise. While this makes the meaning with which 'good' is used in stating the Thesis somewhat stipulative, it does not undermine the truth of the Thesis.

(d) The good-making features of an action can be relational, as when it is instrumentally good or relationally good (good for the friendship, etc.). As the example of instrumental goods illustrates, they can be contingent features of the action.

(e) The feature that makes an action good may be that it is the action the agent has a duty to perform. It is therefore good because it is good to do what you have a duty to do. In other words, the Thesis does not assume what is sometimes asserted or denied as 'the primacy of the good over the right'. It is neutral regarding that matter. The controversy, as I understand it, is whether there could be actions that are the right thing to do, actions that are one's duty, that one morally must do, etc. that have these properties not because they are good in some way. The Thesis is silent on that issue.

(f) Moreover, the Thesis does not assume that all people capable of intentional actions believe that when they or others act intentionally they do so in the belief that there is some good in their actions. That is a philosophical thesis that can be and is denied by many people capable of intentional action. The Thesis is that, regarding any intentional human action, it is performed by the person who performs it in the belief that there is some good in it. People who have that belief regarding each of their actions need not believe that the same is true of others, nor that it must be true of themselves or of others.

4. The Difficulty

The Guise of the Good Thesis implies that if an act is intentional it is done because of a belief that the action is good in some respect. The Guise of the Bad says that one can act intentionally because of a belief that the action is bad in some respect. While an action can be both good in some respect and bad in some respect, and it can be believed to be both good in some respect and bad in some respect, its being done because the agent believes it to be bad in some respect cannot make it intentional, at least not if the Thesis is true. For according to the Thesis, what makes a human action intentional is that it is done in and because of belief that there is some good in it.

5. Conciliation?

Perhaps, appearances to the contrary notwithstanding, the two guises are not in conflict; perhaps the Guise of the Good is a true thesis, while acting under the Guise of the Bad is possible.

Perhaps, the Guise of the Good is not strictly universal. Rather, it will be said, it is to be understood as an ordinary generalization, which like all other generalizations allows for exceptions. But the conciliation does not succeed. The Guise of the Good Thesis connects intentional action with (a) action that is taken by agents in light of their view of their situation, and therefore with (b) actions for a reason—namely it holds that agents acting intentionally act because they think that their action is worth doing—that there is a reason for it, and therefore with (c) that to be worth doing the action must have something good about it. Thereby it sees intentional actions as intentional because they can be given normative explanations, showing that the agent is trying to do something good.

Actions under the Guise of the Bad, too, are subject to normative explanation: they are actions taken because of, and guided by, the action being—as the agents see things—bad. That is why they are problematic. They are problematic because the Thesis makes action under the Guise of the Bad, if it is possible, not merely exceptional but incomprehensible.

The Thesis as presented ties up with reason explanations. Successful reason explanations have to explain why features of an action are, in certain contexts, reasons for it, and why some features can be thought to be such features. The brief explanation, though crude and requiring elaboration, is that features of the action can be reasons for it if they show it to be good, in some respect, and therefore worth doing. Normative explanations need not be successful reason explanations. But they depend on understanding the agents as taking themselves to be acting for reasons. Action under the Guise of the Bad is also susceptible to normative explanations: it is action for the (believed) reason that the action is bad. But for action under the Guise of the Bad to be possible we need to understand how something bad in an action can be thought to make it worth doing. Failure to do so—it can be claimed—establishes that there cannot be actions under the Guise of the Bad. Success in providing such an explanation will refute the Thesis of the Guise of the Good. Either way, conciliation fails. Either the Thesis is correct or there can be action under the Guise of the Bad, but not both. Or at least that is the claim.

6. Narrowing or Revising the Thesis?

Given that there is a strong case for the Thesis, it is unlikely that the normative version of the Guise of the Bad can refute it. More plausibly, either no action under the Guise of the Bad can take place or the scope of the Thesis has to be narrowed to accommodate such actions. I will examine one type of objection to the Thesis, an objection that the case that is presented for it justifies a weaker or narrower thesis only.

First, why assume that regarding each of their intentional actions agents believe that there is some good in them rather than that they believe that each possesses some property that does in fact make the action good in some respect, but that they may be unaware that it makes the action good in some respect? I assume that understanding any of the value-making, that is, good-making, properties, involves knowing that there are others like them—that is, that they are instances of a more general category whose other instances would, among other things, also make the action worth doing.[11] Therefore, if agents believe that the action has some specific feature that is in fact good-making, and they broadly know what that feature is like, at least to the extent that they believe it makes the action worth doing, they at least implicitly understand that it must be of the kind of properties that can have other instantiations that would also make other actions worth doing—namely that it is a good-making property.[12] That is what is meant by the claim that if they believe that the action has a feature that is a good-making one they also believe that it has some good.

Second, these observations assume that in deploying concepts we are, normally vaguely and implicitly only, familiar with their rough interrelations.

[11] Compare: 'Mature conceptual capacities are associated with a capacity for abstraction. By this I mean both the simple capacity to think about objects in their absence...and the capacity to employ a variety of more abstract concepts' (Hawkins, 'Desiring the Bad under the Guise of the Good').

[12] That is not a terminological stipulation. It attributes to agents a substantive belief that what makes actions worth doing is something that makes them (in the extended sense of the word used here, and in philosophical discussions generally) good or of value in some respect.

We know that if we run to the station because the bus will leave in two minutes, then the bus's impending departure is only part of the reason to run to catch it, and therefore that when the other facts that are part of the reason are absent, its departure will not be a reason to get to it, etc.

But circumstances do not always determine what beliefs people have, or do not have. Consider:

> I told him it wasn't long till morning, and how in the morning somebody would find them, and then all of it, me and Dick and all, would seem like something they dreamed. I wasn't kidding him. I didn't want to harm the man. I thought he was a very nice gentleman. Soft-spoken. I thought so right up to the moment I cut his throat.... I didn't realize what I'd done till I heard the sound (Perry Smith as reported in Capote's (1966) *In Cold Blood*).

Did he act intentionally? Did he believe he had a reason to kill? Given that description it is difficult to say, and one possibility is that it was a marginal case: the act was intentional and is subject to a normative explanation, but abnormally so: Smith's control of the initiation and course of his action being limited. He knew not what he was doing in a somewhat literal sense. Does that call for a modification of the Thesis? I doubt it. Psychological theses are always subject to marginal and anomalous cases. That is their nature. It is not part of the content of these theses that they are.

Third, let us return to the case of masking beliefs. Recall failed attempts to be guided by reasons: agents act—as they see matters—for a reason, but their belief that the reason is there is mistaken. Their actions can be given normative explanations, even though they cannot be given successful reason explanations. While they are not brought about by a normative reason, they are brought about by belief in a normative reason. In this they differ from cases in which agents' motives induce a false belief in a reason, as when a desire to revenge an injury induces belief that the person who accidentally and blamelessly caused it is guilty of deliberately causing it, thus leading the agent to believe that he has reason to retaliate. These are cases of self-deception, of motivated irrationality. They are not susceptible to normative explanations. While the belief has a role in explaining the action, its role is limited to disguising from the agent what 'really' brings it about—namely that it is the motive not the belief in the reason, which, being a self-deceived belief, is not a full or regular belief. It does not fulfil the role of ordinary belief in the life of the person.

Do masking beliefs present a case for revising the Thesis? The answer depends on the way we resolve an ambiguity in the Thesis. It sets two conditions: when acting with an intention, people act in the belief that there is some good in the action—that condition is met. The self-deceived believe that there is some good in the action. The second condition is that they act because of this belief. As I remarked earlier, the self-deceived belief is part of the explanation of the action: they need to deceive themselves to allow their motives full reign. But this explanatory role of the belief is not one that renders the action subject to a normative explanation. Should we say, therefore, that when understood as intended the Thesis has to be narrowed down to allow that if agents' belief in the value of the actions is self-deceived then they can act intentionally without their actions being explained normatively by that belief? That is not clear. The self-deceived believe that their actions are motivated by (their belief in) reasons. And that belief, though incorrect, need not be self-deceiving.[13] That shows that they are trying to be so guided. That, as you will recall, was what the concept of normative explanation tried to capture. It turns out that it does not cover all cases of attempts to be guided by reasons. But that may tilt one towards an understanding of the Guise of the Good that applies to their cases as well. The case is moot, and ultimately not much depends on which way we go. So let us assume for the time being that the Thesis does not need to be narrowed.[14]

7. The Luciferian Option

It is time to discuss the Guise of the Bad. But first an analogy and a contrast with weakness of the will. The analogy is limited to one point: weak-willed action both is and is not susceptible to normative explanation. It is, because it is taken for the reason that, as the agent sees matters, the action is good in some respect. The food is tasty, or having it will assuage the pangs of hunger, etc. At the same time, it is not (altogether) susceptible to a normative explanation, for the agent does not believe that there is sufficient reason for the action. In his view, the reason for the action is defeated by reasons against it. That is what makes the action weak-willed and, while the fact that the agent acted akratically may be explained, the explanation will not be a normative

[13] However in some cases it may be best to narrow it. We need not consider all the possible complexities of such cases.

[14] That reminds us that motives as well as beliefs can identify actions that are to be the object of intentions, enabling those intentions to guide the performance of those actions. What they cannot do is replace the Thesis and establish another route to forming intentions—that is why we need to deceive ourselves into believing that there is some good in the action.

explanation. It will be an explanation of why normative explanations fail to apply in this case.[15]

By its very identification, action taken for the reason that it is bad (or has some bad feature) is subject to normative explanation: it is an action for a (believed) reason. But the explanation cannot be complete, or completely successful, at least not if the Thesis is correct. The agent attempts to act for a reason, but fails. He fails because that the action is bad is no reason to take it. But there is more to his failure. It differs from that of a person who mistakes a poison for wholesome food. The agent acting for the bad makes no mistake about the character of his action, except for those that are entailed by his main mistake, which is about the possibility that a bad feature of the action would make it worth doing.

Is it possible to make such a mistake? Do those who act under the Guise of the Bad make it? It is possible to be mistaken or confused about concepts. But not all mistakes about a concept are consistent with being able to deploy the concept. Those, if there are such, who act under the Guise of the Bad deploy the concept of a reason, whether or not they would express themselves in these words. They take the badness of an action as favouring the action. That is, they act for a reason, and to do that they must have some mastery of that concept, or of closely related ones. They have the concept to the extent that their thoughts and words can be described using it. Given that they have the concept of a reason, is it possible that they believe that the badness of an action favours it?

Suppose that one performs an action, believing it to be bad, and saying or thinking that one is taking the action for that reason, yet, while employing the concept of a normative reason, having no thought about that concept. Perhaps in that case it is impossible to understand the agent to be taking the badness of the action as his reason. We are forced to understand his reason in a way that avoids attributing to him this incomprehensible thought: he may take the fact that it is bad for someone as his reason, for he may enjoy harming that person, or he may take the fact that it is thought by some or all to be bad as his reason, for he aims to shock them. But in such and any other case we may imagine there is, in the agent's eyes, some good in the action, and that is his reason.

Are matters different if his thoughts that lead to the action are, in part, about the concept of a normative reason, or about the Thesis? There is a

[15] However, it is worth remembering that the fact that the action (or any other condition) cannot be normatively explained, or the fact that it is irrational, does not entail that it is necessarily bad all things considered.

traditional explanation of an affirmative answer, a secular version of the Luciferian motive. One may have an urge to defy the limits of thought, the limits of what we can do or think, limits that are expressed in our concepts. Ordinarily, the drive to extend boundaries is different. It is the drive to create things of new kinds, requiring new concepts for their description. One may wish to write a narrative text that is neither fact nor fiction, and people who had that desire created a new genre of writing that is sometimes called 'nonfiction novel' or 'faction'. Things are different when the desire is to defy basic concepts: to produce an object that will not be an object, to add one to one without their sum being two or to take the badness of an action as something that is a reason for doing it. Alternatively, and another way to try to defy the Thesis, one may want to do something for a reason but not by taking anything to show that it is worth doing. To do that, one could perform the action because it possesses a feature that does not make it good. It need not be one that makes it bad. One chooses a bad feature as one's reason just to make abundantly clear that one is acting for a reason but without anything assumed to be good about the action being one's reason, and therefore without taking the reason to establish that the action is worth doing in any respect at all. There are probably other variants of Luciferian motives.

Some people may deny that there can be Luciferian motives or Luciferian goals. Stating them does not make sense. To be sure, they will say, one would be using grammatical sentences, but they have no content. One is merely verbalizing, and perhaps getting some feeling of satisfaction or comfort from one's own thoughts or words. But there is no content to those thoughts or sentences. But it is generally recognized that in some sense we do understand some kinds of nonsensical motives and goals. They are stated in sentences that do not give rise to the incomprehension of the famous 'Green ideas sleep furiously' or 'Saturday is in bed'. We do not need an account of what sense they make and how. We can assume that people can have these motives and goals. The question is to what extent one can succeed in them.

We do not expect complete success. Lucifer cannot win. But he can have something that can be thought of as a partial success. Like the weak-willed, the Luciferian aspires to both eat his cake and have it. The weak-willed aims, metaphorically speaking, to satisfy reason while flouting it. He succeeds in acting for a reason, and to the extent that he does that his conduct is subject to normative explanation. But he knowingly follows a reason while acting against reason, and that cannot be given a normative explanation. All we can do is explain (non-normatively) the motivation that leads him to attempt the impossible.

The Luciferian aspires to act for a reason by taking something that cannot be a reason for a reason. He knows what he is doing. By definition the Luciferian aspires to break the mould, so he knows what it is. In effect he is trying by his action to *make* the bad a reason for action, knowing that it is not, or has not been so far, or cannot be for beings lesser than he is.

I said that he could not succeed. But it may appear that he succeeds in something. He does not make the bad into a reason. But he performs the action that is bad because it is bad. Does that not show that he is guided by it and that his action is susceptible to a normative explanation—namely that he showed that it is possible to think that the bad is a reason?

Assume that he succeeds in that. I mean: he really acts out of a belief that the badness of the action is a reason for it. In itself that would not be remarkable. Many act out of a false belief that they have a reason when they do not. In the case of the Luciferian, the belief itself would be irrational: he irrationally believes—on our supposition—that by his choice he makes the badness into a reason, and that is irrational. But, even so, his action is susceptible to a normative explanation, though his having that irrational belief is not. It can only be explained non-normatively, by reference to his motivation. If this is how to understand the Luciferian, then action under the Guise of the Bad is possible and the Thesis has to be scaled down to allow for the Luciferian exception. This exception itself may be unexceptional. It is but one way in which theses about what can and cannot be thought are subject to exceptions, including exceptions through defiance.

But is this really how the Luciferian has to be understood? We have already encountered, in another context, the alternative. In discussing masking beliefs, we saw that motives can lead to intentional action in a way independent of a belief in there being something good in the action, provided they can induce an irrational belief that there is some good in the action. Perhaps the Luciferian action is similar: the bad action is to be explained non-normatively by the motive, but the rationalization is the irrational belief that the bad can be a reason. That belief does not explain the action, but it enables the Luciferian to believe that he achieved his goal. He is self-deceived, and the Thesis is intact. The Luciferian is acting intentionally but not for a reason, let alone the reason that the action is bad.

But does the Luciferian act under the Guise of the Bad? He does in the motivation version. Does he in the normative version? I suppose that the answer is: yes and no. As he sees matters he does. But that is due to his self-deceived belief that the bad can be a reason. So, in the objective sense, from an objective perspective, he does not. Which is the more important of these perspectives? Clearly, the subjective: being the perspective of the agent, it affects his actions and impact in the world. The objective perspective is only conceptually important.

7

Normative Powers

1. Normative Powers: Wide and Narrow

Powers are abilities or capacities to bring about a change or to prevent a change from taking place. It seems plausible to define normative power as a power to change or to prevent a change in a normative condition. Two quick clarifications: First, a normative power is exercised by a single act (as is typical of promising) or a relatively short series of actions (e.g. legislation[1]) and, second, its impact, the change it effects, is not causal (as when one person becomes fond of another through extended acquaintance) but normative (as when undertaking a vow or reciprocal vows generates rights and duties).[2]

The definition yields a concept so wide-ranging that it has little if any use. For example, according to it, killing and promising are both examples of exercising a normative power. I suspect that often thought and discourse about normative powers, whether or not they use the expression 'a normative power', refer to and use a narrower and more useful concept. Many years ago, I suggested something like the following definition:

[1] Among many other matters requiring further clarification, one problem is whether the exercise of the normative power effects normative change on its own, or whether it does so only in combination with other factors, i.e. only if other conditions are met. An example would be a case in which an act creates an obligation but only if another person exercises a power of his in an appropriate way. I tend to favour a wide definition including combinations of an exercise of power with other conditions. But I will not explore the limits of such possibilities.

[2] Some people seem to take 'normative power' to mean power (to change or prevent change) that is authorized by some normative condition (by a rule or another power, etc.). In that usage normative powers include also permissions to perform an action. For example, if I am permitted to move the chair then I have a normative power to move the chair. Needless to say, a permission (to move a chair, etc.) does not imply that I have the power (i.e. that I am able) to move the chair. And, I may have the power to move the chair even though I am not permitted to do so. This suggests to me that this sense of normative power is liable to breed confusion. However, the important point is not to confuse it with normative powers discussed in this chapter. In recent times the realization that power, roughly meaning influence, is sometimes caused by or sustained by common views and social conventions that are open to criticism (e.g. that people who speak with lower voices and an authoritative manner may silence others from expressing their views) encouraged some writers to elide the difference between normative and causal power. Important as the exploration of the ethical implications of such social practices is, it should not lead one to confuse these two kinds of power.

The Roots of Normativity. Joseph Raz, Edited with an Introduction by Ulrike Heuer, Oxford University Press.
 DOI: 10.1093/oso/9780192847003.003.0008

> a person's act is an exercise of a normative power if it brings about or prevents a normative change because it is, all things considered, desirable that that person should be able to bring the change about or prevent it by performing that act. Those who can exercise a normative power have a normative power to do so.[3]

I will call this the narrow concept of normative powers, and generally, when discussing normative powers, I have in mind those that fall under the narrow concept.

A prominent feature of the definition is that it identifies normative powers by the considerations that establish the justification for their existence (to be distinguished from the justification of their use), taking their justification to be sufficient for their existence. Some may have preferred explanations that focus on the characters of the acts that exercise normative powers, defining promises by defining the promising act or legislation by defining the act of legislation.[4] While the current paper does not explore the nature of power-exercising acts, it would be a mistake to assume that my account has nothing to say about the subject. Rather, the conditions on the exercise of normative powers follow from the definition of such powers, possibly with additional premises. Later, I discuss the considerations that require that many normative powers be exercised by communicating certain intentions. Another, even more general condition: given that a normative power exists if and because it is desirable that those who qualify to hold it be able to choose whether to exercise it or not, it is desirable that there will be no reasons for or against the act exercising it other than the normative change it brings about.

This chapter develops and modifies the definition of normative powers, casts some doubts on whether the wider powers are normative powers at all, and proceeds to locate normative powers in a general conception of normative justification.

3 I refer to the desirability of the power-holder having that power. In many contexts we would use a different term, often stating something stronger than 'mere' desirability: the power-holder may have a right to have the power, or s/he may deserve it, or it may be to the great advantage of humanity or of some part of it that s/he should have it. In some, but not all, such cases these considerations establish that the normative power exists: they establish the existence of the power if the right, duty, etc. establish the all-things-considered desirability of the power-holder having that power. So, the definition uses the broader concept, in order to capture all the cases that can sensibly be included among normative powers. This definition, like many philosophical definitions, is meant to capture, in an illuminating way, the nature of the phenomena defined. As such, it deviates from the ways the concept 'Normative power' is sometimes understood, a deviation that is justified on the ground that those other uses commonly mistake the nature of the phenomena they are intended to catch.

4 Currently the best attempt to do so is D. Enoch, 'Giving Practical Reasons', *Philosophers' Imprint* 11/4, March 2011. It is effectively criticized by E. Monti, 'Against triggering accounts of robust reason-giving', *Philosophical Studies* March 2021 and 'On the Moral Impact Theory of Law', *Oxford Journal of Legal Studies* October 2021.

2. Chained Narrow Normative Powers

The narrower concept I have provided does not apply without modification to normative powers within social normative systems, like the law, the constitution and rules of the university, etc. There are normative powers in such systems, and arguably their use is essential for the emergence and continued existence of such systems. But while, as I will claim, the concept of normative powers is the same when applied to powers existing within social normative systems or independently of them, its definition requires modification to apply to powers within such systems.

Let me call the narrow normative powers that meet the definition just given basic normative powers (NP). We know that basic NP are powers to change some normative conditions. But which ones? Can any normative condition be changed by the use of some normative powers? Is it at least possible that this is so?

There is no need here to explore what are normative conditions. They are conditions or situations of having a right or a duty or obligation, or indeed a power or a status, or a liability, etc. What is clear, when exploring the nature both of normative conditions and of other aspects of these concepts, is that we are likely to encounter many borderline and undetermined cases. To mention one extreme example: does the act of giving birth change a normative condition? If so is it the exercise of normative power? Another extreme example is that of a custom: given that customs are created and sustained by human acts and omissions are they the exercise of a normative power? Clearly not when it is the custom of a large country, but what of a family custom? The reason borderline cases and indeterminate cases are likely to proliferate is that to the extent that people's attention is drawn to normative powers it is drawn by an interest in some paradigmatic cases. We start from them, trying to understand a more general concept that is not in fact widely used. Hence it is unlikely to be completely formed.

However, some questions force themselves on us. One is whether there can be (valid) normative powers that enable their possessor to affect the normative powers that he or others have, namely to remove some of their powers, diminish their scope, or to add to them or enlarge their scope?

The obvious answer: 'it depends on whether there is an all-things-considered value in people having such powers'. Whether or not this test is satisfied may, of course, vary from case to case. The general question remaining is whether there is a case for thinking that the test for the existence of normative powers will never authorize the existence of a power to grant or modify powers. The answer must be negative. For example, by every valid promise, as well as undertaking an obligation, the promisor invests the promisee with a power to waive the undertaken obligation. So, if one can never have a power to create other powers then promises are never valid, and never bind the promisor. In fact, powers to create powers are common, and useful. My power to manage my property includes a power to endow some trusted person with power to manage all or some of it on my behalf, etc.

I will call a power that is created by the exercise of another power a chained power. And an originating power that is not itself a chained power is a basic power. Basic powers are valid only if they meet the test with which this chapter started: only if there is an undefeated value in the person whose power it is supposed to be having the ability to change at will the normative conditions that that power enables him to change. Call this the basic test.

Are chained powers valid only if they meet the basic test? At first blush we may think that they are not, for they are simply created by the holder of the originating power, who could create them at will. Except that that need not be the case. Assuming that the originating power is a basic power, it is valid only to the extent that it meets the basic test, which can impose limits on the use of the power. So, to revert to the routine example, a promise to commit genocide is not binding. Could it be that the basic test also, necessarily, requires that any chained power generated by the originating power would itself meet the basic test to be valid? That seems unlikely. What is true is that the basic test will impose some restrictions on the scope of valid chained powers. They too will not be able to impose an obligation to perpetrate genocide and so on. But I doubt that the basic test itself can apply to all valid chained powers. We recall that the point of basic normative powers is to extend the options of the power-holder to the extent of allowing him to make mistakes. Regarding certain matters, the basic test implies, it is more valuable to enable the power-holder to act on his own judgement, than to make sure (if this were even possible) that his decisions are always sound. The inevitable result, given human nature and the conditions of our life, is that the holders of originating powers will make mistakes, including mistakes in deciding when and to whom to give chained powers. Requiring too much perfection in their exercise of their powers will fail to achieve its aim, and will generate a host of undesirable consequences, such as increasing surveillance and interference in the life of power-holders to excessive and self-defeating degrees.

The conclusion is that the test for the existence or validity of a normative power sometimes yields the existence of powers to make and remake powers, and when it does, the validity of the chained powers so created[5] depends not on there being an undefeated reason for their holder to have them, but on a modified test that relies on the basic originating power being valid by the basic test, and on the chained powers being authorized by it.[6]

Chained powers are created by the use of other powers whose existence depends on their value. Chained powers are, therefore, social powers, the products of human actions and the actions of social institutions, which derive their own powers, ultimately, from the value of their existence. The validity of chained powers depends on value considerations indirectly, through the value of the powers whose exercise created the chained powers.

Normative conditions can change in ways other than by the use of normative powers. For example, social customs change them. Interestingly, normative conditions that come about through custom or through the use of normative powers share an important feature. They may be normatively binding, valid, and yet it might have been better had they not come about, and/or better that they be repealed. So, some specific social conditions may give rise to a valid, binding, duty whose existence or continuation is undesirable. I will call such conditions normative social conditions, and I shall call other normative conditions basic. Note that basic does not mean unchanging. The fact that normative social conditions can be deficient, in the ways indicated, implies that chained NP do not conform in all details to the account of normative powers that I gave at the outset. This is because such powers are given to agents to use as they see fit, and they may use them unwisely, granting powers when none should be given, etc. Therefore, chained powers exist not because it is desirable that their power-holder should have them, but because the normative system in which they are generated, or the agents creating them, take them to be desirable.

Chained powers are as normatively valid and can be as important as other powers. They should not be confused with claimed but normatively invalid powers, for example those claimed to be created by an illegitimate government, or by an individual who did not have the NP to create them.

[5] Though one should be careful not to assume that the chained powers are terminated when the powers that created them come to an end.

[6] Chained normative powers can be parts of complex structures of normative conditions. They may be constituent elements of status, or of rights, etc. The complexity of such structures makes it difficult to determine the value (and therefore the validity) of an existing or proposed single normative power. We modify the way we do so: we ask, given all the other existing elements in the structure to which this power belongs or will belong, will it be better if modified or avoided altogether?

3. Are There Wide Normative Powers?

This chapter focuses for the most part on narrow normative powers (chained or otherwise). What is the main difference between them and wide powers? Many and perhaps all NP in the wide sense, which are not narrow powers as well, can be called directing powers. They are powers one is (normatively) required to use or to refrain from using in specific ways (ways that determine their content). You have the power to kill but you are directed not to use it.[7] You have the power to make your tax returns by the appointed date and you are directed to do so. Directing powers are derivative powers in that what matters normatively in the first place is the outcome of their use: that people should not be killed, that taxes be paid. The purpose of the power is to secure the value of people using their powers as directed. Like everything else, these powers may be used for other useful, or undesirable purposes. Just as a book can be used as a door stop, so the directing powers can be used, say to promote reconciliation and trust between wrong-doer and wronged, or, on the contrary, to extract revenge, etc. In such cases, the direct purpose of the power, achieved when it is used as directed, is the occasion to serve other goals. However, there is no other, direct, value in having the power. Assuming that all killings are wrong, if people simply could not kill and therefore would not have the power to kill, which is a normative power, nothing would be lost (though its use to achieve indirect goals may make its loss regrettable or welcome, depending on the situation). But if people would not have the power to make promises or to get married, or to make laws for their communities, much would be lost beyond the value accruing from their use of these powers. The further loss is of the value of having these powers in expanding the range of free choices that people have. Because the value of the narrow normative powers is, in part, in the ability to use them, in the ability to choose to use them or to choose not to use them, and not only in the consequences of those choices. Perhaps this difference justifies taking the narrow concept of normative power as the core case; while other normative powers are only derivatively normative.

Narrow powers belong to such a great variety of kinds that it may be impossible to provide a comprehensive tabulation of their characteristics. I tended to think that they may be placed on a scale from content-determined

[7] Just to remind ourselves: while killing is just a physical act or activity, ending the life of a living being, it is also the exercise of a normative power in that it changes one's normative standing, making one liable to being treated in certain ways by the authorities and others.

to content-undetermined.[8] The powers to make promises or to legislate are examples of the second: those who hold such powers have considerable freedom to determine the content of the change their use of the powers brings about. I can promise to bring flowers to my mother and I can promise to look after a friend's child until his maturity, and so on and so forth. Naturalization, on the other hand, is the power to acquire a fixed set of rights and duties, or to bestow it on the person naturalizing. The newly naturalized cannot change its content. S/he can only accept (or not) the status of a naturalized person with all that it implies. Many powers can be placed on this scale of more or less content-determined. But others do not fit the scale, sometimes because of the great complexity of the implications of their use.

4. An Objection

The definition of normative powers is open to many possible objections. For example, some writers believe that the application of a concept should be value-neutral. Obviously, the correctness of the application of unchained narrow normative power to any instance depends on whether it is desirable that the agent should be able to effect that normative change at will, thus depending on the normative consideration. However, the value-neutrality requirement is misconceived and can be ignored here without argument. The arguments against it are available elsewhere.

I will focus on one important objection to the definition of basic normative powers: how can the existence or occurrence of a normative condition, like having a right or duty or a status, depend on the desirability of someone having the power to bring it about at will? It may be desirable that this car we see out of the window be yours if I say so. But it is not made yours by my say so. At the very least it has to be admitted that the desirability of the existence of a normative condition does not guarantee its existence or bring it about. What distinguishes cases in which the desirability is, as it were, self-fulfilling, from others? The definition I gave suggests an answer: it may be desirable that I should be able to make John's car yours, but there are also reasons against my having that power. It is not all-things-considered desirable that I should be able to give it. That may be a good answer, but doubts linger and require

[8] The terms were suggested to me by Sebastian Lewis.

further examination.[9] The difficulty is that what is presented as an objection is no more than a doubt or a question, and not at all an objection. No fault in the argument is suggested, and therefore none can be refuted. Being a question, it suggests no mistake that can be discussed. It has to be approached in a more roundabout way.

One popular way of arguing for one's view is to show that all alternatives to it are false. I have little trust in that way of arguing. But I will mention a few alternatives to my approach that have found considerable support, primarily to indicate points of difference that require further argument.

Buck-passers are likely to object that my definition gets things the wrong way around. Extreme buck-passers remind one of semantic phenomenalists who insist that the meaning of every term can be stated in an expression referring to sense data only. Non-reductionist buck-passers look for more complex ways of getting round taking value as grounding anything. I mention the fact only to concede that the defence of the definition I proposed involves some fundamental issues that cannot be discussed here.

An assortment of objections relies on the role of conventions in establishing normative powers, claiming that the account presented in this chapter is mistaken, because it ignores the role of conventions. Some such claims, whether true or false, are consistent with the definition of normative powers given here. One may point out that the use of normative powers typically affects people other than the power-holder, and that it would be odd to think that they can meaningfully be exercised when those affected by them are unaware that they are so affected, or that anyone may think that they are. Can Jane promise Rose to do her shopping next week unless Rose too understands what promises are and that they bind (or at least that that is a common view)? Such thoughts may encourage the view that normative powers exist only when there is, in the relevant population, a common understanding that they do. True or false, variants of this view are consistent with the definition here offered, being claims about some of the conditions that have to exist for the definition to apply.

'Institutional conventionalism' may be a suitable name for a more radical conventionalist view. Noticing that the origins of discussions of normative powers are in legal contexts the institutional conventionalist maintains that normative powers exist only in institutionalized settings like the law, the

[9] One question not addressed here is whether the existence of an unchained narrow power requires that the case for its existence defeats all competing reasons, or, whether it is enough that it is not defeated by them.

constitutions and rules of corporations, non-governmental organizations (NGOs), etc. We need to distinguish two questions: (1) Do normative powers exist in a certain domain? (2) Assuming that they do, is there a case for talking of normative powers when talking of that domain? The institutional character of a domain makes it helpful to talk of normative powers within it. For example, the accountability of institutions invites one to be careful and explicit in describing their activities. Contrariwise, the informal character of the domain often makes it better to avoid applying a formal and explicit analysis to its normative phenomena. Doing so may introduce a formalistic aspect to the understanding of relationships that should be kept fluid, and informal. For example, some people think that when one requests something of another one gives that other a reason to accede to the request. If this is so, then requesting is an exercise of a normative power. It may, however, be advisable not to discuss requests in these terms, except in the most abstract academic contexts.

I see no reason to accept institutional conventionalism. A more radical and difficult challenge is posed by what might be called 'pure conventionalism'. It understands conventions to be patterns of conduct ('most people wash their cars on Sundays') and takes such patterns to be reasons for action. So, the fact that when saying that they will do something most people do it, is a reason for any person to do what he said he will. Why? I know of no answer. Nor, it seems, can there be one, given that the pure conventionalist denies that there can be a normative explanation of normative facts. It is too far reaching a challenge to be discussed here.

Some writers may object to my definition in some of its applications only. Some think that consent, even when it is the use of a normative power, is a special phenomenon, manifesting the normative power of agents' will. People can impose duties on themselves by consenting to having them, directly or indirectly, explicitly or implicitly, that is by accepting them, embracing them, by their will. Desirability, they think, is neither here nor there. It is, however, known to all that in the practice of our societies, consent is taken to have normative significance almost always only when expressed in an act of consent. On the one hand, acts of consent that are taken to bind do not always express the will of the consenting agent. On the other hand, some consents that express the will of the agents are not taken to be binding. It is open of course to will-theorists to be reformers who denounce many of our common practices. But, those who believe that there is good sense in some of the common conditions under which consent is given normative force, face the difficult, I suspect the impossible, task of distinguishing between cases in which consent is normatively binding and those in which it is not, without appealing to the value of treating some cases as binding and others as not binding. Furthermore, will-based accounts even if successful in some cases, do not show that other accounts fail either in the same or in different cases. So, the success of my account has to be judged on its own merits.

Not all exercises of normative powers are examples of consent. Public authorities have, where appropriate conditions are met, the power to deprive some people of some of their rights and award those rights to others. But, supposing I am such an authority, it would be wrong to say that by decreeing that Charles's car shall belong from now on to Susan I am simply consenting to this change of ownership. I am using a different kind of power. It is also implausible to think that such change of ownership can be normatively justified by being the will of a stranger.

The need to distinguish between cases in which consent changes the normative situation and those in which it does not, by appeal to considerations other than the will, supports the attempt to provide a unified explanation of the normativity of all normative powers. One attempt to do so is presented by a communication account of normative powers. To be sure, some writers regard cases in which consent is binding only if communicated as a mere subordinate condition to the will-based account of normative powers, designed to protect third parties. Of course, that the communication requirement may protect third parties, does not save the will-based account, which is still unable to explain why only some consents bind. Protecting the will of third parties does not explain why consent to slavery, say, is not binding. In denying it validity the consenter is protected from himself. So, the question remains whether the normativity of normative powers can be accounted for by these powers being used by acts of communication? True, common practice includes normative powers whose exercise does not involve communication. But as so many normative powers do involve communication, perhaps those that do not are either a mistake or a special case enjoying separate justification. The problem facing a communication account is not that it doesn't match actual practice, but that it is not clear why anyone communicating an intention to assume a duty or to confer a right on someone else should be taken to have changed a normative situation. To explain that, we are likely to revert to a will-based account: my communicating to you that my car is from now on yours transfers ownership in the car because it expresses my will to do so. And we are back with the deficiencies of the will-based theory.

It should be clear that I am not contesting that many, perhaps all, exercises of normative powers are binding only if they express the will of the power-holder or only if they involve communicating the change they are meant to effect. My claim is merely that if they do, that is because it is desirable that normative powers be subject to such conditions. Indeed, in writing about promises, I endorsed the claim that promises are made by communicating an intention to undertake this specific obligation by the very communication.

Yet, it would be a mistake to think that the exercise of normative powers always involves communication. Of the various considerations that require that the exercise of power will involve communication perhaps the following two are the most common and important. First, when the powers used are partly content-undetermined, the content of the duties, rights, or the other conditions created using the power is determined (at least in part) by the power-holder when using the power. Among other things, the content of the communication determines what normative change has been created. Second, making a normative change by communicating it enables people to learn of it, thereby helping them to protect their interests, and often also helping a power-holder to protect his interests. Paradigm examples are content-undetermined powers, for example promises, contracts, general legislation, judicial decisions, in all of which both factors are present, and some content-determined powers, for example gifts, other unconditional transfers of title, getting naturalized, getting married, and other changes effected at will, but where the agent can only choose to accept or reject the new condition and has no power to modify its content. In these cases only the second condition is present.

However, there are many ordinary uses of normative powers to which neither consideration applies. These include many cases of consent, for example consenting to and thus agreeing to conform to the, clearly and visibly stated, rules of a restaurant or a theatre, etc. upon entering them. In cases of this type, when the consent is expressed by an open public act that is not an act of communication, neither factor applies, and the use of a normative power may properly not involve any communication.[10]

5. The Ultimate Self

The picture of the possibilities and limits of human agency that underlies the views explained in this chapter (and much else that I and others have written)

[10] This example, like many of my examples, is informally stated, relying on the reader being able to supply the required context in which they apply. It is not, e.g., my intention to claim that one who enters a restaurant carrying a poster saying I do not consent to the house rules of this restaurant, is consenting to them, nor that one who is forced to enter with a gun to his head is consenting to the house rules.

takes being guided by values as the mark of self-mastery and control of one's life. Humans can act for no reason, following urges and incomprehensible passions, anxieties, or frights, but central to their sense of who they are, and what their lives are about, is their ability to act for reasons, and direct their lives to the realization of goals that there are reasons to pursue. Admittedly most of the time when people have various options, those reasons do not direct them which specific option to pursue. Most of the time people have good reasons to exclude some options but also adequate reasons to choose among a number of rational (i.e. acceptable by reason) options, and their actual choices are guided by preferences for kinds of content that are admitted as rational but not required by reason. These choices contribute importantly to the development of individual tastes and lifestyles, all backed but not required by reason. So far this picture, while radically incomplete, may appear to be reasonable. The doubts with which I will finish this chapter arise for those, and they include me, who think that the values that provide more or less all the practical reasons that should guide our lives are themselves the product of the nature and activities of human beings. The theoretical background can be stated simply: what has value are either beings of certain kinds, those whose life and character can have value, or other things, experiences, activities, or whatever, that can be good for beings whose life or character can be valuable. If human beings are such beings then what is good for them can be valuable, and that will be determined by its possible role in their life. Hence, the nature of humans and the cultures that shape the character and opportunities of their life are a major factor in determining what is of value (and so are the nature and cultures of other beings whose life is of value).

Let us assume for the sake of the argument that many values depend on human nature, activities, attitudes, and practices, so that they would not exist without them. We will assume that when our actions can be guided by values, namely when values indicate which of the options open to us we should choose and pursue, we should do so. We should do so even if at the time we do not feel like doing so, even if at the time we feel that we would rather do something else. But given those assumptions why are we unable to create reasons for ourselves at will when there are no other reasons applying to the options available or when the reasons supporting none of the options defeat the reasons supporting each and all the other options?

The puzzle begins to clear when we reflect on the explanation of the dependence of some values on human nature and human cultures—they are among the factors that determine what makes human life rewarding and worthwhile, and what makes human activities enjoyable and worth doing: the beauty of a poem makes it worth reading, the value of being an eye surgeon makes it worth being one. These are but examples, helpful in pointing to the relations of actions, reasons, and values: values identify what is worthwhile for beings whose existence is or can be valuable. That is why values depend on the nature and practices of such beings. Values constitute reasons for those who can be guided by them, enabling them to choose what is worthwhile.

The examples may be suggestive, but they do not replace a systematic account: the existence of which beings is of value, and what follows from that fact (why does it not follow that it is better to have more rather than fewer of them?); why and when is the good of such beings a good for other beings? How to reckon with the different time dimensions of various goods—those that make one's life as a whole better and those that make a short period, or even a very short one, good or wonderful, etc. to have? And there are many others. But assuming that these questions can be answered, the sketch my examples provide holds good, and they enable one to resolve the puzzle that led to them. It is obvious why value depends, among other things, on human nature and culture, as they are among the determinants of what makes life and action worthwhile, and therefore obvious why values provide reasons for those who can follow them, for that is how they can enrich and improve their lives and actions.

When at any given moment reason underdetermines which of several options available to an agent is best, this is because none of those options would make the action better, more worthwhile, either in itself or in its contribution to the value of life generally. Given that nothing makes any of those options superior, the agent cannot make one of them superior just by declaring that it is. When—as with promising—agents can make some options good, that is because of the value those options have, and are known to have, before they are chosen. When agents choose them, they do not make them good *ex nihilo*, they merely realize the value of the options, a value that gave those agents reason to choose them.[11]

But, one might ask, could it not be that a person would just act arbitrarily, namely choose arbitrarily what to do? And that there would be nothing wrong, no fault or shortcoming in doing so? Yes, we should answer, subject to

[11] This is consistent with the possibility that the value of the option is conditional on its being chosen. The crucial point is that being chosen confers value only under some conditions, which are themselves independent of any choice. It is also consistent with the truism that every action may change the reasons one has before performing it. It may cause offence, requiring recompense, it may yield, intentionally or otherwise, a gain or a loss, to the agent or to others, which affects the balance of reasons now confronting him and other people.

interpreting 'arbitrary' in an appropriate way, that is possible. Just as the reason for an action may not be in the value of the consequences of the action but in the value of the action itself, so the reason for an action may be in neither the action nor its consequences but in the manner in which the agent comes to be resolved to do it. Therefore, it could be in the fact that an arbitrary process leads to its performance. When it is so, there is at least some value in acting and choosing arbitrarily. Of course, in some circumstances it may be impossible to deliberately act arbitrarily, for it may be impossible to devise such an arbitrary decision procedure or to follow it. It is not the case that if some choice is of value then any agent, or any agent for whom it is of value, has a reason to choose it. To have a reason it must be possible for the agent to choose the option for that reason, and that is not always possible.

In other words, the impossibility of people creating reasons when there is no value that enables them to do so is not a natural limitation on their powers or motivations. It is a necessary limitation, which is the result of the nature of value and of reasons: whenever a person can create a reason for himself, as in the case of promising, there is an explanation of why that is so, an explanation that consists in pointing to the possible value of his doing so.

However, none of this denies the possibility of people acting for no reason, yielding to caprice, surrendering to panic, or phobia, etc. On many occasions such actions will be irrational, but not always, hence not necessarily. The most common cases of acting for no reason are probably the innumerable cases in which people mistakenly believe that there is a reason for their actions or that they are acting for such a reason, and the cases in which people try but fail to do what they intended to do. Common to the numerous instances of such actions is that they are not fully controlled by the agents, frequently being actions they take against their will, or against their better judgement. Nonetheless the actions may turn out to be good, their desirable aspects may be more significant than the undesirable ones. That does not, however, make them actions that create reasons for their own performance where there was none before. Far from manifesting the self in its purest or deepest form, they manifest failure of self-control, or they are some peripheral cases of agency.

6. Normative Powers in the Larger Picture

Earlier in the chapter normative powers were defined by reference to the value of possessing them, which includes the value of the use likely to be made of them, but crucially also the value of having the choice whether to use them and how, including the expected value of refraining from using them on various occasions. That definition did not commit to any view of the nature of value generally, or to the character of the values establishing the existence of normative powers. The definition of normative powers does not stand or fall with the success of the view of value that I sketched in the previous section. However, if that view is correct it can apply to normative powers, and shows how their definition is but a special application of that general account of values.

However, as was briefly indicated earlier, some normative powers, namely chained and non-basic powers, belong with a class of normative conditions that can be both normatively binding and yet normatively defective to the degree that it would have been better had they not existed. For example, wills, gifts, marriages, agreements, patent rights, laws, administrative regulations, as well as customary rules whose existence is not owed to the use of normative powers, could all be valid and binding yet so defective that it would have been better if they had not been created, and sometimes, it would be better to terminate them.

The very possibility of things that are binding because it is good that they should be and yet are bad and should not be binding appears paradoxical. In that, it is unlike the apparently similar cases of things that are both good and bad in that some of their features are good and others bad (as in tasty but poisonous). There is no appearance of paradox in such cases. Nor is it like cases of things changing their value over time: they were good but are not so any more, because of changes that deprive them of their value (as when a new tower blocking the view from a flat reduces the value of the flat).

A natural suggestion is that this dual aspect of chained normative powers and of other normative phenomena like customs has to do with the fact that they are exercised by acts intended to exercise them. That is, however, a mistake. The definition of normative powers does not require them to be exercised with the intention to exercise a normative power, though often this is how they are exercised. The mental state required for their use is determined by the value that establishes their existence. Often it does not require such an intention. That is obvious in the case of the activities and practices that establish customary rules, as well as in the evolution of the common law through judicial decisions that often are not intended to develop the common law. The same is true of some other normative powers. Yet there the suggestion may be close to the truth. Normative powers are almost always exercised by acts that are related to intention to perform some actions, even if they end up being accidental, or if they are motivated by false beliefs in reasons that do not exist, etc. Given that in all these cases they are a successful exercise of power because they meet the value condition that applies to them, that condition recognizes the value of possessing power even when its exercise involves mistakes, misjudgements, etc. That is why chained powers, and related normative phenomena like customs, have that apparently paradoxical dual aspect.

7. How Sharp Can Our Distinctions Be?

One way to object to the sketch offered above is by an example meant to illustrate the creation of precedent as one way of changing reasons that is not backed by value or by a change in value. Think of two good friends, Ben and Jerry. As happens to most of us, Ben repeatedly finds himself in situations dominated by incommensurable options. Even though he has no more reason to choose one of them rather than the other, he tends to choose the same option every time. He does not know why, and he may even not be aware of the fact that he has the habit of choosing the same option whenever this situation recurs. Jerry, a caring and observant friend, does notice the habit, and takes this disposition of Ben's as a reason to make sure that the option he tends to choose is available to him in similar circumstances. After some time, Ben becomes aware of Jerry's actions and their reason. Now he takes himself to have a reason to choose the option he chose unawares in the past, and it becomes a little ritual between them, another way to mark their mutual affection. Ben's habit had, initially, no normative significance either to him or to Jerry. After a while it acquired a normative significance to Jerry. He realized that it is a way of pleasing Ben, in a small way in itself of little significance. But once Ben became aware of Jerry's motivation it became a common ritual providing reasons for both of them to keep it in existence, each of them feeling disappointment and some hurt when the other forgets to play his role, or refrains from doing so because he is upset for some reason.

Here, what started as a non-normative disposition was transformed into a practice enabling both Ben and Jerry to signal something about the state of their feelings or of their relationship, by conforming or not conforming with it. At that stage the practice may be said, perhaps at a stretch, to endow each of them with a directing normative power. The lesson I learn from this story is that the boundary between normative power and mere habit is often obscure to the degree of not existing in particular instances, a fact that does not cast doubt on the distinction between a mere habit and a normative practice. More importantly, the Ben and Jerry story illustrates one way in which the normative arises out of non-normative facts about humans and their relations, thus helping to explain how values can depend on human nature, dispositions, and cultures.

8
Is There a Reason to Keep a Promise?

Recent times have seen the publication of a good number of articles and book chapters about promises and related normative phenomena like contracts, agreements, voluntary undertakings, and consent. Of these one may think that promises are the least important, and if we think of the kind of promises that moral and political philosophers write about this may be so. At least it is true that most undertakings and agreements are much less formally created, arising not so much out of explicit acts of commitment as out of the implied meaning and consequences of an interaction over time. Discussions of promises commonly aim to illuminate much more than promises. They aim to explain voluntary undertakings in general, and to shed light on consent, hypothetical consent, and agreements. That promises are undertaken (or are at least discussed by philosophers as if they are undertaken) in an act of commitment merely makes them clearer and easier to discuss, but *mutatis mutandis* they stand for the wider class.

But do they? Possibly the paradigm, and therefore the explanation, is radically different. It may be in the web of mutual obligations arising out of stable continuous interactions, of one or another of recognized kinds, among people, as in personal friendship, or in parent–child relations, or the relation between a client and his regular supplier of goods or services.

I will not discuss the claims of this second type of explanation. It seems to be credible, and of great importance to the understanding of social life. I doubt, though, that it can displace the accounts of promises and other undertakings generated by acts of commitment. They require a different explanation, and their explanation is also vital to an understanding of human interactions. The explanation of promises alone is the topic of this chapter.

The chapter discusses the bare bones of promises. Promises are made by acts of communication, but the content of the promise is not the same as what is said in making the promise. Much of it is implied rather than said (did I, when promising to water your garden daily during your trip away, promise to do so first thing in the morning, as we know that you do?), and some of it is determined by the general moral principles governing the conditions that apply to promises (that they lapse if the promisor is paralyzed, that failure to

The Roots of Normativity. Joseph Raz, Edited with an Introduction by Ulrike Heuer, Oxford University Press.
 DOI: 10.1093/oso/9780192847003.003.0009

perform the promised act because it could only be performed by killing someone is not a breach of the promise, etc.). They have different meanings in different contexts, though sometimes made almost useless when the context is too thin (a stranger comes up to me asking for a loan of a dollar, promising to return it the following day—if I give him the money this is only because I discount the promise, though I am unlikely to reject it openly as this would openly display distrust of him). At the other extreme within a close intimate relationship promises may be out of place. Friends trust each other to act sensitively and the very fact that one promises an action whose performance should have been taken for granted may be inappropriate in that it conveys that one does not believe that the friend trusts one. And if one did promise and broke the promise it may be inappropriate for the other to express criticism invoking the promise, rather than the failure to act as one should have anyway, for that would show that one does not count on the other to be sensitive to the situation. I'm writing about the bare bones of promises, ignoring the rich contexts in which they occur, because the richness is based on familiarity with the bare bones and that enables the embedding of promises in the rich fabric of life.

If promises are binding, if they are cogent ways for people to bind themselves, there must be a reason to do as one promised. The chapter is motivated by belief that there is a difficulty, often overlooked, in explaining what that reason is. It arises because the reasons that promising creates are content independent. Similar difficulties arise regarding other content-independent reasons, though their solution need not be the same.

Section 1 introduces an approach to promises, and outlines an account of them, that I have presented before.[1] It will form the backdrop for the ensuing discussion. The problems discussed in the chapter arise, albeit in slightly modified ways, for various other accounts as well. It is, however, helpful to use a specific account as a springboard leading to one explanation of promissory reasons, namely of the reasons that valid promises constitute for performing the promised act (Section 2). We can call it the bare reasons account. Sections 3 and 4 will raise difficulties with that account leading to its abandonment in favour of an alternative in Sections 5 and 6. Throughout I will avoid technicalities except when they matter to the issues under consideration. Thus I will refer indistinguishably to the promise, the promising, or the promising act as the reason or the source of the reason, or something that

[1] See J. Raz, 'Promises and Obligations', in P. M. S. Hacker and J. Raz (eds), *Law, Morality, and Society* (Oxford: Clarendon Press, 1977) 210.

creates or establishes or provides a reason. I will not consider the conditions for a promise to be valid (can young children bind themselves by promising? Are promises to act immorally binding? Are promises binding after the death of the promisee, etc?), and will assume that they are fulfilled in the cases here discussed. And for the most part I will not comment about the special character of obligations, even though promisors have an obligation to keep the promise, and assume no more than that they are reasons. Nor will I say much about the fact that promisees have a right that the promise be kept.[2]

1. Promissory Reasons as Content-Independent Reasons

To see the difficulty think of an ordinary case: I have reason not to hit you, for a number of reasons: it may injure you, hurt you, invade your body, etc. They all depend on the nature of the action, its consequences and context. Now think of a reason arising out of a promise, say my reason to let you use my car tomorrow. The reason is that I promised to do so. But that very same reason applies to all my promises. If I promise to feed your cat next week, to come to your party, to send flowers in your name to your mother on Mother's Day, to lend you my book, or whatever the action I promise to perform (or to refrain from), the reason is the same: my promise. Of course, these are different promises. But normatively speaking they are the same, they all bind me because they are promises I made, regardless of what is the act promised. This is why they are (called) content-independent reasons.[3] There are considerations that make them binding, that account for the fact that the promisor has a duty to perform the promised act. But these are reasons why a promise is binding as a promise. They have nothing to do with its specific content.

[2] Though to avoid misunderstanding it is worth remarking that on my view the right to have a particular promise kept is derivative from the general right to have promises made to one kept, and it is in part grounded on the general interest promisees have to have the promise-generated relation to promisors.

[3] The term was coined by H. L. A. Hart. See H. L. A. Hart, 'Legal and Moral Obligation', in A. Melden (ed.), *Essays in Moral Philosophy* (Seattle: U of Washington Press, 1958) 82–107; H. L. A. Hart, *Essays on Bentham. Jurisprudence and Political Theory* (Oxford: OUP, 1982) 254–5. For my own discussion see J. Raz, 'Authority, Law, and Morality', *The Monist* 68 (1985) 295–324, reprinted in J. Raz, *Ethics in the Public Domain* (Oxford: Clarendon Press, 1995); J. Raz, *The Morality of Freedom* (Oxford: OUP, 1986); J. Raz, 'Reasoning with Rules', in Raz, *Between Authority and Interpretation* (Oxford: OUP, 2009) 203. For some other discussions see P. Markwick, 'Law and Content-Independent Reasons', *Oxford Journal of Legal Studies* 20 (2000) 579, and S. Sciaraffa, 'On Content-Independent Reasons: It's Not in the Name', *Law and Philosophy* 28 (2009) 233. As these discussions illustrate there are other kinds of content-independent reasons. For example, whenever any person or institution has (normative) power to impose duties on some people those duties are content-independent for they are binding not because of their content but because they are the product of the use of duty-imposing powers.

This last paragraph exaggerates. Some acts or omissions cannot be promised. One can mean to and even try to promise them, by communicating an intention that would have made a valid promise had it related to acts or omissions that can be promised, but the putative promise will not be binding.[4] If so, in what sense are promises content-independent reasons?

One simple idea is that promises are binding qua promises (or rather that that is the only ground for their binding character of relevance here), and that they are promises because they are communications of an intention to undertake an obligation by that very communication, regardless of their content, regardless of which act or omission they are about. I suggested that there are exceptions; acts that one cannot promise to perform. For example, a promise (given in current circumstances) to exterminate *Homo sapiens* or all primate species would not be binding. One may think that so long as such exceptions are rare they do not undermine the suggestion that promises are content independent. Such classifications are commonly subject to exceptions. For example, most of his readers do not think that Nozick's idea of side-constraints is undermined by the fact that, as he allows, side-constraints are not exceptionless.[5]

We have, however, to explain further the kind of reasons we are talking about, on two grounds: (1) if the exceptions are not to undermine the cogency of the classification, there must an explanation of what it is that makes them exceptional. This may not be necessary when the suspected exceptions are borderline cases. But many, including my examples, are not. (2) The acts for which we have content-independent reasons are acts for which we have such reasons because of some of their features: they bring the acts within the ambit of those reasons. So in classifying the reasons as content independent we mean that some aspects of (the content) of the acts are irrelevant to the fact that they fall within the ambit of those reasons. But that is true of all acts: reasons apply to them because of some, not all of their features. We need an explanation of the special way in which these reasons are content independent.

We can proceed on the assumption that all content-independent reasons are generated by the use of normative powers. This is not entirely true but the explanation of why the other cases are cases of content-independent reasons

[4] 'Promise' and its cognates are used to refer both to what I here called a putative promise, and to a binding promise. As is common I rely on context to disambiguate their meaning.

[5] See R. Nozick, *Anarchy State and Utopia* (New York: Basic Books, 1974) 29ff.

is analogous to explanations that apply to reasons generated by the use of normative powers.[6]

Normative powers are the abilities of people (or institutions) to change normative situations or conditions (i.e. to impose or repeal duties, to confer or revoke rights, to change status, etc.) by acts intended to achieve these changes, where the ability depends on (namely is based on, grounded on, justified by) the desirability (the value) of those people (or institutions) having them.

In the case of promises the value of the power is that it expands people's ability to fashion their lives, or aspects of their lives, by their actions. Through their promises they commit themselves to others. Up to a point, promises are analogous to decisions that constitute reasons for the deciders to perform the act they decided to perform. Both are ways of opening up options through closing other options, normatively speaking. Decisions, as well as having goals, facilitate undertaking complex activities (giving a ball, writing a symphony, etc.) that require a series of actions or concerted actions. Promises, being commitments to others, facilitate cooperation, the forging of relations that presuppose dependence, trust, and joint actions, and more. For the sake of brevity I will refer to the value of having these powers as the value of enhanced control (of one's life),[7] though a somewhat different explanation of their value is required when the powers are held by institutions.

Now we have the answers to our questions: The claim that some (putative) promises are not binding presupposes a distinction between binding promises that are overridden by conflicting reasons, and promises that are not binding,

[6] A typical and relatively well-known example concerns the making of the first laws of a new legal system, e.g. of its first constitution. In all respects it is just like the use of legislative power, except that as the original lawmakers established the first laws of the system there was at the time no law that conferred legislative power on them. They may or may not have had mere moral power, but they did not have morally valid legal power to make the laws that they did.

[7] Note that no claim is made that trust or cooperation, etc. require promises. They do not, but often the ability to promise makes it easier to facilitate them, as well as—by refraining from promising—to make clear that they are not sought. However (these observations are prompted by a question of Selim Berker), would not the value of enhanced control be equally served if people believed that they have the power to promise even though they do not have it? False beliefs always lead to the conduct that the same beliefs would have led to had they been true until they collide with reality, a collision that if circumstances are propitious, leads to their abandonment. The same is true of normative beliefs. Those who know that they do not have the power to promise will not be able to make promises (unless they are willing to mislead the promisees) and those who discover that there is no power to make binding promises will realize that all the promises made to them are not binding, and the trust and reliance they inspired are ill-founded, or depend on the promisers remaining ignorant of the truth. Not only does the vulnerability of the falsely secured enhanced control lead to it not being as valuable as the one provided by the power to promise. It is also misguided to think that a significant good is systematically secured by continued false belief, especially when this implies, as it does here, that people unknowingly rely on the other not knowing the truth.

and therefore do not constitute any reason at all. The difference is that the former do, and the latter do not serve the value that grounds the power to promise, giving promises their normative force, making them reasons for the promised acts. The assumption is that there are some undertakings, ability to make which does not serve the value of having enhanced control. Ability to promise to become a slave may be an example, as is a promise to destroy all primates. If the assumption is mistaken, and that is a substantive moral question, then we have power to make such promises, and when made they are binding and constitute reasons.[8]

The crucial point is that it is not having the obligations one undertakes by promising that is valuable, in enhancing people's control or in some other way. These obligations may or may not be valuable. Even when they are, their value does not establish the existence of a normative power to undertake them by a promise. The power is grounded in the desirability of people being able to commit themselves by the relevant act of communication. For example, it may or may not be desirable that Jean will have a duty to serve in the army, or to do jury service. It is a separate question whether it is desirable that she should be able to undertake such obligations by promising to serve. So the value of the ability to promise to help a neighbour, for example, is the value of being able to fashion one's life in one's relations to one's neighbours, and it is as important to people to be able to decide to keep a distance from their neighbours as to get involved with them. The value is in being able to decide *whether* to commit to the neighbours, not in the value of committing to them. When you can commit, not committing is itself significant, and the ability to commit at will makes it so. And indeed, we know that people can gain by avoiding commitment (but only when that avoidance is optional,

[8] These considerations help with the question what intention is required for the promise to be valid. Clearly, an intention to keep the promise is not a condition of its validity. But is an intention to undertake an obligation by the act of communication such a condition? Is an intention to communicate an intention to undertake an obligation? Some would argue that the value of having the power to promise is served only so long as one is bound only when the promising is done with the intention to thereby undertake an obligation. But arguably an intention to communicate, by the conduct that constitutes promising, an intention to undertake an obligation is sufficient for the promise to be binding, according to the explanation I gave. Others say that neither intention is needed for a promise to be binding. Promises are binding if the promisee would reasonably assume that the intention to undertake (or to communicate an intention to undertake) is present. This, if unqualified, goes too far. The consequences of even reasonable mistakes may justly have to be borne by those who make them. However, when a reasonable mistake is due to careless or negligent conduct of the promisor, the promisor will have a duty to compensate for any untoward consequences of the mistake, and that would often be the same as a duty to keep the promise (or to compensate for its breach). It would be pedantic to expect our concepts to be clear about whether that duty is the promissory duty or a separate one.

when they could have committed). For example, one person may reward an agent for not committing to another.

Therefore, if one does not have a power to promise to extinguish all bird species, that is not because it would be bad to extinguish them. That would only show that the obligation that the promise would have generated had it been binding, is overridden. What explains the absence of the power to make such a (binding) promise is that it is not desirable that one should be able to decide whether or not to undertake such a commitment.[9]

That is why the value of the ability to bind oneself to others, in identifying the range of acts performance of which we have the power to promise, establishes the sense in which the reasons to perform them are content independent: it is not independent of their character as promised acts (whose performance was undertaken in binding promises), but it is independent of all their other features. The fact that they depend only on this one external property makes the use of the term content independence natural.

2. Promissory Reasons as Bare Reasons

Does this explanation of why promises constitute content-independent reasons answer the question of the title? It appears to do so: we have reason to act as we promised because we promised, and promises are such reasons because they are the product of the use of a valuable normative power. This may be true, but it also generates a puzzle.

Given that normatively all promises have the force of a promise, it must be, the argument goes, that their strength or stringency is the same. It does not matter whether the promise was to look after your children while you are away on a work-trip next week, or to lend you a copy of the new Murakami novel. The reason to keep either of these promises is the same because they are both promises, and have the so-called weight that all promises have. This may appear absurd. But perhaps it is not. Arguably as promises they all have the same force or weight. But once given they may affect the course of events in different ways. In the children promise my friend forgoes making alternative arrangements for looking after his children in his absence, in the Murakami

[9] How broad is the category of cases regarding which it is not desirable that one should have the power to bind oneself? It may relate to types of acts (self-enslavement, etc.) or duration or other aspects of the promise (cannot promise to obey forever, etc.), and it applies to the largest class of cases that does not include a subclass (demarcated in universal terms) such that it is desirable to have the power to promise regarding it.

case he forgoes buying the novel in a book sale. Given these facts the results of breaking the promises will be very different, and therefore the force of the promise is different, much greater in the children promise than in the Murakami one. But the difference in the strength of the reasons for keeping the promises is due not to the bare facts that I made the promises, but to events that happened as a result of promising, and for which I am responsible. Qua promises my reasons to do as I promised are indeed the same, the appearance of the difference is due to other events for which I am responsible. Of course, one may point out that the additional reasons, the ones that depend on the consequences and/or context of the promise, would not constitute the reasons that they are but for the promise. Therefore, they are promise-generated reasons. But they are contingently dependent on the promise. Let us call them secondary strength-affecting factors. The bare fact of the promise generates a reason of the same strength in all cases, never mind what is the content of the promise.

This argument is reinforced by the fact that what I called secondary strength-affecting considerations need not even be present. Possibly the promise was not relied upon and did not affect the course of events in any way. Nevertheless, even such promises are binding. That shows, the argument proceeds, that the very reason to keep a promise is independent of these strength-affecting factors. The strength-affecting factors are indeed secondary. The bare promise, shorn of all these contingent additions, is the reason to do what I promised, and it always has the same strength.

Perhaps this conclusion is premature. Perhaps the strength of the promise is determined by the promisor in the act of making the promise. 'Why can't the promisor communicate an intention to create an obligation specifically of strength S?'[10] Perhaps promisors do so explicitly: 'I promise to lend you my book, and that promise will have the strength S', but more commonly they may do so by their demeanour, or by making the promise in circumstances that imply that it has a certain strength.

The answer lies in the nature of promises. By promising we create a reason to act as promised. The nature of the promised act contributes to the determination of how much I am willing to give up to keep it. If I promise you $1,000 I create a reason that requires a greater 'sacrifice' from me than if I promise you $1. I indicate that the promise has greater strength.[11] As each

[10] A question urged on me by David Owens.

[11] I have argued (J. Raz, 'Reasons, Decisions and Norms', *Mind* 84 (1975) 481–99) that promises have exclusionary force: They are reasons not to act for some reasons that apply to the promisor. More specifically, they are reasons not to act on some reasons that arise out of the promisor's convenience or

promise defeats 'ordinary' self-regarding reasons against keeping it, the more it costs me the stronger it is, that is, it can defeat more weighty reasons against keeping it. So by making that promise I determine its strength at least to that extent. If promises are ever binding that is because of the value of people having the power to determine (up to a point) the strength of the promised act relative to their other interests. But that does not mean that there is value in people being able to determine the strength of the reasons that promises generate, or the strength of any other reasons, relative to the strength of reasons that arise out of the interests of others. There is not. I cannot make a binding promise to come to your party even if this will require me to injure or rob someone, or not to help a person just injured in an accident, etc. While it is, I assume, desirable that I should have some control over the strength of my promise relative to some of my own other interests, and the very making of a promise does just that, there is no case for letting me determine its strength relative to other people's needs, interests, etc.[12]

The strength of a reason is its standing when conflicting with other reasons. Assume that G has a general power to determine the strength of his promises. He can (a) promise to perform some action, and (b) determine that the promise will have a certain strength, and he can do both by communicating an intention to do that by that very communication. He can of course promise to perform an act without determining what strength that promise has (beyond what is inherent in making a promise to perform that act). Can he also determine the strength of existing reasons without creating a new reason? Why not? He could, for example, do that by making the following promise: 'Tomorrow I will do whatever serves my self-regarding interests regardless of whatever other reasons apply to me.' That promise does not constrain him to perform any act he would not have reason to perform anyway (one's interests are reasons anyway). Its effect is merely to reduce to nothing the force of all reasons that derive from the interests of others applying to him. How much strength, if any, does this declaration have? I find nothing to suggest that there is any value in people having that power.

his personal interests. That is why the reasons they provide are duties (roughly, exclusionary categorical reasons). This is consistent with the fact that the duty to act as promised can be overridden by some considerations relating to the promisor's interests or well-being.

[12] As always there are exceptions that confirm the underlying principle. Some promises are made in response to a request by the promisees that their interests or concerns shall not stand in the way: I may promise my partner that when choosing my next employer I will not be affected by her convenience, but by what is best for my own career. That promise binds me to downgrade reasons that concern her, but only in response to her own wishes.

Two additional clarifications may be useful here. First, I ignore informal aspects of the manner of promising, those that convey sincerity, assurance of performance, etc., as they may affect trust in the promisor, but not the strength of his obligation. Second, different considerations apply to undertakings of different kinds, marked by their formal features. There are oaths of office (as a judge, etc.), and of loyalty (upon naturalization, etc.), vows of marriage, and more. These are voluntary undertakings that do or purport to affect the relative strength of reasons arising out of interests of people other than the person who undertakes them. Not all of them are normatively sound, and not all do yield valid undertakings. But some do, and those that do differ from promises in many ways, among them the fact that as they are established by law or custom: (a) people committing themselves do so in public; (b) they undertake duties whose content is determined by law or custom rather than by them; (c) there are restrictive qualifications for being able to undertake these obligations; and (d) strict conditions for being released from them; and all of these help explain why they do affect the strength of other people's interests. They establish, when sound, valuable optional patterns for structuring one's life, and relationships.

Back to the bare reasons account of promissory reasons. Though the reasons for embracing it may differ, it is often implicitly assumed, and has recently been explored by David Owens,[13] who traces it back to Hume's discussion of an analogue of the issue, applying to motives rather than to reasons.[14] According to it promising (when creating a binding promise) generates a bare promissory reason, which is the same reason with the same strength (relative to reasons relating to other people's interests and concerns) regardless of the promised act. However, the overall force of a promissory reason may be affected by secondary strength-affecting considerations, so that the case for keeping promises varies with these considerations.

3. What is the Strength of Bare Promissory Reasons?

Later on I will argue that (a) while the reason for performing the promised act is the promise, (b) the strength of that reason is varied by factors that are not

[13] D. Owens, 'The Possibility of Consent', *Ratio* 24 (2011) 402–5. Rather than write about the obligations and reasons promises create he writes about the wrongings that (presumably only some) of their violations constitute. See his explanation of 'bare wrongings' on 404 and on the relations between them and secondary reasons for keeping promises on 405. These matters are explored in greater breadth in his *Shaping the Normative Landscape* (Oxford: OUP, 2012) pt. II.

[14] David Hume, *Treatise on Human Nature* (1740) (P. H. Nidditch (ed.), Oxford: OUP, 1978) 482–3.

contingently related to the promising in the way that the secondary weight-affecting considerations are. But first, what is actually wrong with the thought that all promises qua promises have the same strength?

Imagine that I promised to do something today, and imagine that no secondary strength-determining factors apply. The promise was beyond doubt a binding one. Therefore, it constitutes a reason for performing the promised act. As is common, there are, however, also conflicting reasons. At the very least if the promise is to act, but sometimes even when it is to refrain from action, behaving as promised requires attention and effort that one could usefully put to other use. Hence the question: what is the strength of the promissory reason, how does it fare against the conflicting reasons?

Why not consider a case where there are no conflicting reasons? Would not that reveal the true strength of the promissory reason on its own? No, is the answer. That would only establish whether the promise is binding at all. The strength, stringency, weight, importance, call it what you will, of a reason just is the case for conforming to it rather than to conflicting reasons.

So, what determines the bare strength of the promissory reason? As with all other practical reasons, it must depend on the considerations that make promises binding. At this point the content-independent character of our case complicates matters: The case for any particular promise being binding, thereby being a reason for the promised act, does not depend on the specific character of the action promised, but merely on the fact that it was promised. Therefore, it would appear that the case for keeping a promise must rest with factors that unite all binding promises regardless of their content. So, plausibly the factors that determine the strength of the reason to promise are to be found in the case for, the value of, possessing the power to promise. For example, given that I promised to let you use my car today, I have reason to let you use my car today. That reason does not depend on the wisdom or value of having made the promise, nor of your using the car, of having the chance to use it, nor of that chance being provided by me, nor on anything else to do with this particular promise and its content. It derives from the power to promise. Needless to say, I would not have the power if my promises did not bind me. They bind me because I have the power to bind myself, and I used it to make them.

Here finally is the puzzle: I have a reason to let my friend use my car because I promised, and the promise is binding because that is the consequence of having and using the power to promise, and I have the power because of the value of the enhanced ability to shape my life that it provides. The value of that power should, I suggested, determine the force of the reason to keep the promise. But it does not seem to do so. My enhanced ability to control my life manifests itself in having the power to promise and in using it by promising. How does it reflect on the reason to keep a promise, and on its strength? Keeping the promise will not further enhance that ability, nor will breaking the promise undermine it. The normative case is a case for possessing the power to promise, not a case for keeping a promise, unless that is constitutive of or conducive to having the power. But is it? People who break their promises do nevertheless have the power to promise, as is evidenced by the fact that their promises are binding. If they were not there would be nothing wrong in breaking them.[15]

It is true that sometimes breaking promises will reduce the value of having the power to promise. Generally speaking the value of the power depends on the degree to which some people (those to whom we may wish to make promises) trust us to keep our promises. Sometimes, though far from always, breaking a promise undermines that trust. In such circumstances the case for protecting the value of the power to promise is one of the secondary strength-affecting considerations I referred to above. But in no case does it affect the strength of the bare reason to keep a promise, because it does not affect possession of the power to promise and the case for the power is the only resource that can provide bare promissory reasons for keeping promises.

It would, by this reasoning, appear that the value of having the power to promise is realized, and exhausts itself, by making binding promises. It does not determine the strength of the reason to keep one's promise. Worse still, it appears not to determine the strength of promissory reasons because it is powerless to give one a reason to keep promises.

4. Is There a Bare Reason to Keep Promises?

I began with a puzzle about the resources available to determine the strength of the bare reason to keep a promise. In exploring it we discover that it goes further. It raises a question mark on the very existence of a reason to keep a promise. Earlier I assumed that the value of enhanced control over one's life,

[15] Some people think that habitual promise breakers lose the normative power to promise. I think that they lose trust of others, and with it much of the value of having the power to promise, but they lose that power only if it is impossible for them to regain trust, and only if having the trust of others is the only way in which the power to promise is valuable to those who have it. Both conditions rarely materialize. It is true, though, that if a promise-breaker loses the confidence of people they may refuse to accept, or they may rescind, any promise he may make.

by providing an adequate case for having the power to promise, also constitutes an adequate case for the binding force of promises, for the power cannot exist without it, and thereby it establishes that there is a reason to keep them. But that may have been premature. Without resolving the puzzle about the force of bare promissory reasons, one may claim, there is no case for holding that there are any reasons for keeping promises. If so the reverse of the original argument holds: if one has power to promise one has reasons to keep one's promises. Therefore, since one does not have reason to keep promises one has no power to promise. Can it be that we have reason to keep our promises even though they do not have any strength? I doubt it. Here is an argument supporting the doubt:

First premise: The secondary strength-affecting considerations apply only if there is a bare reason to keep promises. Of course there may be other reasons for performing the promised act. Letting you have my car today may express friendship or good will and trust, and there may be a case for lending you the car for reasons to do with these or similar considerations. But these are reasons to perform the promised act independently of whether or not there is a valid promise.[16] The same is true of reliance. Some writers have maintained either that people would not rely on promisors to perform the promised act, or that such reliance will not constitute a reason for promisors to perform it unless promises are binding and constitute reasons to act, at least if they were relied upon. But that is not true. People rely when they expect their reliance to be vindicated. This may be because they believe that binding promises were made, or more likely because they believe that the people on whom they rely think that they are bound by promises they made, but it does not presuppose that promises are binding. Nor is it the case that one has no reason to fulfil another's expectations when the other acted on them unless one made a valid promise to that person. The results of frustrating the reliance may be such as to require avoiding them. Besides, in many situations if the other innocently believed that I am bound by a valid promise that is a sufficient reason to behave as I would had I really been bound by such a promise. So, reliance can be an independent reason to behave as one promised. So can various other secondary reasons: where there is no binding promise they may be independent reasons in their own right. But they cannot be considerations affecting the strength of the reason to keep a promise,

[16] In saying that I am not denying that where there is a valid promise and a promissory reason to keep it some such considerations may affect its strength, may constitute strength-affecting considerations.

unless there is a binding promise that constitutes a reason, whose strength they affect.

Second premise: A reason that has no strength-determining factors is no reason at all. First, an aside: Could it be that it has some strength that we simply cannot know? Even if it has, the point is irrelevant here. The premise is about factors that make the strength what it is, regardless of our ability to know the strength. But throughout the discussion I assume that factors that ground reasons can in principle be known because reasons are factors that one can be guided by, one can act for, and that requires that they will be—in principle—knowable.[17] I further assume that not only can they be known, they can be understood. They are intelligible considerations, ones whose force and binding character can be understood.

Given that assumption, if a reason has strength or stringency there are grounds determining its stringency that can be known. And if there are none then either there is no reason or there is a reason whose degree of strength or stringency is zero. That possibility can be ruled out, given that the very idea of a reason is of a factor that militates in favour of some action (or omission), namely that lends some support to the possible conclusion that that action is the one to take.

But perhaps we should distinguish between two aspects of the normative force of reasons: the first is that they favour an action (or omission), the second that they have some strength or force. The first aspect is essential to all practical reasons, but the second is not. In its absence the reason cannot defeat any conflicting reasons, but it can (a) determine what is to be done in the absence of conflicting reasons,[18] and (b) be a tie-breaker. Can there be such reasons? They will be reasons that will be defeated if they conflict with another on their own,[19] however insignificant that other reason is. I find that hard to envisage: what could make it understandable that a consideration that militates for an action so that in the absence of any conflicting considerations one would have conclusive reason to perform it will nevertheless be defeated by even the most insignificant conflicting reason? I suspect that the distinctions on which we rely in deliberation and in reasoning cannot cut that fine.

[17] See Chapter 3 above and J. Raz, *From Normativity to Responsibility* (Oxford: OUP, 2011) Chap. 6.

[18] I suggested above that that is hardly ever the case with actions. But perhaps it is not that rare with omissions.

[19] Note that the claim that any reason has some strength supporting the conclusion that the action is to be done is consistent with allowing that its existence makes no difference to the conclusion that the action is the one to be undertaken. It is possible that whenever that reason for doing Φ is present so is another reason for Φ-ing, and that the combined strength of both is no greater than the strength of either one of them in support of the action.

Therefore, I am inclined to conclude that: Unless there are factors that determine the strength of a bare reason it is not a reason, and we have discovered no such factors. Indeed, if all promises have the same strength it is difficult to see what could determine it.

This argument does not contradict any of the premises of the earlier argument that seemed to establish that there are binding promises. Rather, it points to a missing step: that argument relied on the fact that it would be good if people had the power to promise, and that there is no conflicting normative case sufficient to show that on balance people should not have that power. But that is not enough to show that people have the power to promise. It is impossible to have the power to promise, however good it may be to have it, unless that one promised is a reason to do as one promised, and it is impossible for there to be a reason to keep a promise unless it has strength. If promissory reasons have no strength they do not exist and however desirable it is to have the power to promise one cannot have it.

Yet we do have it. It would seem that I have failed to notice some factor that connects the case for the power to promise with the reasons to keep promises in each case in which one has promised. The fault may be in looking for too direct a connection. Here is one different approach, based on considerations of integrity: the power to promise serves and expresses one's ability to have some control over one's normative situation. Having exercised that power by making a promise it would show lack of integrity to deny that one is bound by the promise. Possibly, the degree to which denying that a promise is binding compromises one's integrity varies with the content of the promise, and therefore while the reason is always the promise its strength varies with the damage to one's integrity of denying that it is binding.

But the argument is suspect for it merely shows that the promisor has reason not to deny that his promises are binding. Is that enough to show that they are binding (even assuming that the reasons not to deny that they are are conclusive)? Besides, the argument is guilty of *petitio principii*. Integrity is involved only regarding people's attitudes to obligations they have. It cannot establish the existence of those obligations, and therefore it cannot establish that promises create reasons.

The conclusion towards which we are driven is that there are no bare promissory reasons, and therefore no considerations that determine their strength. The thought that there are misunderstands promises because it misunderstands the point of promises. This conclusion can be reinforced by examples.

Consider the car-lending case with some additions. Abby promised to bring Ben her car and leave it in his garage for his own use for the whole of today. Yesterday Ben, who lives alone, was taken suddenly ill and is now in hospital unconscious, where he is expected to stay for at least a week. The example is meant to be one of a bare promise in that no conditions that could qualify as secondary strength-affecting considerations obtain.[20] Would Abby be breaking her promise if she fails to leave the car in Ben's garage, and instead uses it to do her shopping? Could it be that she would be breaking the promise and violating her duty to Ben, but that she is justified in doing so because the reasons to use the car for her shopping defeat the reasons for keeping the promise?

It is hard to think of any reasons that would not defeat the promising reason. Suppose it is just to save her the expense on petrol of driving the car to Ben's place, or suppose it is just saving herself the bother of getting out of bed in time to deliver the car. It appears that any reason against keeping the promise would in the circumstances override the promising reason. That makes it virtually impossible to maintain that the promise is a reason to perform the promised act. As we saw, to be a reason the promise must have some strength or force, and strength just is resistance to conflicting reasons. A reason that is defeated by any possible conflicting reason is (possibly apart from some exceptional cases) one without force and therefore is not a reason. That conclusion generalizes to all promises. The reason we are investigating is the reason provided by a bare promise according to the account that takes the strength of that reason to be the same regardless of the content of the promise. It is determined just by the fact that it is a promise, and is the strength of all bare promissory reasons (promises to counteract climate change, to provide pensions for the elderly, etc.). It appears that the bare reason account must be mistaken.

The way out is to deny that in the circumstances Abby is bound by the promise. Promises, like intentions, decisions, orders, vows, permissions, and the like are subject to conditions. These can be described as part of the content of the promise (I will give you the car so long as there is the slightest chance that having it will be of use to you, or something along those lines) or they can be described as part of the ground rules that limit the kind of promises people can make: the limits can be conditions under which promises lapse, etc. (rather than merely specifying kinds of promises that can never be binding). In some cases one of those ways of perceiving the situation is better

[20] That means that it is assumed that Ben intended to use the car himself, made no arrangements for others to use it if he is prevented from doing so, that there is no one with the right to make such arrangements in his stead, etc.

than the others. In some cases it matters not which way it is taken to be. What matters is that in some kinds of circumstances, and Abby's are one such kind, promises that appear to apply to them do not in fact apply.

This seems right, but it is also right that these background conditions eliminate the possibility of bare promissory reasons. It is plausible to think that in all situations to which no strength-affecting considerations apply there is no valid promissory reason. That casts doubt on the bare reasons account. It is time to consider an alternative account.

5. The Point of Promises and the Interests of Promisees

We have some building blocks: The point of the power to promise is to expand people's options by enabling them to undertake obligations at will, more specifically by communicating to the promisees an intention to undertake those obligations by that very act of communication. It is a valuable power, which is used (or not used) for many purposes. The value of having the power, and the fact that that value defeats contrary considerations, constitute the case for the existence of the power by showing that its existence is desirable.

The difficulty we encountered is that it is impossible to have the power unless promising creates a reason to perform the promised act. And so far we have found no way in which the value of having the power by itself generates such a reason. We need an account that shows how the exercise of the power changes the normative situation, most likely in different ways on different occasions, and how through that the value of the power to promise can explain why one has a reason to keep promises, the same reason, but possibly with a different strength on each occasion.

To find it we have to describe more fully what we do when we promise. One way to think of it is to think of the point, or purpose, of promises generally, meaning here not the point of having the power to promise (discussed earlier) but the point served by promises made. Different promises or classes of promises have, no doubt, different specific points or purposes. But all of them are particular instances of the general point of promises, and it determines what we necessarily do when we promise. For example, that general point cannot be to confer an advantage on the promisee, for while often this is the whole or part of the point of a promise, it need not be. It need not even appear or purport to be. I can promise my mother that I will look after my health, or that I will give money to Oxfam, or that I will never give her interests precedence over the interests of my father, for example. But something about promises being obligations undertaken *for the promisee* must be right. The question is how to understand the phrase '*for the promisee*'.

But why must it be that promises are obligations undertaken *for the promisee*?[21] There are two defining features of promises whose explanation establishes the point. First, obligations are binding only once communicated to the promisee. Second, the promisee has a right that the promise be kept, and a right and power to waive his right,[22] releasing the promisor from his undertaking, at any time and at the promisee's complete discretion. These features are not necessary elements of all undertakings. Vows do not require a recipient in the same way (though some have recipients). Undertaking an office, say of a judge, is not open to revocation at will by some recipients, etc. But the two are defining features of promises. Some writers add a third pointer in the same direction: the promisee, they say, has to accept the promise for it to be binding. This may be an exaggeration. I may promise someone in person, face to face, to come and visit him in hospital tomorrow. He receives the promise stone-faced, saying nothing and moving not a muscle. My promise is binding, and it requires some imagination to claim that it has been accepted. It is merely that the promisee can release me from the obligation, at any time, including when it is undertaken. He did not do so, which is why I am bound by it.

That the promisee has a right that the promissory duty be kept, and a power to waive it and terminate the duty, reinforces the thought that the obligations are meant to be for the promisees. However, as we saw, being *for the promisees* does not mean conferring on them an advantage. It has to be understood more broadly, perhaps something like responding to something they are interested in or have an interest in, or may become interested in or develop an interest in (by relying on the promised act, betting on it, or some other way) once the promise is made.

The combination of the two factors, (a) the obligation is *for the promisee* and (b) he has the power to rescind it, implies a third (c) that the promisor relinquishes control over the question of whether it ever was or still is or is

[21] There are marginal cases, but probably not clear counterexamples. I can promise my friend to diet if he sets me a weekly eating menu. Clearly that is a promise meant to help me rather than him. But it presupposes that he cares about my state of health, or just about me, and would be gratified if I keep my promise.

[22] Does it include the power to vary the terms of the promissory obligation? Possibly the matter is not completely determined—there may well be variations about which there is no fact of the matter whether the promisee has power to make them. But generally speaking promisees have the power to change the terms of the promissory obligation in ways that are clearly to the advantage of the promisor. But what these are may be very context dependent. Even a simple extension of the deadline for performance of the promised act will sometimes be against the interest of the promisor.

likely to become of interest to or in the interest of the promisee. It is up to the promisee to judge that and cancel it or not cancel it. Promising, we may say, relates to the self-governing ability of the promisor and the promisee alike, though in different ways. The promisor's interest in enhanced ability to control his life establishes his power to promise, and promising is an exercise of the power. On the other side, the promise once made enhances the power of the promisee by giving him *the normative assurance* of the promised act. I will use this expression to refer to the assurance, which can be overridden and is therefore not absolute, that a promise gives the promisee. It is normative for it is provided by the normative structure of a promise. It consists of (a) the obligation the promisor undertakes plus (b) the power of the promisee to terminate that obligation, plus, (c) the disability just noted of the promisor to terminate the promissory obligation on the ground that it is no longer in the interest of the promisee, and I will return to this point.

We can highlight the role of the promisee by contrasting a promissory obligation to my brother, with an obligation to do something for him arising in some other way. Suppose that my mother told me, and that I should obey her in this matter, to do something for my brother, who is finishing a gruelling task at work. I intend to buy him a week in an Alpine hotel, judging that to be an appropriate gift. Until I actually buy the holiday (and possibly even for some time after that) I should change my intention the moment I realize that it never was, or no longer is, a suitable gift. But if I promised my brother the holiday (thinking that it is an ideal gift) I cannot change my mind. He has the normative assurance that he will have the holiday, and it is now up to him to decide whether to release me from the promise or not.

The general point of promising, I conclude, is to give promisees the normative assurance of the promised act. If that is *for the promisees* it must relate to their interests (in both senses of the word) that promises serve. The power to promise serves the interest of promisors in enhanced control. When wisely used, and subject to luck, etc., both making a promise and refraining from making one serve an interest of the promisor (or the one who might have been the promisor). Given that promises are *for the promisees* promisors are served by serving the promisees. They may do so in one or both of two ways. First, the promise or the keeping of the promise may serve, directly or indirectly, an interest of the promisee, or something the promisee is interested in, cares about. Second, the promise gives the promisee (as it were as a gift) an opportunity to develop an interest, one that it may not be sensible to develop or to have without the promise or the performance of the promised act being there.

I dwell on the second way of being for the promisee not only because it is sometimes ignored, but also because while it is contingent whether the promisee has an interest in the promised act, and whether it serves his interests, it is in the nature of promises that they (to use metaphorical language) extend an invitation (not always trustworthy) to the promisees to develop an interest that depends on the promised act. A book I will lend you may lead to developing new interests, as may a game of chess or an hour on the tennis court, or the loan of a sum of money, and so on. To the extent that a promise provides an opportunity, the opportunity will be there unless the promise is not kept. Often it can be used after the promises are kept. These opportunities may range from being of little value to being of very great value. The crucial point is that normally opportunities, options, for things or actions that may be of interest to a person have some value in themselves, that is qua opportunities, regardless of whether they are made use of or not. And it is that option that the normative assurance that the promise gives assures. It may do more, much more, but the rest is both specific to individual promises and contingent. If we are looking to what interest the normative assurance the promise just about always serves—that is it.

Admittedly, even that option may be without value to the promisee. However, promises do not expire once they no longer serve the promisees. As I noted above, giving promisees the power to terminate the promissory reason implies that the continued normative force of the promise depends on the promisee's action—it is not merely that a promise may have lapsed, but the promisor may not rely on his judgement on the matter. It does not lapse merely for the reason that it no longer serves the promisee, and the promisor is unable to terminate it on that ground. Its continued existence is now in the promisee's hand. It binds so long as it was not rescinded, provided that the power of the promisee to waive it has not lapsed as well.

The promisee's power is neither unconditional nor absolute. For one thing, the reason to keep the promise may be overridden by conflicting considerations. Furthermore, if the promisee is disabled in a way that makes it impossible for him to waive the promise then if the promise no longer serves the promisee it lapses. That was the case with Abby's promise to lend Ben her car. Once he became ill in such a way that he could neither make use of the car, nor waive the promise to lend him the car, the promise lapsed and Abby had no promissory reason any more to lend him her car.[23] Finally, it is arguable that

[23] Two clarificatory points: First, that Ben's condition is not permanent does not matter. What matters is his ability to waive the promissory duty before or at the time its performance is due. Second, nor

the power to rescind lapses if abused, that is, if exercised for immoral purposes, or in an arbitrary way.

Is the power to rescind the promissory obligation a third kind of promisee's interest (in addition to the interest served by the performance of the promised act and the opportunities to develop new interests that it provides)? David Owens goes further. Seeking an explanation of the way promises are for the promisees, he claims that their function is to enhance an important individual interest: the interest of gaining authority over another.

> [P]romising exists because it serves our authority interest, our interest in having the right to oblige others to do certain things. My claim will be that human beings have an interest in the possession of authority for its own sake, regardless of any further purpose this authority might serve, and that this fact accounts for the distinctive features of a promise.
>
> The authority interest is a normative interest: it is an interest in the possession of a certain right, the right to impose an obligation.[24]

I doubt that there is such an interest, and if I am mistaken and people have that interest I doubt that there is a general reason to protect or serve it. But that is beside the point, as its existence is irrelevant to promises. Owens maintains that the fundamental promissory interest is an interest of the promisee ... namely the promisee's interest in gaining authority over the promisor.

This suggests that the function of promises is to endow promisees with that authority. While not all promises are made in order to serve their function, given that they are made intentionally by people who know what promises are, it seems to follow from Owens's view that standardly promises are made when people intend to endow others with authority over them and they make them in order to endow those others with power over them, in order to submit themselves to such power. This is of course consistent with maintaining that promisors make promises in order to serve a goal that they themselves are interested in. They aim to serve it by making the promise, namely by subjecting themselves to the power of another.

According to the account offered here matters are very different. The point of promises is to provide promisees with normative assurance that the promised act will be performed, thus enabling them to get the advantages and

does it matter that Ben has an interest in being able to control the duty in the sense that it would have been good for him be able to waive it. The control or power to waive that we are concerned with is the power you have only if you (physically) can use it.

[24] Owens, *Shaping the Normative Landscape*, 146.

opportunities that that assurance can provide. Again, promises are not always made to serve the point, but standardly this is the intention with which promisors make them: to provide that normative assurance and enable the promisees to have those advantages and opportunities. The power to rescind is merely part of the normative structure that creates the normative assurance: promisees have a right that the promise be kept, and (as with many rights) a power to waive it, to terminate the promissory obligation. Furthermore, the promise can neither be cancelled by the promisor when it no longer serves the promisee, nor does it then lapse. The normative assurance would have been less secure if the promisor were free to conclude that in the circumstances the promise serves no point and is not (or no longer) binding.

In some cases one can imagine that one's interest in having power over another is not purpose specific. A hostage taker need not have an idea how to use his power over the hostage before capturing him. Once he has that power he may make the hostage clean his house or aim to secure some political objective by holding him, or releasing him, or just get ransom to release him, etc. With promises this is an implausible account. The power the promisee has is merely to rescind an obligation whose content and creation were not up to him. His interest in it is almost entirely derivative from his interest in the normative assurance of the promised act, and the advantages and opportunities that it serves. Hence the conclusion that the power to rescind is but an ingredient in securing normative assurance, which itself serves the point and purpose of the promise, rather than being an independent interest that promises are there to serve.

One final point before moving on: In asserting that promisees' interests are served by having the power to rescind the promise I was implicitly assuming that the case for that power is analogous to the case for the power to make promises. But there are important differences between them. We all have the power to promise. It merely depends on basic mental competence. But the power of promisees is had only by promisees, who are invested with it by promisors. Furthermore, in a significant number of cases, keeping promises disadvantages promisees. This need not be by damaging their independent interests. It may be because as things turn out keeping the promise imposes a considerable burden on the promisor, while doing little for the promisee. Promisees may prefer not to be in the situation where they impose the burden of keeping the promise on the promisors. But given that they have the exclusive power to release the promisor from the promise they find themselves with the burden of deciding whether to release the promisor and of communicating their decision to him. Most of the time this is hardly a burden at all, but at times it is. Can we still say that having the power to rescind the promise is of value to promisees? I think that we can. Considerations like the one I mentioned show that it is not an unmixed blessing. But it is of value on balance. Those who deny that do not believe that promises are normatively sound.

6. Promissory Reasons

The explanation of the point of promises, the interests they serve, and the way they do so, when applied to each promise, yields an explanation of the reason to keep that promise and of the strength of that reason. The puzzle we started from resulted from the fact that as regards any promised act, the reason to perform it (the reason that applies to each and all of them) is that it was promised, namely the same reason in every case. However, initially we failed to find factors that determine the strength of the reasons and establish how they differ.

Promises are binding because there is normative power to make them, which is grounded in the interest for enhanced control. The question is how can that interest, seemingly affecting all promises uniformly, provide reasons of different strength regarding different promises, or indeed how does it provide any reason to keep promises, given that breaking the promise does not threaten that power?

There is, however, an inevitable and obvious connection between the value of the power to promise and the reasons to keep a promise: to repeat a triviality—the reasons are a result of the use of the power to promise, a result of the making of the specific promise made. All valid promises change the normative situation because they are the exercise of the same power, but they change it differently because they are different promises. In one regard promises are analogous to gifts: they give promisees the normative assurance of an action (or omission). Whenever I give a gift I change the normative situation by using the same gift-giving power, yet I change it differently by giving different gifts. My exercise of my power of making the promise changed the situation. Now the promisee has that normative assurance, namely I have a promissory reason to perform the promised act. Of course, gifts and promises are fundamentally different in other respects: When giving a gift I give the recipient something I had before. The gift was mine, now it is his. When making a promise I grant the promisee a right that did not exist before to a duty that did not exist before. There is nothing that was mine and is now his.

Promises may, in themselves or in combination with other factors, provide reasons, or affect the strength of reasons, for or against the promised act. But only those that relate to the point of the promise are promissory reasons, and these are the factors that make it a normative assurance meant to be for the promisee.

So that is how we can have our cake and eat it too. Promissory reasons derive from the value of having the power to promise, through its exercise. The exercise of the power introduces variability. All promises are the normative assurance of an act or omission, but the value of that assurance varies.

It is tempting to equate the strength of the reason to keep a promise with the value to the promisee of the promised act. But we already know that that is a mistake. For example, the promisor may perform the promised act anyway, regardless of whether the promise remains binding or whether it is waived by the promisee. The value of the promise is the value of the normative assurance it provides. In a case where the promised act will take place anyway that may be much less than the value to the promisee of the promised act. Besides, the promise is binding even if the promised act is of no value to the promisee. So, where performance of the promised act because it was promised serves the promisee, its value to him is just one consideration that affects the strength of the promissory reason. The opportunity value that the promise provides, its 'invitation' to the promisee to developing interests based on the assurance of the promised act, is an independent consideration that is present in almost all promises, and affects their force. Yet there must be other strength-affecting factors present in all cases in which the promise is binding. This is where the power to terminate the promissory obligation, coupled with the fact that it does not lapse unless waived, are relevant. They exist in all binding promises, and their existence is of benefit to the promisee, enabling him to rescind the promise when it is to his advantage to do so, and disabling the promisor from escaping his promissory obligation without the promisee's consent.

As was explained, the promisee's interest in the power to rescind is secondary, being merely protective of the main ways in which the promise is for him. Only in exceptional cases would that be the only aspect of a specific promise that serves his interest, and thereby keeps the promise binding. There is, however, another doubt as to whether that interest can affect the strength of the reason to keep a promise (and if it cannot then in those exceptional cases just mentioned there would be no reason to keep it, it would not be binding). Does breach of the promise deny the promisee the power to terminate the promissory obligation?

I wish to avoid technicalities, and at this point they are hard to ignore altogether. I will simplify. We have to distinguish between a repudiatory breach and a non-repudiatory breach.[25] Now consider the difference between a one-shot promise and a continuous one: between promising to water your plants tomorrow and promising to water them once a week for the coming year. Failure to water them once in the second case is a partial breach. Partial failure is possible regarding some one-shot promises as well: for example, when time is not of the essence watering them a day late is not a complete breach. A complete breach is always repudiatory whereas a partial breach may or may not be, depending on the circumstances, including the intentions of the promisor. A repudiatory breach terminates the promissory obligation. It may give rise to a new duty, a duty to compensate for the breach.[26] In cases of non-repudiatory partial breach the power to waive or rescind the promissory obligation lapses regarding the partial breach, and in repudiatory breach it lapses with the termination of the promissory duty altogether. Hence, even in the marginal cases where the only promisee interest a promise serves is due to the promisee's power to waive his right and terminate the promissory duty, breach affects that interest, and therefore there is reason to keep the promise.

[25] Which can be anticipatory, i.e. occurring before the time to keep the promise arrives, and can be by declaration: 'I will not keep this promise'; such declaration deprives the promisee of the assurance that is the point of a promise, and is therefore a breach of the promise.

[26] The new duty comes with new powers to the promisee. But while they include a power to waive the duty to compensate that power differs, both in scope (the duty to compensate differs in content from the promissory duty) and in conditions of its exercise (communicating the waiver to the promisor is not constitutive of it). Hence its existence does not undermine the point in the text.

PART III
THE NORMATIVE IN OUR LIVES

9
The Role of Well-Being

'Well-being' signifies the good life, the life which is good for the person whose life it is. Much of the discussion of well-being, including a fair proportion of my own,[1] aims to explain what kind of life is good for the people whose life it is, what constitutes well-being. I have argued that well-being consists in a wholehearted and successful pursuit of valuable relationships and goals. This view, a little modified, is part of the background to the discussion to follow. However, my purpose here is to consider the role of well-being in practical thought. In particular I will examine a suggestion, which I will call the radical suggestion, which says that when we care about people, and when we ought to care about people, what we do, or ought to, care about is their well-being. The suggestion is indifferent to who cares and who is cared for. People may care, perhaps ought to care, about themselves, and they may care, perhaps ought to care, about people with whom they have, or ought to have special bonds, and finally they may care, perhaps ought to care, about other people generally (I will refer to this as caring about strangers). In all cases what they care, or ought to care, about is the well-being of the relevant people, themselves, or others.

The radical suggestion is not as radical as some. It allows that the reasons or duties of care, and their stringency, may vary depending on the relationship between the carers and the cared for. Besides, it does not include the claim that moral reasons or duties, or self-regarding reasons, or reasons or duties of friendship, or of other relationships, are reasons, duties of well-being, and nothing else. The view that this is so will be neither assumed nor examined here.

My impression is that the concept of well-being has become increasingly prominent in discussions since the 1960s, in the hope that it would help with pressing philosophical problems, primarily ones encountered by people

[1] See J. Raz, *The Morality of Freedom* (Oxford: OUP, 1986) Chap. 12; J. Raz, *Ethics in the Public Domain* (Oxford: OUP, paperback edn. 1995) Chap. 1; J. Raz, *Engaging Reason* (Oxford: OUP, 1999) Chap. 13. Scanlon's position in T. Scanlon, *What We Owe to Each Other* (Cambridge, Mass.: Harvard UP, 1998) Chap. 3 is in many ways similar to mine. This chapter ties up this conception of well-being with the account of value I offered in some other writings, especially in J. Raz, *Value, Respect, and Attachment* (Cambridge: CUP, 2001) Chap. 4.

The Roots of Normativity. Joseph Raz, Edited with an Introduction by Ulrike Heuer, Oxford University Press.
 DOI: 10.1093/oso/9780192847003.003.0010

sympathetic to the ethos of utilitarianism. First, it became clear to many that the claim that what matters to people in their life is either pleasure and the avoidance of pain, or preference-satisfaction, is unsustainable. Other things matter too. Second, Rawls gave expression to a vague concern that utilitarianism, while intending to be concerned with people, manages to miss out on the importance of people. In its classical versions, for example, it virtually regards people as repositories of pleasure. We should (according to some versions) maximize the total or the average (per person) amount of pleasure, never mind where it resides. It is pleasure which matters, not people.

The concept emerged or re-emerged in recent times with the claim that it is helpful in both an explanatory (designating what people care about when they care about themselves or others) and a normative role (what they should care about when they care about themselves or others). The phrase 'well-being' is used in philosophical writing in a meaning different from its meaning in ordinary English.[2] Hence an examination of the concept cannot be entirely separated from examination of the role which it emerged to play in philosophical discussions. We cannot understand it otherwise. It is meant to play this role through having two basic features. First, it is a property of a life. Second, it is a property a life possesses in virtue of its character, taken as a whole. Of course, we can apply it also to periods in a life. However, the concept plays its pivotal theoretical role, as expressed in the radical suggestion, when applied to life taken as a whole.

In Part One I will defend the concept against some criticisms of its coherence or significance. In Part Two I will reject the radical suggestion and propose an alternative understanding of the role of well-being. My purpose is primarily to sketch a position, whose defence requires more extensive and far-ranging arguments than can be offered here. All I can hope to do is to indicate the direction of some of them.

Part One: The Concept

1. The Objective Value Component

The radical suggestion is that caring for people is (a) caring about the quality of their life, (b) in its entirety, and (c) that that means caring that they should

[2] It rose to prominence in part because its philosophical use is more remote from its 'ordinary' meaning than that of its likely alternatives such as 'happiness' or 'welfare', and therefore less likely to mislead.

have a life which is good for them. A person enjoys a high degree of well-being if his life is good in a way which is good for him, as against just good (perhaps morally good) or good in ways which are good for his dependents, or for his country, or for his employer, etc., but not for him.

One possible objection to the radical suggestion says that we should distinguish between a happy life and a good life. A good life is one of rectitude, propriety, moral good deeds, of integrity and adherence to standards of personal morality, or devotion to one's family or to one's friends, or of contribution to the arts, sciences, or other admirable branches of culture, or whatever—always provided that it did not include lapses that negate the significance of the good activities or events. A happy life is one of contentment, of ambitions and aspirations realized, etc., always provided that it did not include frustrations and sufferings which negate those satisfactions. The concept of well-being is a hybrid, an attempt to find a concept that is half one and half the other. A good life may be a happy one, but such coincidence is contingent, and should not encourage the emergence of, or assigning any theoretical role to, the hybrid concept of a life which is good (borrowed from a good life) for the person whose life it is (borrowed from happiness).

There is a thorough subjectivist understanding of the objection, according to which one necessary condition of the happy life is that it is one the person whose life it is is happy with. Happiness on this view is transparent to those who are happy. We need not accept that view. We may believe that people may be unreflective about their own life, be neither happy nor unhappy with their life, and yet be happy or unhappy. We may also believe that sometimes people think they are unhappy or that they are happy when they are not. We may understand people correcting their view of past periods of their life, saying 'I thought then that I was so happy. Now I realize that it was merely an illusion, or that I was deceiving myself'. The point remains that the objective element in happiness, the element that makes it possible for people to be mistaken or self-deceived about their happiness, is not a value element. The happy life remains, even on this more objective understanding of happiness, distinct from the good life, and requires no goodness at all.

The problem with this view is that a happy life cannot be devoid of valuable activities. First, a happy life, as well as one that is good for the agent whose life it is, is marked not only by satisfaction with occasional specific events or activities. It is marked by a general attitude to oneself, and specifically by whole-hearted acceptance by the person of himself, of who he is. Second, both the general attitude to oneself, and the specific satisfaction with events and activities, depend on the agent's belief that these actions and events are worthwhile. One cannot be completely and unreservedly satisfied with an activity or an event that one believes to be meaningless, demeaning, worthless, etc. One cannot whole-heartedly accept being what one is if one believes oneself to be evil, depraved, lacking in integrity, etc.

But this may be too hasty. Several questions require careful consideration. First, can one be satisfied unreservedly and contentedly with what one takes to be worthless or base? Second, if not, is this an empirical generalization or a necessary truth? Third, assuming that the answer is that there is a necessary connection between whole-hearted (undiluted, unambivalent) acceptance and belief in that attitude or its object being well-deserved,[3] the question remains whether one needs to have any view of the value of what gives one pleasure. Do I need to believe that a song is a good song to enjoy it? Or that an ice cream is a good one in order to take pleasure in it? These questions cannot be explored here. But as the last one is crucial to my argument let me say something about it. Knowledge of logical and conceptual truths that can be known a priori (e.g. that if P and If P then Q then Q, or that Yellow is a colour) is rightly attributed to people who may never have consciously entertained them provided that (a) these truths can be expressed in concepts that are understood by these people, and (b) the people use these concepts in ways that conform to the truths we attribute to them. The second of these conditions is part of the grounds for attributing possession of the concepts.

Possession of a concept requires some, though not complete, understanding of it, a degree, though not the highest degree, of knowledge of the rules that govern its correct use. We can attribute a belief in a conceptual truth to people who mastered the concept, however imperfectly, provided the imperfections in their understanding do not consist in contradicting the belief attributed.

So, if there is a necessary connection between accepting or taking pleasure in something and beliefs about one's attitude or its object having an appropriate value, then it would be right to attribute knowledge of that fact to people who have the concepts and use them without contradicting it. Is there such a necessary connection? It is based on the Socratic-Aristotelian view that actions, desires, and other aspirations are rational only to the extent that they are believed to be worthwhile, which often means that they have

[3] I will assume that one can take pleasure in what one believes to be bad, unworthy, or worthless, but that such pleasure is exceptional, not statistically, but in being parasitic on the normal case, i.e. where it is believed to be worthwhile. The poignancy of the exceptional derives from the flouting of the normal, in a spirit of defiance, rejection of common opinion, self-hatred, self-loathing, self–punishment, etc.

worthwhile objects. None of this can be established here.[4] Two comments about its basis are, however, helpful in clarifying the view: First, desires, aspirations, and actions are open to criticism. Criticism which if justified would require abandoning them. That is a necessary truth. But then does it not follow that in acting, intending, or desiring one assumes that the criticism does not apply, that is, that they are worthwhile? Second, the very attribution of intentions, intentional actions, desires, etc. depends on criteria such as that the fact that one does not take an action when one could take it at no cost or sacrifice, would indicate, other things being equal, that one did not intend to take it, and that one did not want to take it. But the criteria cannot be one-dimensional: we can criticize people for being irrational in not doing what they intended when they could, etc. The criteria are multifaceted, so that attribution is warranted even when agents fail on some criteria, a failure which will often show that they are irrational. For criticism of this kind to be possible, and for the multifaceted criteria to relate to rationality, then desires, intentions, etc. must relate to rational factors, namely beliefs in their worthwhileness.

This is as much as I can do here to defend the view that normally people can be happy only if they believe that their life, activities, etc. were worthwhile. It does not show that happiness requires that they actually were worthwhile. This may indeed not be so. The question we face is whether happiness that is based on a mistake about the quality of the life concerned is an ideal to any degree at all? This does not seem plausible. It is not relevant that under some circumstances it is good to have an experience based on false belief: to experiment, to learn how to tell it from its twin true belief, to save one's life, or that of others, and so on. What we are asking is whether it can be intrinsically, not instrumentally, valuable, and whether it can be valuable as the rule, rather than as an exception. That is improbable. Not because there is value in having true beliefs or true experiences. Rather, whatever value is in an experience depends on its character. The false experiences, that is, the experiences based on false beliefs, which one is supposed to assume make for happiness, are not the experiences the people who have them think they have, nor the ones they want to have. They want to experience being loved and admired and they experience being flattered and used. What is there about the experiences that they have which makes them good and valuable? Possibly, nothing; possibly they are not valuable at all. But if they are, this will depend on some

[4] See Raz, *Engaging Reason*, Chap. 1.

understanding of the value of experiences which makes it independent of what the people who have them think they have or want to have.

The emerging conclusion is that the criticism of 'well-being' as a hybrid concept cannot be sustained. The notion of 'happiness' even when understood as involving nothing more than a state of the person whose happiness is in question involves reference to values, if only in the form of believed valuables. If happiness matters, if we should care about our or other people's happiness then it must consist in the satisfaction of worthwhile desires, or, more generally, whatever mental states happiness consists in must have value, usually through their objects being worthwhile.

2. Good for

Another, almost exactly opposite, objection denies that there is a coherent concept able to play the role that the concept of well-being is supposed to play, because the reference to 'a life good for the person whose life it is' makes no sense. To be sure a life could be good or bad to various degrees. But that, the objection goes, is so in virtue of the life including good or bad, valuable or worthless episodes or actions. Saying that they are good for the person in whose life they occur adds nothing, and misleads us into believing that there is something added. There is no sense in which episodes in a life, or the life as a whole, can be good for the person whose life it is beyond just being good.

If this objection is right we are back with the sort of value theory exemplified by versions of utilitarianism, which fails to find value in human beings as such. They are locations of valuable episodes. What matters, what we should strive to pursue or promote, are valuable events or episodes such as pleasure, or discriminating or refined aesthetic appreciation, physical accomplishment, or making scientific discoveries.[5] The people who manifest them have no distinctive claim on our attention, or, indeed, on their own attention.

The same is true if value inheres not only in episodes in the life of people, but also in a person's life itself. Even then the value is not the personal value of the people themselves: their existence is simply impersonally good. It is so, for example, if the existence (namely life) of people or of anything that is not a copy of another thing, but distinctive, is important because it adds variety to

[5] This is the way in which Regan understands the implications of Moore's conception of the good. For a powerful presentation of the case for it, with which he challenges those who argue for the promotion of well-being, see D. Regan, 'Why am I My Brother's Keeper?', in R. J. Wallace, P. Pettit, S. Scheffler, and M. Smith (eds), *Reason and Value* (Oxford: OUP, 2004) 202.

the world. But are intrinsic values, or some of them, personal in the required way? Is 'non-instrumentally[6] good for X' different from 'is good and resides (or can, will, etc. reside) in X'?

An initial, partial, answer is readily available. There is a difference between different ways in which a person may be involved in a valuable event or state. Contrast the following two pairs of examples:

(1.1) Mary is photographed without her knowledge, and the photograph is used to become a vital element in a great work of art.

(2.1) Rather drunk, Mary falls asleep with her body blocking shut the (fire) door, thus saving many people from the fire which erupted accidentally on the other side.

(1.2) Mary takes a photographic self-portrait and incorporates it in a great work of art she was creating at the time.

(2.2) Aware of the danger the fire poses, Mary stays by the fire door pressing it shut, thus saving many lives.

In all examples a good or valuable episode involving Mary occurs. The material difference is that the first pair is of things which happen to Mary. She is active in the episodes of the second pair, while passive in those of the first. That difference explains why neither episode in the first pair can be good for her,[7] whereas those in the second list can be.[8] Episodes in which we are passive, as well as ones in which we do not feature at all, can be good for us only indirectly, through their contribution to another valuable aspect of our activities. Only active episodes can be directly good for us.[9]

What explains the connection between activity and being (directly) good for a person? The answer requires sketching, in the briefest and crudest of outlines, a couple of fundamental distinctions in the basic modes[10] in which things, events, or states can be good or have value. The first distinction is fairly familiar, and is best illustrated by the way one thinks of the value of

[6] Well-being can be enhanced by the pursuit of both instrumentally and intrinsically valuable goals. But for the most part my discussion will disregard instrumentally valuable pursuits. Some of the conclusions are restricted to intrinsically valuable relationships and pursuits.

[7] At least not in themselves. They may be causally relevant.

[8] It is tempting to say that the difference is between episodes in the life of people and episodes in which they figure, but which are not part of their life. Only the latter can be good for a person. This may be true but is not in itself very illuminating, as the division we draw, for this purpose, between what is part of the life and what is not is tailor-made to respond to certain normative concerns. It cannot be used to explain them.

[9] Oddly, the same is not true of what is bad for us. Events in which we are totally passive can be directly bad for us. They can violate our integrity, dignity, etc.

[10] That is, excluding being good conditionally or instrumentally.

natural features, like the Grand Canyon. Some people think that the value (aesthetic or other) of the Grand Canyon is totally independent of its appreciation or the possibility of its appreciation by anyone. Others think of its value as fulfilled only if it is appreciated by valuers, and wasted or pointless otherwise. Some values, for example friendship, cannot be instantiated without being appreciated. One cannot have a friendship without the friends being aware of the fact, and valuing it.[11] For our purposes, however, they can be treated together with, for example good novels which must be written, but need not be read, and either way their value may remain unappreciated. What is common to friendships and novels, and much else that is of intrinsic value, is that they are fully realized only when appreciated and engaged in in the right spirit, in the right way (in this case: read with understanding). To facilitate expression I will call such values 'personal values'. On some views the value of the Grand Canyon is personal, on others it is impersonal. Similarly, on some views the value of valuers, for example of persons, is impersonal. But arguably their value is purely personal,[12] that is, it is not fully realized unless they bond with others who, one way or another, appreciate their value.

For present purposes I will proceed on the assumption that all values are personal. I will take it to entail that anything which is of value can be good for someone. Some take anything which has (personal) value to be good because it is good for someone. According to them, 'good' is short for 'good for someone'. I believe that this is neither true nor an implication of values being personal.

If something is intrinsically good for me it is so because it is good—'it would be good for you to read this novel. It is really excellent'—and it is that very quality which makes it good for others too. It would be good for you to read the book for the same reason it is good for me, that is, because it is an excellent book. Of course, not everything good is good for me. I need to be able to appreciate it and engage in it. (I may be tone deaf. Music is not for me.) It has to fit in my life (I may be set on becoming a weightlifter, which is inconsistent with being a good long-distance runner), and there may be other conditions. But whatever is good (unconditionally and non-instrumentally) for one person can be good for others, and will be good for them for the same reason—because it is good. This primacy of 'good' over 'good for' is consistent with values being personal, for it is consistent with it being a condition on

[11] At least *pro tanto*. Sometimes we say 'she is your friend' just to indicate that she is well-disposed towards you, a fact of which you may be unaware. This is not friendship as a relationship, of which alone I write above. There are false friends, etc. but I disregard these nuances.

[12] Obviously, something can have both personal and impersonal value.

anything being good that it is capable of being good for some valuer. It cannot be good if its value cannot be appreciated and engaged in by some valuer.

There are three kinds of personal values. Things having personal value can be intrinsically good in the way in which good paintings, good novels, or beautiful landscapes are. Or they can be good in themselves (according to one use of this phrase) in the way in which persons are, that is, beings who can appreciate value and respond to it, be guided in their actions by it. They can also be intrinsically good in the way in which my listening to the Emersons playing the Second Razumovsky Quartet can be good. This last category is of valuers responding to value (intrinsic or instrumental) in appropriate ways. The value of things provides us with reasons for appropriate responses, in action, emotion, or thought. As mentioned, metaphorically speaking what is of intrinsic value is wasted if not responded to in the appropriate way. Correspondingly, valuers are diminished if when it would be appropriate to do so they are unable to respond to what is of value.

I do not know in what way the instantiation of an impersonal value can be good for anyone. Personal values, on the other hand, are there to be appreciated and engaged in. The ability to be good for people or other valuers is central to their nature as personal values. In general, any appropriate response to value out of appreciation of its value, is good for one. The common exception is when it conflicts with stronger reasons one has. Broadly speaking two kinds of responses are appropriate. I will refer to them as engaging with the value and respecting it. Appreciating or enjoying a good painting, a good drink, participating in an appropriate way in a good party, dance, or discussion are examples of engagement with value. Protecting or restoring a good painting, protecting the party from hooligans or other interferences, are examples of respecting value.

Beyond the fact that engaging with something of value involves appreciation of its value in some way (e.g. taking pleasure in it) and to some degree, not much can be said in the abstract about what constitutes engagement with a value. It depends on the value concerned. The actions required by reasons of respect for value too are diverse, but united in being aimed at protecting that which has the value. In one sense of the term we respect something if our actions and attitudes conform to reasons of respect, whatever the reasons for which we act. In another, stronger sense, we respect something only if we do what respect requires out of respect. Of the two engaging with value is primary. Respect is due in recognition of the fact that the value is there to be engaged with. Its point is to keep open the opportunity to engage with what is or may become of value.

Because episodes that are good for us directly (i.e. among other things, non-instrumentally) consist in an appropriate response to value, they are episodes in which we are active. Needless to say, while only what is good for me can directly contribute to my well-being, not everything that is good for me does so. As will be explained in the next section, it may be good for me to watch some TV programme tonight, even though it will have no bearing on my well-being.

Establishing the distinctiveness of the concept of a life good for the person whose life it is does not yet meet the objection. Admitting that whatever is good for one is good, it remains a puzzle why my well-being should carry any normative weight, or have any normative force beyond the value of the actions and events in my life. What is good about well-being as such? Why should caring about people consist in caring about their well-being? This seems to require that their well-being has value that is distinct from the value of episodes in their life. If, for example, I am a great educator, or sportsperson, then many of my actions are valuable independently of whether I hate myself for engaging in them, or have other of the negative attitudes that affect well-being. Does it mean that my actions or my life have less value than those of someone whose life differs from mine just in that he accepts who he is and what he does? If not does it not follow that well-being is not valuable in itself, and that we have no reason to pursue it for its own sake?

That way of putting the objection may make it sound like an objection to the thought that there is any reason to care about people, rather than about valuable episodes, which may or may not be good for them, or for the impersonal value of their life. It becomes an objection to the radical suggestion, and to the role of the concept of well-being, only if there is a way of caring about people which does not involve caring about their well-being.

3. 'Life as a Whole'

Suppose we accept that caring about people is caring about their life, on the ground that people have nothing beyond their life. Suppose we further accept that caring about people's lives is caring about the quality of their life, about how good their life is. Even if that is so does it follow that what we then care about is the well-being of the people we care about? One doubt is raised by the fact that the judgements of well-being we are interested in are about how good people's lives are as a whole. There are various ways of understanding this condition. The atomistic view maintains that the contribution of every moment or episode to one's well-being is independent of the content of the rest of one's life. The objective balance view maintains that the contribution of moments in a life to one's well-being is not independent of that of other moments in one's life. It takes the well-being of people to depend in part on the relations between different parts of their life. Possibly for every person, given his talents and tastes, there is a range of experiences such that his life is good for him to the extent that it displays the right balance between them. Having too much of one kind or too little of another makes life worse. Hence if in the past I read lots of philosophy, but never played football, my well-being will get worse if I continue as before, and will improve if I abandon philosophy for football.

Objective balance accounts can be total or partial, depending on whether they hold that every moment of one's life contributes to or detracts from the ideal balance. I know of people who adopted plans of life informed by a desire to have a life that is balanced in certain ways, and whose plans do not appear unreasonable. At the same time I know of no good argument that the absence of some such balance detracts from the well-being of the people whose life it is. So far as I can see, the life of a person whose life is governed by an all-consuming dedication to mathematics, or some other single pursuit, need not be less good for him than the life of those who have a much better balanced life. In ways that need explaining, well-being does not necessarily depend on balanced patterns, though it may be served by them in the life of people who pursue such goals. I will therefore ignore the balance view from now on. Instead I will contrast the atomistic view with another, which seems to me correct:

The variable pattern view denies that all moments in one's life count equally, or even count at all. One's well-being, according to this view, depends in the main on the degree to which one succeeds in pursuing valuable relationships and projects which one adopted as one's own. Subject to an important qualification to follow, episodes in one's life that do not bear on them do not affect one's well-being, and those that do bear on them vary in importance according to their contribution to those relationships and goals, and to the importance of these relationships and goals to one's life.

The atomistic view consists of two claims:

> The independence claim: The contribution of moments in one's life to one's well-being depends on their intrinsic value only, and is independent of their relations to other aspects of one's life.

> The positive correlation claim: The better the quality of any moment the greater its contribution to the well-being of the person whose life it is.

Both are mistaken. There are various possible reasons for rejecting them. Possibly different stages in people's life contribute differently to their well-being. A traditional view distinguishes between a preparatory stage in childhood and early youth, a stage of mature activity, and a stage of relative retirement. Possibly people's years of mature activity count more (minute for minute, as it were) towards their well-being than the early or later stages. We discount a relatively unhappy childhood, or undistinguished decline late in life, if they flank years of successful mature activity.

The claim that all events in childhood, or some other period, must be completely discounted is not credible. Imagine a severe illness which causes great suffering and disables one from pursuing any rewarding activity, other than fighting that illness. There can be no reason to deny that the period of that illness, whenever in life it occurs, matters a lot to the well-being of that person. But one can reject atomism, and maintain that some episodes, periods, or aspects of people's lives do not matter to their well-being, even though they would have mattered had they followed a different course. The variable pattern view, for example, could accommodate this possibility by taking well-being to be, in part, a function of the degree to which the life of the people concerned successfully realizes a pattern, which in turn determines the relative value of different periods or aspects of their life, while in part being pattern independent. Certain modes of conduct or pursuit are—on this view—appropriate for people of a certain age, but not for others, or appropriate for people in certain occupations but not for others, appropriate towards people with whom we have certain relations, but not towards others, and so on. Their contribution to well-being depends on their appropriateness. Other states, events, or their aspects affect well-being in a pattern-independent way. Arguably they include one's basic attitudes to oneself (e.g. unjustified low self-esteem, unjustified lack of self-respect, self-hate, shame about one's looks), occurrence of severe and enduring pain and suffering, and commission of serious wrongdoing. The pattern-dependent elements relate to projects and relationships regarding which people who have them are active,[13] whereas pattern-independent factors may include events in which the people

[13] Of course, even regarding them, events in which one is passive, like being jilted by one's lover, may affect one's well-being, but these passive elements derive their significance from being embedded in one's active pursuits and relationships.

concerned are passive. Arguably, some, perhaps even many actions, states, or events in a life do not manifest any pattern-independent features. Similarly, many of them do not manifest pattern-dependent ones. If so then numerous decisions, actions, or other aspects of one's life have no bearing on one's well-being, and others have variable impact. That is, their impact is not due to their intrinsic character, but depends on how they are situated in one's life relative to certain patterns.

If well-being is pattern-dependent, and the determination of the relevant pattern is contingent, then the relevance, if any, of different episodes, or aspects of episodes, to people's well-being cannot be determined independently of their relations to other episodes. The significance of each episode, if any, depends, contrary to the independence claim, on its relations to others, in light of the direction the person whose life it is gave to his or her life. The relevance and meaning of other episodes is determined by reference to that pattern.

What reasons are there to endorse the variable pattern view? I will use examples to illustrate its plausibility.[14] Here is one:

> In order to participate effectively in a public debate I read about the other participants, and spend a good deal of time considering the questions under discussion. I make sure that I am well rested and untroubled when arriving at the venue of the debate, and that I introduce myself to the other speakers trying to establish a suitably civilized atmosphere even before the event starts. I then perform my role in the debate.

Any action in the pattern derives its meaning from its role in preparing me for the debate, and its value depends on its success in that, coming from its contribution to my performance once the debate takes place, and from its relations to other preparatory events, which may make it more or less redundant or more or less effective, and therefore more or less valuable. Moments of anxiety can be more valuable than moments of pleasure, if, for example, they make me more alert, whereas the pleasure of the pleasurable moments induces an unhelpful over-confidence.

The pattern displayed in this example is instrumental. No less common are non-instrumental patterns. Valuable activities extend over time (though they need not be continuous, nor all absorbing—we may be able to do other things even while engaged with one of them). Think of attending a film, or climbing

[14] To save space I will omit mention of the non-pattern-dependent factors of well-being. Being common to all conceptions of well-being, they are not relevant to this argument.

a rock-face, or just about any other culture-imbued activity some people care about. All of them extend over time, and in all of them the value of the episode as a whole depends on appropriate relations between different moments in time. In all of them, moreover, the value of moments in time depends not only, not so much, on their intrinsic qualities as on their relations to other parts of the episode. Fear and frustration can be more valuable than enjoyment in the context of a patterned valuable activity. They may be the appropriate response to an event in a play, or a novel, or to the experiences of a friend, etc.

The patterns illustrated so far are rather limited in scope and duration. But they tend to be elements of wider, more extensive patterns which determine the meaning of our lives in our own eyes. One person is an ardent lover, a software developer, and a jazz enthusiast, who plays the stock exchange, and spends his holidays surfing. Another is a concerned parent, a social worker, a devoted and loyal friend, etc. Such brief profiles are to a degree part of people's myth-making about themselves or about others. But when true they determine the meaning of people's lives, and the parameters by which their well-being is to be judged.[15]

My suggestion was that the pattern-dependent aspect of well-being consists in success in the whole-hearted pursuit of valuable relationships and goals. There are many relationships which could be, when appropriately pursued, valuable, and many valuable goals and projects to pursue. Sometimes the circumstances of our life dictate that some we must and others we must not pursue, but generally there is a wide area of choice, that is choice among relationships and goals that are worthwhile, and therefore would be good to pursue, but need not be pursued. Others may be adopted instead. Their pursuit determines the contours of people's well-being, they set the standards by which people's well-being is determined. People enjoy a good life to the extent that they succeed in the wholehearted pursuit of their adopted relationships and goals. That they are indifferent or bad in other types of activities and pursuits does not adversely affect their well-being, nor does the occasional success in something that could have been, but is not part of their goals and pursuits add to their well-being.

[15] An extreme example of the dependence on their role in life of the impact of experiences and actions on well-being is the contrast between a person committed to a life of variety and change and a drifter. They may spend a period of very similar actions and experiences, but in the drifter they are meaningless, whereas in the life of the one pursuing variety and change they mark his success in having the life he set out to have, thus, other things being equal, contributing to his well-being.

The variable pattern view encounters two important problems: First, it has to identify which pursuits and relationships are important enough to bear on one's well-being. Second, well-being is supposed to be a property a life has in virtue of its character as a whole, but as according to the variable pattern view not everything that happens in people's lives affects people's well-being, how can it justify regarding well-being as a property a life has in virtue of its character as a whole?

We need to solve the first problem in a way that will solve the second as well. Broadly speaking the aspects of a life that are relevant to its well-being are those that could contribute to people's sense of the meaningfulness of their life, given their interests and tastes.[16]

The sense of meaningfulness is best known to us through its opposite, the sense that one's life is meaningless, pointless. Many people do not reflect about the meaning of their life, nor have any view on the subject. That is enough to say that they find their life meaningful. Saying that need not amount to more than the absence of a feeling that one's life is pointless or meaningless. Much can be said about both attitudes, but for present purposes I will take them to be sufficiently understood, and will only add a few brief clarifications:

First, whatever else is indicated by finding life pointless, or meaningless, it indicates an estrangement, and more particularly, an enervated and depressed mode of being. Those who find point and meaning in their life are fully invested in their life, they address themselves to various relationships and projects with energy and commitment, and these attitudes infect other aspects of their life as well. Those who feel that their life is meaningless merely go through the motions without spirit. Their heart is not in it.

Second, when asked to explain, both those who do and those who do not find meaning in their life will point to the presence, or absence, of certain relationships and pursuits. They find their life meaningful because of them, or would find it meaningful had it included something like them.[17]

Third, whether people's life has point and meaning depends in part on whether they find meaning in it. Perhaps this is a necessary condition of its being meaningful. However, that people find their life meaningful is not sufficient to make it meaningful. Certain aspects of life can give it meaning

[16] I have benefited from an illuminating discussion of the relations between well-being and the meaning of life by Malte Gerhold (unpublished D.Phil. dissertation, Oxford 2004).

[17] Needless to say, nihilists differ from others in thinking that there is nothing that could give their life, or that of others, point or meaning.

and others cannot. The philosophically famous blade-of-grass-counter may think that counting blades of grass makes his life meaningful, but it does not.

Fourth, and finally, not every aspect of our life that can contribute to its meaningfulness does so: aspects of our life that can contribute to its meaningfulness do so only if we take them to do so, not necessarily by reflecting on the question, but in investing ourselves in them, and holding them to be central to our life, to what, as we sometimes say, our life is about.

With these points behind us we can solve the two problems: First, the aspects of our life that contribute to our well-being, in the sense that success in them enhances it and failure detracts from it, are those that could make us feel that our life is not meaningless, whether or not they do so, and all activities and experiences that relate to them contribute to our well-being. Others do not. The fact that those aspects of our life can make it meaningful or meaningless justifies regarding their impact on the life as determining its success as a whole. This claim does not presuppose some priority to 'life not being meaningless' over 'well-being'. These concepts are interdependent. We understand them, and explain them, by pointing to their modes of interdependence.

Part Two: The Normative Role of Well-Being

4. The First Person Case

One view has it that people always inevitably strive to pursue their own well-being, and nothing else. Some used to take this to be a robust empirical generalization, others as some kind of necessary truth. The preceding account of well-being shows this view to be not merely false but necessarily false. Our well-being is constituted by success and failure in our worthwhile relationships and pursuits. And we must have pursued them for reasons other than just to enhance our well-being, because that reason would have been served by many other relationships and pursuits and it beggars belief that we never have any reasons to discriminate between the course we pursued and all its worthwhile alternatives, that we never have more specific reasons bearing on the relative attractions of those different options. Hence, even if the thought that a friendship or a pursuit would, if successful, enhance our well-being may be in our mind, most commonly it affects us only inasmuch as we are moved by some other reason to adopt the course of action in question, aware that if we succeed, it will enhance our life. Besides, many intrinsically valuable relationships and pursuits have to be undertaken for appropriate reasons (fondness of the friend, love of music, etc.), and are beyond the reach of anyone acting for his own well-being alone.

It may appear that while well-being can be achieved only if not aimed at, it is the inevitable result of all successful actions. The necessary connection between successful actions (i.e. ones in which what was intended was done) and contribution to well-being does not exist. The two come apart in a number of cases. First, there are cases where we act intentionally but for inadequate reasons. This can be the case when the action is irrational, for example when it manifests weakness of the will. It can also be the case when we mistakenly think that we have adequate reasons. Many immoral actions are of this kind: those who commit them believe that they have adequate reasons for their actions, but they are wrong. Since well-being is only served by pursuit of worthwhile goals such cases cannot serve one's well-being. Second, and more interestingly, there are numerous cases in which we act for adequate reasons, and yet even if successful our actions do not enhance our well-being.[18] This happens when the action or experience has no bearing on our well-being, but also, more dramatically, when it militates against our well-being. I have discussed the first of these above. There are numerous actions and experiences of this kind, that is, ones involving no significant immorality, nor any of the other pattern-independent factors capable of affecting our well-being, and which are not connected to any of our significant relationships and pursuits. Perhaps less numerous but in various ways more important are choices which we make for adequate reasons, and which jeopardize[19] or directly diminish our well-being. The most often noted examples of this kind are choices that sacrifice our well-being for some moral cause.

Well-being is neither the intended nor the unintended end of all our intentional actions. But is it, for the person whose life is in question, a normative consideration at all? Is it ever an independent reason for an action that that action will contribute to the agent's well-being? It is easy to give both an affirmative and a negative reply. The affirmative reply is supported by the fact that we want to have a good life and are aware of being moved by that desire. The negative reply is suggested by the previous considerations which

[18] I am not claiming that my list of these cases is exhaustive. One example of a type of case that is not covered by it is that of moral dilemmas in which a person has to choose between two evils. There may be a clear right choice—one option may clearly be the lesser evil. But arguably, choosing the lesser evil, even when unavoidable and justified, cannot enhance the agent's well-being.

[19] And obviously I do not mean ordinary risk-taking in actions that would if successful enhance our well-being, and can be known to be so.

show that an act could contribute to our well-being only when there are other adequate reasons for taking it. Hence, possibly well-being does not have a normative force independent of the force of the reason on which it rides piggy-back.

These yes and no answers are compatible. The rules for the correct application of 'reason for action' are flexible, and allow for great redundancy. They do not require that if the fact that P is a reason for performing an action then the case for it is stronger than the case constituted by the other reasons alone, and they allow that one reason (e.g. promoting one's well-being) can be present only if others to which it is logically related are as well. However, this reconciling position is likely to be resisted, and resisted on the basis of two (inter-related) considerations. First, without assuming that promoting one's well-being is a reason (with independent weight) for the person whose life it is we cannot, it may be argued, explain the way in which people are rationally and inevitably partial to themselves. Second, without that assumption one cannot explain the character of conflict-situations in which reason requires people to sacrifice their well-being for a moral cause. I believe that both arguments fail.

The second argument presupposes that when people sacrifice their interests or their well-being for a moral or some other cause they find that other cause a more compelling reason than their own well-being. The facts do not bear out this assumption. Often what is regarded as a sacrifice or a self-denying action has to do with giving up means that one may use for one's own purposes. For example, giving a large part of one's income to charity or handing one's home over to refugees and moving in with one's parents. Reducing the means at one's disposal need not affect one's well-being at all.[20] Those who deny that must think that the richer one is the better life one has—a doubtful proposition. More interesting are cases in which one abandons, interrupts, or jeopardizes a relationship, or a pursuit, for example a career, for a cause. Here too there may be self-sacrifice without compromising one's well-being. One abandons a career in the financial sector for the life of a primary school teacher when one becomes aware of the great shortage of teachers, and the growing rate of illiteracy, truancy, and criminality among the young in that part of the country. Why should that reduce one's well-being? Some abandon life in the financial services, which they find 'relentlessly

[20] Notice that in a society used to charitable giving only disproportionately large giving is considered as a sacrifice. Similarly, where people are commonly moving in with their parents to make their homes available for others' use this is not considered a sacrifice. Such factors militate against understanding sacrifice in relation to well-being, and support my suggestion below.

competitive, forcing one into conspicuous consumption empty of any nourishment to the soul, doing nothing but make the rich richer', for the 'more involving, more varied, more socially valuable', life of a teacher, and they do so just because of these reasons. There is no sacrifice involved, and certainly their life is improved, not sacrificed or reduced.

Well-being is put in jeopardy when people do not succeed in replacing what they abandoned with a new rewarding content, when having abandoned career and friends to volunteer as an aid-worker in a foreign country, they then, when the crisis is over and they are back home, fail to find a satisfying job, fail to pick up with old friends or make new ones, and so on. In the case I imagine, the sacrifice is independent of that failure, of the diminution in the quality of their life. The self-sacrifice consists in the initial abandonment of (part of) what their life was about at the time, of some important elements of it, out of conviction that that is what they should do, whether they want to or not (i.e. for categorical, will- and goal- independent reasons). The loss of well-being is subsequent, it consists in the failure to find equally rewarding and fulfilling substitutes, a failure which many experience when they change their situation, by choice or necessity, which has nothing to do with any sacrifice, but is due to bad luck, bad choices, economic downturn, or other factors. The people who make the sacrifice may anticipate that that will or may happen, and in such cases their decision to make the sacrifice assumes that the cause it serves is more important than their interest that is sacrificed. But that need not be, and is not always, the case.

Is not the view I am putting forward here naïve? Does it not disregard the degree to which we are inclined to favour ourselves, the degree to which we have a special concern with ourselves? This takes us to the first objection I mentioned above, namely that to explain the inevitable partiality to ourselves we need to acknowledge that our well-being has normative force for us. If we all do, inescapably, conduct ourselves as if our well-being has an independent normative force for us, can it be that we are all wrong, and that it does not have such force? I do not deny the force of this thought, of this conditional. What I deny is its antecedent.

There are several aspects to our partiality to ourselves. I will comment on four. First, most humans, like most animals of other species, have a range of strongly preferred, sometimes even instinctive, responses to what are often dangerous situations, responses that tend to keep us out of danger, and they have a preference, again strongly built into animals capable of that determination, for extending their life, in almost any circumstances. This instinct for survival, or desire for ever greater longevity, has nothing to do with well-being. It is not the desire, which many of us also have, to have a good life. In general, the quality of people's life is independent of its duration. The observation 'what a shame he died so young, but at least he had a good life' is as familiar as its converse: 'he had a very long life, but what a miserable one', and is often true. Certainly, sometimes dying interrupts before fruition pursuits central to people's life, and that may indeed affect the quality of the life they had. But such interruptions are only contingently related to death, and affect only certain kinds of pursuits, those that terminate or culminate in some specific accomplishment. Many: friendships, jobs like being a teacher, an interest in the opera, and so on, do not normally have such ends (though one may have some subsidiary ends within them, like striving to see one's friend through a difficult patch). In general, longevity is one thing, well-being another.

The second manifestation of special concern with oneself has to do with the fact that our actions and experiences are, trivially, our own. Hence while I may find no more reason why I should have a certain enjoyable or otherwise valuable experience than anyone else, my relation to it will be different. The same is true of my actions. The reason for me to do something appealing may be the same as the reason for you to do it. But my doing is special to me simply because it is mine. The significance of this triviality is that concern with the successful completion of an action I am engaged in or of an experience I am having is part of what it is for the experience and action to be mine. I may lose heart, change my mind, and abandon an action midway. But so long as I am acting I want the action to succeed—not a desire additional to my action, but one which is what makes this (i.e. given the character it has) action mine. The same is true of my welcome experiences: part of having them is caring about their proper completion (which may be wanting them to last long, or to follow their proper path, depending what kind of experiences are in question).[21]

It is a mistake to think that this form of partiality to self, the difference between my caring about my actions and experiences, and caring about those of others, essentially involves caring about one's own actions and experiences more, or that it essentially involves thinking that, or behaving as if one thought that, one has more reason that one's own action or experience succeed than that those of others should. I will turn to such undoubtedly familiar preferences next. Here I simply point out that they are not to be identified with the necessary asymmetry between our concern for our own actions and

[21] Likewise when they are unwelcome we want them to end.

experiences and our concern for those of others. This asymmetry, part and parcel of what it is to be an agent and to have experiences, does not stand in the way of knowing that one's actions and experiences are no more valuable than those of others, and that, where this is the case, one has as much reason to see to it that others act successfully and have rewarding experiences as that one have them oneself. I may be in the middle of taking the remaining free seat when I perceive someone else trying to take it, and if I recognize that he has a better claim on it than I do (being older, for example) I will abort my action. Lovers know the need to make their partner's experience as pleasurable as they can, even if this involves moderating their own pleasure, and so on and so forth.

These comments relate to present activities and experiences. In less obvious ways, which I will not be able to elucidate here, the same is true of past and future acts and experiences. Being a person (the same person) essentially involves different attitudes to one's own past actions and experiences, or to those one intends, or plans, or foresees having, than to others. This is part and parcel of what it is to be the same person. Yet again, these asymmetries do not essentially involve belief in, or conduct as if one believed in, either the greater value of one's own actions and experiences, or a greater reason to care about them, or to succeed in them.

The third form of self-other partiality is more difficult for me to characterize. I do not understand it, and that is probably partly due to the fact that I am not sure what instances such partiality. Perhaps it can be described as a tendency to act as if one has more reason to care about one's own experiences, actions, and goals than about those of others, when this is not the case. It is this last 'when this is not the case' which makes the class of cases hard to identify. Some people believe that whenever I have something which someone else wants more intensely than I do then it is better that he have it than that I do. Others believe that if I have something the loss of which will affect me less than the benefit it will bring to another then I should give it to the other, and so on. This is the ground of much moral reflection. The difficulty is that without having fairly definite views on what people ought to do it is very difficult to understand what sort of systematic preferences cause them to fail to act as they should.

The difficulty is not due to a doubt regarding the existence of such preferences. It is probably true that concerning any remotely sensible view of our obligations to others it is fairly easy to find types of situations, within our experience, where it would be generally agreed that people often disregard those obligations and behave in ways that would be justified only if they had more reason to care about their own concerns than they do. I suspect that people will agree that they themselves are prone to the same biases. The difficulty is not that the existence of the preferences is in doubt, but that without knowing their scope it is difficult to know their origin and nature. They may be due to being socialized in societies with prevalent practices that militate against conformity to some moral obligations, while acknowledging their validity. Or they may be due to social factors that encourage the emergence of certain psychological tendencies which make, in some cases, for psychological conflicts when conformity with acknowledged moral obligations is called for. In other words, these biases may be due to contingent social formations, rather than inherent in our nature as some would have it.

It is a moot point. What seems less problematic is that these preferences cannot be explained as favouring one's own well-being. The preference manifests itself in petty meanness, as when we become attached to objects with little value to our life, and are reluctant to part with them when we ought to for the sake of others. In general, it seems to me to be a bias arising out of obsessive attachments to objects, or to options or prospects, surrender of which sometimes may affect our well-being, but often will clearly not, and sometimes the very attachment prevents us from advancing our interests. There is no evidence here of a general tendency to believe, or behave as if one did, that well-being is of independent normative force.

Some cases of partiality to self may be different, possibly constituting a fourth category. Suppose that in today's world it is more valuable for a person to have primary than university education, and that I have a choice between spending money on my own or my child's university education or using it to enable a stranger to have primary education. Arguably, everyone would be strongly inclined to use the money for his own or his child's education, rather than for the stranger. Arguably, this manifests partiality to oneself, and that is so even if morally or rationally one should spend the money on one's own or one's child's university education. In cases like this the sources of partiality are not obsessive attachment to one's possessions or to one's established routines. But nor are they to be explained by concern for one's well-being. Rather, they express concern for one's ability to develop and pursue goals successfully. These may advance one's well-being, but they may sacrifice it for moral or other causes. Generally speaking,[22] one's own well-being is not an independent normative consideration for the person whose life is in question. This is consistent with people caring about their well-being, for what they then care

[22] I have suggested that one can make the advancement of one's well-being one of one's goals, and in that case it has such additional normative force as one's goals have. See Raz, *Engaging Reason*, 328–30.

about is what their well-being consists in, that is, their success in their adopted valuable (as they see matters) relationships and pursuits, and in those they may adopt or pursue in the future. People may care about various aspects of their life. They may care about their service to their communities, to their families, about their success in leading a moral and upright life, and much else, and among other things they may care about their well-being. (Even when they do it may not be seen by them as the most important aspect of their life. It can be a consolation for failing to achieve what they did care about most: I wish I were a really good scientist, one may say, but at least I had a good life.)

Whether or not people care about their well-being depends partly on whether their culture made the concept available to them, and partly on whether they came to focus their concerns in that way. Many people do not. They may care about their virtue or about some accomplishments they have set their heart on, rather than about their well-being. But even they must acknowledge that having a good life is a good, even if it is not one they particularly care about.

That having been said, well-being enjoys a special position among the different perspectives from which to judge a life. The factors that determine people's well-being do not include everything in their life, and need not coincide with the factors those people care most about. But they do include everything of importance.[23] This makes well-being the most comprehensive perspective from which to judge a life. It is, therefore, a natural default perspective—when there is no special reason to think of a life from another perspective (because of its moral importance, or special achievement in some area, or because the person concerned cares so much about that aspect of his life) the way by which we, who have the concept, will judge how good people's life was for them, is by their level of well-being.

5. Respecting Strangers

The conclusions of the previous section constitute a rejection of part of the radical suggestion. The suggestion says that when we care about people, and when we ought to care about people, what we do, or ought to, care about is

[23] To clarify, consider, by way of illustration, an ocean-going sailor. He judges himself only by his record-breaking attempts. But he has friends and family, and other interests, and they too contribute to his well-being (even if less than his sailing), as do the non-pattern-dependent factors. Sailing matters to him most. But well-being is the most comprehensive perspective on his life, taking account of everything of importance, and leaving out only episodes that are insignificant for any of the determinants of well-being.

their well-being. I argued that this is not necessarily the way in which people care about themselves.[24] But if so, if people's concern about themselves is not necessarily concern about their well-being, why should our concern for others express itself as concern about their well-being? Similarly, if we do not have an independent reason to promote our own well-being why should we have any reason to care about the well-being of others?

The symmetry that the radical suggestion offered between caring for oneself and caring for others was a source of strength. It fulfilled two functions. First, it showed the point of caring for another's well-being. If this is what people care about when they care about themselves then this must be what matters when we care, or should care, about them. To deny that is to assume that people are always wrong in their concern for themselves. Second, it provided an argument why we should care about the well-being of strangers. Since my well-being is not more valuable than that of anybody else, if I care about my own well-being, holding it to be of value, I should also care about the well-being of others.

Once we reject the radical suggestion inasmuch as it applies to people's attitudes to themselves the two questions: 'Is there any point in caring about the well-being of another?' 'Do we have a duty to do so?' become moot. If there is no point in caring for the well-being of another then when we care about people because we like them, are attracted to them, but owe them no special duty, it is pointless for our concern for them to express itself by caring about their well-being. Likewise, if I do not take my own well-being as an independent reason, realization that my value, or the value of my well-being is no greater than that of anyone else cannot yield an argument that I have a duty towards others' well-being, since I have none towards my own.

The first question 'Is there any point in caring about the well-being of another?' is easy. An affirmative answer does not imply that there is no point in caring about other aspects of people's life (similarly an affirmative answer to the second question does not imply that we do not have other duties towards strangers). Clearly, having a good life is a good thing, and that is all it takes to show that there is a point to caring about the well-being of another. We can express concern for others in a variety of ways; concern for their well-being is one such way.

[24] Thus it is also a critique of views like Darwall's that the welfare of a person is what 'it would be rational to want for him for his sake': S. Darwall, *Welfare and Rational Care* (Princeton: Princeton UP, 2002) 9.

But do we have a general duty to be concerned about the well-being of people in general, given that we have no 'special'[25] reason to be concerned about our own well-being? The issue is complex. All I can do here is sketch the outline of a view which gives well-being a central, albeit indirect, role in our general moral duties towards strangers. The outline will leave both the content of the duty, and the arguments for its existence more hinted at than spelt out.

Ethical doctrines that take a duty to promote the well-being of people (and of other animals) to be a core moral duty often seek to derive it directly from the value of the life of people (and of other animals). The value of those lives is a reason for the promotion of the well-being of those whose life it is. There is however a gap between the value of life and a duty to promote the well-being of others, a gap that some sought to fill with the inference from the supposed necessary truth that people seek their own well-being through the fact that no one's life or well-being is more valuable than that of any other, to a duty to promote the well-being of all. Having abandoned that argument what can replace it?

That question is misleading, for the conclusion I will advance is not that of the discarded argument. I do not think that we have a duty to promote the well-being of others. Rather, we have a duty to protect their ability to forge a good life for themselves. But before we examine the conclusion we should turn to the argument. It derives from a general view of rational agency, that is, the intentional actions of creatures capable of acting in light of a view of how things are in the world.[26] Rational agents, even when acting intentionally, do not always deliberate prior to acting. But their capacity for rational agency plays a part in all their intentional actions in a variety of ways. Some of their intentional actions are parts of sequences of actions each one of which is more or less automatic, where the sequence as a whole is adopted for reasons. Besides, most of the time when rational agents act intentionally their capacity to deliberate is a controlling background presence, so that even if it plays no, or only a limited role in initiating the actions, they will be interrupted or modified if feedback indicates that they do not 'go well', and that background presence justifies describing all intentional actions as actions for a reason. The reasons are perceived features of the world which tell in favour of the action. Such features, when really present, are value properties. Value properties are

[25] I am using this hedging expression to allow for the fact that because having a good life is a good thing some people may be 'unhealthily' concerned with it, as explained in Raz, *Engaging Reason*, 328–30.

[26] Several of the points sketched in this paragraph are further explained and refined in the first part of this volume.

normative properties, and they play an essential role in explaining intentional action, for they render action in pursuit of value intelligible, and they play an essential role in the ability of rational agents to form intentions and to act intentionally. That something has a value property favours (or disfavours) actions which relate to it in appropriate ways. As discussed in Section 2, values provide two kinds of reasons. The value of anything is a reason to engage with it, and it is a reason to respect it.

Regarding people we also have both reasons for engaging and reasons for respecting them. We engage with them when we strike up a friendship, or when we have some other special relationship with them. We engage with them as creatures with their own tastes, their own ways of understanding the world and of reacting to it. That capacity colours many aspects of our relationships with others. It makes our engagement with people reciprocal in a way in which our engagement with a painting, a novel, a mountain, or animals with much more limited ability to understand themselves and the world, is not. We may express affection towards them, when it is welcome, try to lead them towards having a correct understanding of what is important in life, join them on common adventures, holidays, or other joint activities, and much more. Many such manifestations of a caring attitude presuppose reciprocity between persons who can share activities, conversations, and experiences.

We have no duty to engage with others. But we have a duty to respect them. People may be of value in a variety of ways, all calling for appropriate forms of respect. But central to our duties towards them is the duty to respect them as rational agents, who can engage with value, and with whom we or others can engage in reciprocal ways. One question that has to be postponed concerns the stringency of the reasons we have to respect people. But we have to say something, however sketchy, about the content of that duty of respect, as I shall refer to it. As mentioned, respect calls on us to protect what is of value. It therefore imposes different requirements when we respect a person for his beauty, or for being a caring parent, etc. The duty of respect we have towards people qua rational agents is to protect their capacities as rational agents, and the conditions for their successful exercise.

That latter point is, of course, crucial. Am I not overreaching here: let it be conceded that the capacity for rational action is valuable and therefore we have a duty to respect it. Duties of respect, however, consist in protecting what is respected from harm and decay. Should not that mean protecting people's powers of rational agency, but not providing them with any special conditions for their exercise? This suggestion misunderstands the value of capacities. Capacities are valuable only if their exercise is, under some conditions, valuable. A capacity that can never be put to use has no value. Hence just as valuing a capacity entails valuing its exercise and the opportunity to exercise it under certain conditions so respecting it involves a duty to protect the appropriate conditions for its use.

Here we have to acknowledge another implication of the duty of respect. In general respecting something of value, say a painting, involves not only refraining from damaging it, but also taking steps to protect it from decay, for example by constructing a display case with regulated temperature and humidity. The point of respect is to make engagement with value possible, and the protection of the painting has to assure not merely its continued existence, but the possibility of appreciating it. Respecting persons requires more than refraining from unduly limiting their opportunities to exercise their powers of rational agency. It requires making sure that such opportunities are available. This too follows from the fact that the value of a capacity is in its proper exercise. Protecting it involves insuring the availability of adequate opportunities for such exercise.

Those conditions, I am suggesting, are the conditions that enable people to have a good life. The suggestion is consistent with my earlier conclusions, and does not take well-being to be the end of our powers of rational agency. A person who sacrifices his well-being for a moral cause, for example, may be a perfect exemplar of the successful exercise of our powers of rational agency.

I do suggest however that those powers are valuable because they enable us to determine, through both small decisions and large, the course of our life, in conditions that make a meaningful and rewarding life possible. Contrast them with a person trapped in a confined space, two metres by two, with water and food readily available, but with nothing else he can do. Assume that he has no language, no skills other than drinking and eating, etc. That person has no use for his capacity for rational agency. Had he been a slug he would have done just as well. The capacity for rational agency is of value only if it can be used in conditions that enable people to make something of their life. The measure of that is a controversial matter. I tend to be a minimalist. I believe, for example, that in the Stone Age it was possible for people to have rich and rewarding lives, in which their capacity for rational agency enabled them to express the emotional, imaginative, creative, physical, and other aspects of their nature. But we need not take a position on this issue. It becomes a debate about the conditions under which people have a fair chance to enjoy a good life, if they sensibly try. My point is only that the conditions under which people have such a fair chance are the conditions which make for a successful exercise of their capacity for rational agency, and therefore that protecting those conditions is part of the duty to respect people because of their capacity for rational agency, and that that does not require belief that the proper use of their rational agency is to pursue their own well-being, or that their capacity for rational agency will fail or remain unfulfilled if they do not enjoy a considerable level of well-being.

My suggestion is not that there is no other way to delineate the conditions that respect for the capacity for rational agency calls on us to protect. That is highly unlikely. My suggestion is that for us, for many of us, today, it is natural to identify those conditions in part by the fact that they are the same conditions needed for people to have a fair chance to enjoy a good life, if they make a decent go of it. Two factors make this way of identifying some of what the duty of respect requires instructive:

First, the good life is for each of us to live. It is not in anyone's gift. It consists, I have argued, in the wholehearted and successful pursuit of worthwhile relationships and goals. They are goals we have to adopt and pursue. This requires the use of our powers of rational agency. We may, as we saw, take decisions, even wise and necessary decisions, that sacrifice our well-being, and we may do so with open eyes, but we can do so only when those options are open to us. The conditions for having a good life are conditions in which we can use our powers of agency to forge a life for ourselves. The reference to the conditions of well-being highlights the importance of agency.

Second, the connection to the conditions of well-being relates the duty of respect for people to welfarist thinking and policies. But it would be a mistake to read this as suggesting that we can derive specific personal or social policies from a statement of the fundamental duty of respect, any more than we can determine what personal actions or social policies are mandated by concern for the conditions for well-being, taken in the abstract. The second advantage of pointing out the relations of a duty of respecting persons to welfarist considerations is that it brings out ways in which what the duty of respect requires is socially relative.

This is due to at least three factors. First, the ability to forge a life for oneself depends on one's ability to take advantage of the opportunities available in the society in which one lives. Arguably, in medieval Europe illiteracy may not have jeopardized most people's ability to enjoy a good life, whereas today it does. To be able to act as rational agents we need access to an adequate range of those opportunities that are available here and now. Second, respecting people's rational agency involves protecting their self-respect as rational agents.[27] People's ability to enjoy self-respect depends on social recognition, and social status, and that too expresses itself in different ways in different societies. The duty to protect for people conditions that give them a fair chance to lead a good life, should they sensibly try to do so, helps in shaping personal decisions or social policies only when its application to the social conditions in which one operates is carefully considered.

Third, the connection between respect for people and the conditions for well-being brings out the complex interplay of factors that characterize friendships and other personal relations. The duty of respect is categorical and applies to friends and strangers alike. In itself it implies distance. It is a duty to protect conditions for the successful exercise of rational agency, conditions that make for the real possibility of a good life, leaving the respected people free to lead their own life as they see fit. Friendships break down this barrier of distance. Typically, our friends get involved with what we care about. To a lesser or greater degree we can expect them to help with what we are trying to achieve, because that is what we are trying to achieve, regardless of whether pursuing our goals or relationships will be good for us. Friends are caught in a dilemma that strangers are spared, the dilemma of whether to engage with us as we want them to do, or whether to protect us from ourselves. Different friendships often define themselves by the way they negotiate this tension. Different people determine themselves by their capacity to accept different degrees of involvement of others in their lives.

Several writers expressed concern that a moral outlook which requires us to promote the well-being of others is 'too demanding' and is at odds with what can be expected of people given our social or biological nature. That concern does not apply to the view I am advocating here. We cannot make others have a good life. They have to lead their own life. We can and do affect the way our friends' lives go because our friendships make us part of their life, the success of our friendships is part of the success of our life as well as of the life of our friends. Friendships involve engagement with, partnership in, various aspects of the life of our friends. But regarding strangers our duty to respect them as persons requires a certain distance. It requires protecting the conditions that enable them to have a good life, and that may be demanding. It imposes constraints on how we may lead our lives. But it also sets limits to what we owe strangers. In being a duty of respect for their capacity for rational agency it requires us to leave them alone to lead their life. It protects them

[27] Here again there is a complex argument to unfold, with qualifications and elaborations.

from excessive interference with their life, and it protects us from getting too closely involved with the lives of strangers. It protects our ability to lead a life of our own.

6. Conclusion

The preceding discussion took no account of instrumental considerations, or of considerations arising out of special national or societal bonds, and of much else. It aimed at the most abstract case for duties or reasons to care about people. I rejected the radical suggestion. Agreeing that well-being is a good thing to have, I failed to find a reason with an independent force to care about people's well-being. Given that well-being consists in successful pursuit of valuable goals and relationships there is an obvious reason to pursue whatever it consists in, that is, those valuable goals and relationships. But I could not think of a general reason for pursuing well-being, one's own or that of others, beyond that.

I do not believe that there is one way in which caring about people does or should manifest itself. In particular, it seems natural that different people will care about different aspects of their life, and so long as they do not value the valueless or denigrate what is valuable there is nothing amiss if they value their life for their contribution to their country, or for their relations with their family, or for the fun they had, or for having had a good life, etc. Several of these dimensions of one's life may coincide, but they need not.

Caring about people consists in respecting them and engaging with them in various ways. What people care about in their own life is an important guide for their friends, for those who care for them by engaging with them. When it comes to strangers the dominant duty is one of respect for others, and that includes the duty to secure for people opportunities that give them a fair chance for having a good life if they make a decent attempt at it.

10
Attachments and Associated Reasons

Over the years we form attachments and lose them—if 'lose' is the right word. Much of our emotional life revolves around them, is focused on them. The very term 'attachment' connotes an emotional connection, and I am using the term in a common, non-technical way. It is not confined to any specific emotion, or range of emotions, nor is it confined to happy, or willing attachments. There are ones we have in spite of ourselves. And there are ones we struggle to free ourselves from, or are ambivalent about. But they are connections we have to people, or objects, places, or groups of which we are aware. I will not be concerned with attachments to ideas, or theories. To simplify I will not consider complex and multifaceted attachments, such as religious ones, and will spend more time on attachments to people than to other objects. We may not understand our attachments well, nor know much about their scope and reach. But we are aware of their role in our life. Therefore, however anxious we may be to end them, and however aware we are of their negative aspects, and of the negative emotions they raise within us, unless we hate ourselves thoroughly we have towards them some positive feeling, as they are part of who we are and part of our lives.

Given the emotional aspects of attachments it is inevitable that they affect our concerns, and that means that they affect our perceived reasons, the reasons we think that we have. My purpose in this chapter concerns the proper understanding of how it can be that our attachments affect the (non-instrumental) reasons we have. I will neither seek to justify the belief that attachments affect (non-instrumental) reasons nor endorse beliefs about the reasons they constitute or provide. Given the inevitability of attachments for beings with our psychological make-up, justification does not seem to be needed. But uncritical endorsement of our beliefs about what reasons they provide would be rash—while often they provide some reasons there is no general ground to think that we are correct whenever we assume that they provide this reason or that. For the most part my discussion will not reach the question of what reasons they provide, being concerned with understanding how it is that they can provide any reasons.

The Roots of Normativity. Joseph Raz, Edited with an Introduction by Ulrike Heuer, Oxford University Press.
 DOI: 10.1093/oso/9780192847003.003.0011

In many ways my concern merely echoes Barbara Herman's concern in the paper on 'Agency, Attachment and Difference'.[1] Our approaches may be thought to be radically different. She, while not meaning her article 'in the spirit of endless defense of a favourite system' (776), is trying to show that attachments are not inconsistent with Kantian ethics. I, on the other hand, ignore Kantian or any other constructivist metaethics, and consider the issue on the assumption that practical reasons, that is, reasons for actions, intentions, and other attitudes, are given by the value of performing them, or of having them. Yet, we share an understanding of where the difficulty lies.

This chapter will unfold in five sections dealing with five questions: first, does the partiality of attachments present an obstacle to their being or giving practical reasons? Second, given a value-based approach to practical reasons, can universal values generate reasons that are specific to their subjects, reasons—say—towards my friends that only I have? Third, do attachments affect what we do independently of any reasons that they provide? Fourth, in what ways do attachments constitute or provide normative reasons, and briefly, how do attachment-related reasons relate to other practical reasons? Finally, I turn to the question of the nature of and justification for partiality to oneself.

1. The Partiality of Attachments

1.1 Partiality and *Pro Tanto*

Do attachments give one reasons? 'Why not?' you may ask. 'What is the problem?' Some perceive the difficulty in reconciling the partiality imported by attachments with the impartiality of morality.[2] 'Partiality' in the sense relevant here designates either an action or a motivational disposition to favour someone. Favour him compared with what? If the possibility that partiality may be justified is not to be ruled out by stipulation, the basis of comparison cannot be 'favour him more than one should, or more than one may'. So I will take partiality to be acting or being disposed to act in ways that

[1] B. Herman, 'Agency, Attachment, and Difference', *Ethics* 101 (1991) 775.

[2] One view that I ignore here is that morality consists of those considerations that can be established from the moral point of view, which is inherently impartial—that is what makes it moral. Constructivists are committed to something like this. Without a constructivist foundation a point of view is simply a partial view, defined by what it excludes. If one defines morality as sound reasons other than reasons of partiality then obviously morality conflicts with reasons of partiality. But being interested in the way sound reasons cohere we do not need to attend to such an artificial restriction.

favour one person more than others (whether more than some others, or more than all others), when doing so expresses favourable attitudes and emotions one has towards that person.

Given the complex emotional aspects of some attachments, and especially given that they may carry negative emotions, like resentment or anger, they are sometimes perceived to give rise to reasons that do not favour their objects. Partiality[3] implies a favouring, so the question of how attachments give rise to reasons is wider than the question of the possibility of justified partiality. There may, however, be special difficulty with the justification of partiality. Such difficulties also affect matters other than attachments. Possibly we have reasons to be partial or to act in ways that are partial to our relations or to our country or to our employer, whether or not we are attached to them.

But is there a difficulty about reconciling partiality with morality? There would be if one thought that reasons that display partiality always override those that do not, if one thought, for example, that one's duties to one's children always override those owed to strangers. But this supposition is mistaken. Reasons displaying partiality are, like most others, *pro tanto* reasons. Barbara Herman expresses what is essentially the same thought as follows:

> What the Kantian requires is only that he not view his desire to save his wife as an unconditionally valid reason.[4]

As desires are not reasons, I feel that the point is better expressed by saying simply that even given the agent's attachment to his wife, the reason to save her is not necessarily conclusive. It is unconditional and valid, but it may be defeated by conflicting reasons. Though my way of explaining how it is that reasons that express partiality are *pro tanto* differs from Barbara's, the two ways are fundamentally at one. She explains:

> In the wide range of cases, the role of the Kantian motive of duty is as such a limiting condition: it expresses the agent's commitment that he will not act (on whatever motive, to whatever end), unless his action is morally

[3] According to the Oxford English Dictionary 'impartiality' means 'Not partial; not favouring one party or side more than another; unprejudiced, unbiased, fair, just, equitable. (Of persons, their conduct, etc.)'. Needless to say morality does not sanction prejudice, bias, or unfair, etc. treatment. So if morality is impartial that must mean that it does not sanction favouring some people or their conduct, etc. over others.

[4] B. Herman, 'Integrity and Impartiality', *The Monist*, 66 (1983) 234, 246.

> permitted. Thus, in the case of bringing aid to someone in need, it would be quite ordinary for the action of the normal moral agent to be overdetermined:[5] he might act from the emotion-based desire to help (meeting the other's need would thus be the direct object of his action), *and* he would act from the motive of duty (the permissibility of what he was doing would be a necessary condition of his acting to help).[6]

Here is how I see the case: in acting to help a person in need, for a reason that expresses the agent's feeling for the other, the agent at least implicitly endorses the view that the reasons for his or her action are not defeated by conflicting reasons. As you see I am avoiding here the question of what actually motivates, that is, causally explains the action—a matter to be dealt with later—and most significantly I do not suggest that the agent acts from a motive or reason of duty. It is merely that he or she would not have acted as they did if they thought that the reason for the action is defeated. That is, of course, not a point about their moral dispositions. It merely expresses the fact that the action is not irrational, not akratic, the agents are not acting against their better judgement. Whether this aspect of the nature of rational intentional action gives succour to the Kantians is not for me to judge. It does, however, help remove some suspicion about the relations between reasons that express partiality or attachment and moral concerns. Herman observes:

> [E]ven when morality permits mothers to act for their children first among others…I do not act for my child because morality permits it, but because I am his mother.[7]

Well, yes and no. The mother is acting *because* of both facts, in that she would not have acted if the reasons for the action were defeated by moral reasons against it.[8] But things being as they are, the fact that there are no decisive moral reasons against the action is not and cannot be her reason for the action: the absence of a reason is not a reason. The only reason for her action is the undefeated reason to act for her child.

[5] In commenting on the passage I will ignore its description of the situation described as one of over-determination. That idea implies two independent routes, each one sufficient in itself for the same outcome. But that is not what Barbara has in mind. She describes a situation in which two components generate an outcome, each being necessary and neither of them sufficient to bring it about.

[6] Herman, 'Integrity and Impartiality', 236.

[7] Herman, 'Agency, Attachment, and Difference', 780.

[8] It is worth noting that if moral reasons are a distinctive set of reasons they may militate against the action without defeating the reasons of partiality or attachment for it.

1.2 Partiality and Moral Impartiality

Given that reasons, actions for which express partiality, are merely *pro tanto*, are they suspect in any way at all? Perhaps the difficulty is in the claim that morality is impartial. Herman thinks that impartiality consists in observing the maxim that enjoins people to treat like cases alike.[9] However, she believes, as I do, that that requirement is empty.[10] I will dismiss the pedantic observation that since all cases are alike in some respects and different in others the maxim requires one to treat all cases in the same way, but that is an empty requirement because all modes of treatment are likewise alike in some ways (while being different in others). It seems natural to understand the maxim as requiring one to treat alike cases that are alike in that the same reasons for action apply to them. So understood the maxim avoids the pedantic objection. But so understood the maxim does no more than enjoin us to act for reasons that apply to us. We need no maxim for that to be true of us. That follows from the very idea that reasons apply to us. Therefore, unlike Herman, I do not see the rejection of the maxim as a challenge to the claim that morality is impartial, as I do not think that the maxim is about impartiality. Being empty it is not about anything.

Partiality, to repeat, is favouring. It is possible that one has reasons to favour one person over another. But do such reasons conflict with morality? No doubt, we should be impartial or act impartially in some contexts, and sometimes that would involve a conflict with reasons believed to be generated by our attachments. A teacher whose daughter is one of the children in his class should act impartially towards all his students, and that may be difficult. There would be occasions in which one should avoid being in a situation in which these difficulties are encountered. But is morality impartial in the stronger sense, meaning that all moral reasons are impartial?

Given that there is no theoretically significant body of considerations that constitutes morality[11] one may, as we inevitably do, draw the boundaries of morality in different ways on different occasions, and none of these ways has claim to be *the* correct one. So, for example, some may conclude that duties to one's children, demanding partiality towards one's children, are not moral duties, though (they may say) they are valid, binding duties. Those who take

[9] Herman, 'Agency, Attachment, and Difference', 776.

[10] There are other ways of understanding it, some making it too weak, others too strong. They cannot be considered here.

[11] For my own explanation of the matter see J. Raz, *Engaging Reason* (Oxford: OUP, 1999) Chap. 11.

this line will then proceed to provide an account of when moral reasons (or duties) are defeated or overridden by non-moral ones. Others may take parental duties to be moral and interpret or qualify the thesis that morality is impartial to allow for that kind of partiality. Such disputes about the nature or boundaries of morality seem to be pointless.[12]

It is worth examining, however, one proposed way of reconciling reasons of partiality with the alleged impartiality of morality. According to it considerations that permit or require agents to be partial are moral if derived from, or grounded in considerations that are impartial. For example, it may be claimed that:

(1) Favouring one's children is (a constitutive) part of, or contributes to, a parent-child relationship that is valuable or good.

(2) The value of that relationship yields a reason for parents to favour their children.

Therefore

(3) One has reasons to favour one's children.

The argument from (1) to (3) seems to me sound and helpful. I will refer to arguments of this form as the standard arguments. They point to the way reasons that express partiality can be established. But do the standard arguments show that the more basic moral considerations are impartial? It is claimed that they entail conclusions like:

(4) The reason all parents have to favour their children is itself impartial.

But do they? (1) and (2) are about the value of a type of relationship rather than about partiality or impartiality. The reason asserted in (3) is universal, in that it applies to anyone who is a parent. But it simply calls for partiality to be displayed by all. If partiality has something to do with agents showing favour to some over others and if reasons of partiality are reasons for conduct that favours some over others then (3) states that all parents have reason to be partial. There is nothing impartial about it (the proposition itself is not impartial as propositions can no more be impartial than partial). Universal partiality is not a form of impartiality.

[12] And by the same token I do not see room or need for a doctrine about the conditions under which moral reasons are defeated.

1.3 Partiality and the Value of Persons

Could it be that some writers think that morality is impartial because morally all people count, they have value as people, because they are people? And therefore no one is more valuable than any other? It is not easy to know what to make of this proposition. The value of people as people is a reason to respect them. It does not follow that I should respect my grandmother or that I should respect a great novelist just as much as I should respect a complete stranger who accomplished little in his life. I should respect all of them equally as persons, but not as great artists or as my grandmothers. How much should I respect each of them all told? Respect does not always aggregate, but sometimes the reasons for respect that I have towards some people would require me to do more for them than for the others. By way of contrast, we can expect that in some other contexts the cumulative strength or importance of reasons to respect some people will not be greater than the strength or importance of the most important of these reasons. So that taken together, so long as the strongest reason applies to each of the people, they will yield reasons for the same conduct regarding each of them.

Some may object that I have misrepresented the principle that all persons count and count equally. It is not to be understood as saying that apart from their other evaluative properties: being (or not being) beautiful, generous, wise, conscientious, and the like, people also have value simply in virtue of being persons. Rather the principle states that persons enjoy a special status, that of beings that count.

How does that differ from saying that they possess worth in virtue of being persons, as well as worth in virtue of being creative, funny, and the like? Is it that having this moral status is a precondition to be met before any of the other value properties can apply to them? This may be true of some properties. One cannot be a good mathematician without being a person, for example. But there are beautiful, loving, creative, and funny animals that are not persons. Could it mean that even though non-persons can have those evaluative properties they do not provide reasons for actions relating to them because they are not persons? I see no justification for such a view, and will continue on the assumption that the value-based approach is so far intact.

The preferential treatment respect may require is not normally thought of as favouring. 'Favouring' connotes action out of a special favourable attitude to the person or object favoured. We may have such an attitude towards people or objects we have reason to respect, but the reason to respect them is typically independent of the attitude. The doubts about the moral permissibility of favouring actions arise when we act as we do because we favour the objects of our actions. Our attitude is somehow taken to give us a reason to act as we do.

This last point may suggest another source of unease about attachments and favouring. Favouring someone because he is *my* son appears to fail the test of universalizability, because an essential part of the reason can only be stated using a singular reference. Favouring someone for the reason that he is John, or Joseph's child, and the like, is favouring them for non-universal properties they have, or for being a particular individual. Moral reasons, we have been taught, cannot be like that. Of course, when we deal with people we deal with particular people. We often must identify the individuals whom we have reason to treat one way or another using singular reference. But when we have reason to deal with them as we do that is because their case falls under a reason whose content can be stated without the use of singular reference.

The obvious reply is to invoke again the standard arguments:

(3) One has reasons to favour one's children

because

(1) Favouring one's children is part of, or contributes to, a parent-child relationship that is valuable or good.

(2) The value of that relationship yields a reason for parents to favour their children.

That NR is my child is a reason for me to favour him because this is an instance of a reason, namely that parents have reason to favour their children.

2. Personal Value: The Irreplaceability Problem

The standard arguments show that the partiality of attachments is not in itself suspect. It raises no doubts about their ability to provide reasons. But it leads us straight into the real problem. Herman states it thus:

> When I attend specially to the needs of my children and friends because I am partial to them, either I have acted as I ought not (morality requires that I count their needs no more than others'), or I have done what I ought to do, because there are obligations to one's children and friends, but I have

> done it the wrong way: my actions were expressions of my partiality, not of my moral understanding and commitments. (776)

We can dismiss the first horn of the dilemma. Morality does not forbid us to favour our children and friends, or so I—along with Herman—shall assume, meaning that while some forms of favouring are immoral, not all are. The difficulty is understanding how it can be right to express our partiality not as an instance of doing our 'moral' duty.

At least part of the problem is with the way the standard arguments were presented. It seems to explain the value of—say—parental relationships. That value provides reasons for everyone, not only for parents and children. For example, strangers should respect the relations between parents and children. Sometimes, when the relationship is in trouble they should help parents and children repair the ruptures. Governments should help people sustain close relations with their children, and so on.

The standard arguments can explain how the value of an attachment provides universal reasons of these kinds. But can they explain, for example, the value of a friendship to the friends? Assume that the friendship between Abby and Betty is good for both. Values being universal, the objection goes, it follows that there can be someone else, call her Carol, such that if Abby were friends with her their friendship would have the value to Abby that her friendship with Betty has. In that case, Abby has no reason not to replace her friendship with Betty with a friendship with Carol, assuming that she can do so. But that is clearly false, and it shows that universal values cannot account for the value or practical importance of relationships and attachments. It follows that universal values cannot explain the reasons attachments give to those attached. Friendships, one is inclined to say, are with a particular person, not with the bearer of some good qualities. For Abby her friendship is with Betty—with that individual person, not merely Betty as a bearer of some good qualities that Carol may also have, or come to have.

It is not easy to make sense of the objection. Of course, the friendship is with a specific individual, but Abby cannot even recognize her friend except through some of her features, features that may well be shared by others. All her beliefs about her friend, everything she feels her friend to be or have, can be expressed as ascribing to her friend some properties that can (in an a-temporal sense) be possessed by other people. Perhaps the objection is that it is wrong to think that the significance of the friendship for Abby is exclusively in Betty's good qualities. She may like Betty because of her awkward gait, her bent legs, her infuriating contrariness, etc. To be sure, people's affection for others, and whatever dependence on them evolves through their common history, does consist of reactions to features that are not themselves evaluative, and not necessarily commonly seen as endearing.[13] But if the friendship is good, and if the affection and mutual dependence contribute to its significance, then those features are themselves good in one way or another.

It is time to address directly the issues of uniqueness and non-fungibility. Our friendships and other attachments are unique to us. That, however, is consistent with the fact that they are made unique by universal properties. It may be that for Abby her friendship with Betty is special because it was with Betty she had her first satisfying sexual experience, or because it was Betty who nursed her back to health when she had pneumonia, the first serious illness of her life, etc. In each case what makes Betty special and important to Abby is that she relates to her in a way in which many people can relate to one another. Many people were someone's first satisfying sexual partner, many people nursed someone to health from their first serious illness, and many others could have played these roles. Nevertheless, so far as Abby is concerned Betty is unique. She relates to Abby in ways in which now no one else can. And these relational properties are, to Abby, significant. They are part of what makes her friendship with Betty unique, and uniquely valuable.

That means that no other friendship will be the same, will have the same good aspects as the friendship with Betty. It does not mean either that that friendship is the best there can be, or that it would be wrong to end it in order to have another friendship, when the two conflict.

I have illustrated the point using the example of dramatic events in people's lives. Many friendships and other attachments do not share such dramatic events, and for those who share them such events need not be the most important aspect of the meaning of the friendship. With time more and more is shared among people, and some of it becomes—for one reason or another, and they need not be important reasons—significant for them, changing, cementing, or undermining the ties among the friends. Uniqueness is created by the significant historical-biographical features of the friendship. And the role of all the significant historical features of a friendship or other attachment, is explained by theories that fall within the value-based approach.

The objector may reply that while it is true that such historical properties make the relationship unique to the friends, and while they may be valuable

[13] A non-evaluative property may be said to be positive if its presence contributes to the explanation of the fact that a good-making evaluative property is instantiated in the conditions then existing.

properties, they are not the reasons people have for valuing their friendships, at least they are not always among the reasons people have for valuing the friendship. That may be so. The observations above address the familiar tension between the feeling that attachments are valuable because of the evaluative properties that they or their objects have, and the feeling that each attachment is in some sense unique and irreplaceable—we can lose one attachment and acquire others that are no less good and enriching, but they will be different. In some significant dimension we will not be replacing like with like. We may, for example, while conceding that the new attachment is no less valuable than the lost one, and that it enriches our life no less than the lost one did, nevertheless mourn the loss of the lost one (and not merely the circumstances of its loss).

My view of the matter as outlined above is almost entirely consonant with Herman's *deliberative field model* which defeats 'a picture of an autarchy of ends slotted into a legalistic or merely formal deliberative framework and,...[replaces] that picture with the idea of the Good as a constructed object of practical agency',[14] replaces it with an account of how the attachments are integrated within the agents' lives. The main difference between us is the absence from my account of a constructivist understanding of that process, an understanding that implies that the value of the attachment is entirely due to (a) its being embraced by the agent and (b) its not falling foul of moral constraints. On my account, expressed in the standard argument, the attachment has to be valuable and its objects appropriate independently of the agents' embracing them. However, they acquire a personal meaning or value to these agents through their biographical place in the agents' lives and that, those biographical properties of the objects of attachments, makes them unique to the agents, in a way that is consistent with the universalizability of value properties, because there could be similar attachments in the life of other people.[15]

[14] Herman, 'Agency, Attachment, and Difference', 788.

[15] Another difference between us is that I do not share Herman's view that there is a problem with the plural value view. She writes that the 'problem arises when it looks like "over here" is what I most care about, what I want to happen (and cannot not want to happen), but "over there" is what impartial morality demands. There is then deep conflict and tension. And when impartial morality wins, it is not only at the expense of what I most care about, it provides no deliberative space even to acknowledge my concerns. The fact that I care about my son is in no way to affect the deliberative outcome' (ibid. 783). It is part of growing up to realize that some things are not up to us, and they can be the weather, other people's behaviour, or our moral duties.

3. Attachments and the Right Reasons

The conclusion of the discussion so far is that if there is any puzzle about the possibility of reasons that express attachments it is not because they favour some over others, and therefore not because they express partiality to some over others. Such partiality and such favouring are not always defensible, but they are not suspect in themselves. When vindicated, the standard arguments show them to be valuable because they are instances of universal values that have acquired a special significance in the life of the people whose attachments they are. I will therefore now return to an examination of attachments only. The puzzle about them (though not only about them) is that the standard arguments that establish which attachments are valuable seems ill suited to provide the reasons that those attachments appear to provide.

To begin we should examine the ways in which attachments affect our reasons. I will consider only one type of attachment, though a large and varied type: friendship.

The problem we face now is how to understand personal meaning or value, and how it affects the reasons we have. I will first emphasize ways in which attachments affect our reasons without being themselves normative reasons. These are cases where they explain actions and emotions that are rational and permissible, without being constituent parts of normative reasons for them.

3.1 Incommensurability of Reasons and the Impact of Feelings and Attitudes

Two broad situations present different problems. In the first, one acts to cultivate a new friendship or to enhance the significance of an existing one, or one acts to protect an existing friendship from ending or deteriorating. In the second, friendships exist that do not need repairing, enhancing, or defending. The first category involves actions for the sake of the friendship, whereas the second does not. There, when actions affect the friends one can be said to be acting out of friendship, one is acting as a friend.

Let me start with a story. Suppose you ask me about Jack: 'Isn't he an interesting person? Good natured? Fun to be with? A good and loyal friend (to his friends)?' I agree with all of that. 'Why don't you befriend him?' you ask. 'I don't know. I just don't feel like it,' I reply. About a week later you ask me about Jill, and it turns out that I have the same positive opinion about her. 'How about befriending Jill?' you ask. 'Interesting suggestion,' I say, 'I had not thought of it; but now you mention it I think that I will try to become friends with her.' 'Why do you want to be friends with Jill?' you ask. 'You know,' I say, 'she is interesting, and easy to get on with, etc. etc.' 'But so is Jack,' you say. 'I know, but I just do not feel like being friends with him.' 'Do you mean,' you ask, 'that you like Jill better than Jack?' 'No,' I reply, 'I like them both.' 'Do you suspect,' you ask, 'that you will be more successful in establishing a lasting, rewarding friendship with Jill than with Jack?' 'No, I have no reason to think so, nor the opposite.' 'So why?' you finally ask. 'I do not know. I just want to.'

I do not suggest that this is a typical story. Often, probably most often, people drift into friendship gradually, not deciding to form a new friendship deliberately as in the story. Nor, when aiming to forge a new friendship, do people typically act in the way the story describes. It is, however, a possible story, and it brings out an important point, a point that is typically present in all deliberate forging of new friendships. It is that people have reasons for their choice of friends, but those reasons are not unique to the people they choose to be friends with, nor do they fully explain their choice of friends. Typically, they just go for one person and not for another. There are no normative reasons for the preference, though of course there are psychological or other explanations, or if you like, non-normative explanatory reasons.

Another story illustrates the point: It starts the same way, with that conversation about Jack, except that when we meet again you do not mention Jill. Instead I tell you that I changed my mind and I am now trying to forge a friendship with Jack. 'Why?' you ask. 'Well as we said, he has so many good qualities one wants to see in a friend.' 'But,' you say, 'that was not enough for you last week.' 'Well,' I reply, 'I changed my mind.' 'Have you learnt anything new about Jack?' 'No, it is simply that now I feel like being friends with him.'

It is about the same point: I have reasons, but the complete explanation involves more than those reasons. Similar phenomena will be familiar when friends drift apart imperceptibly, until the friendship ends. There are many different ways of drifting apart—sometimes the reasons for the friendship disappear or there are new reasons against it. But sometimes the reasons for the friendship are still there, but the friendship lost its appeal.

Let us turn now to actions within a secure friendship: often people like being with their friends, doing things with them as well as doing things for them. In all these cases what they do are things worth doing and worth doing with someone, whether or not one does them with one's friends. Social intercourse, going on holidays, going to concerts, dances, discussing philosophy, supporting another person materially or psychologically, lending a listening ear, offering sound advice, and so on are all worthwhile in their own right. In many cases agents have reason to spend time with, do something with or for their friends, and they also have reason to do the same, or to engage in other activities, with others. Often the reasons for none of these various options defeat the others.[16] In some such cases agents will feel disinclined to, and will not choose the option of acting with or for their friends. Sometimes I prefer not to be even with my best friends, and would rather be with people who are not among my friends. And I do not mean just that sometimes the better reason would support such options. I mean simply that faced with incommensurable reasons, and feeling at that time as I do, I would choose an option not involving my friends.

By the same token, on other occasions people will prefer, again faced with incommensurable reasons, those options that do involve their friends. Suppose Jill is now a friend. I may feel like spending time with her, doing something with her. Not because she is a friend, but because she is Jill, though I would not have felt like that had she not been my friend.

So far I have emphasized a number of ways in which friendship may be at work, but not as a normative reason. Rather, the web of feelings and attitudes that constitute its instantiation in this person or that causes people to act intentionally, that is, for reasons, but the reasons do not involve the friendship, and do not fully explain the action. The feelings and attitudes associated with the friendship complement the normative explanation of the action, and it is they that account for the choice to be or act with the friend.

3.2 Friendship as a Reason

You may think that in detailing some ways in which attachments can affect our conduct even when they do not feature among the normative reasons for which we act I am trying to minimize the difficulty of explaining how the value of friendship can be a reason for action out of friendship. But my aim is not that, but the need to identify the kind of situations in which attachments, friendships, not only affect our conduct but do so because we act for (normative) reasons, which they constitute. I described two kinds of situations in which our actions are explained by our friendships but where the friendships do not figure among the (normative) reasons for which we

[16] See my discussion of incommensurability of reasons in J. Raz, *The Morality of Freedom* (Oxford: OUP, 1986) Chap. 13.

act. First, when we act for reasons, but the reasons are not conclusive. They are incommensurable with conflicting reasons, and what makes us choose the option we do are our feelings and attitudes about and to the friendship and the friend, feelings and attitudes that explain our actions without being our reasons for them. Second, there are cases in which we want to do things with or for the person who is a friend but our reason is that he or she is that person: I want to do things with or for Jill, because I take pleasure in doing things with or for her. Not because she is a friend, but because she is Jill. Possibly, I would have felt the same had she not been a friend. As things are, our friendship explains why I feel that way. But that is not part of my (normative) reason. Some of these cases are also cases of incommensurability. But they include cases where the reasons to act with or for the friend are conclusive.

When do friendships constitute or provide normative reasons? Some cases are unproblematic. For example, having moved to a new town in which I know nobody, I may set out to spot possible friends and cultivate relations with them. My reason is the value, the benefits, which a successful friendship will bring. Similarly, even though I am not entirely happy with my friendship with Jack, given that he is my only friend I may try to repair ruptures in the friendship in order to keep it alive, for the sake of the value it has for me. Some reasons of this kind are frowned upon as mercenary (forging a friendship with someone one dislikes to gain promotion at work, etc.). But they are not all objectionable. However, they do not exhaust the ways attachments provide reasons. The other ways are the problematic ones.

Even when one's action is not taken for the reason that it is directed towards a friend, even when it is merely caused by feelings and attitudes associated with friendship, it does express the agent's friendship with the other. That an action expresses friendship does not mean that it was taken to express friendship. But that an action would, if taken, express one's friendship makes it possible to take it in order to express the friendship, an act that can reinforce the friendship and reassure the friends of their continued closeness.

Moreover, friendship, like other attachments, is a socially constituted relationship, or rather a range of relationships, as there are so many kinds of socially recognized friendships. To be sure, people mould their friendships to suit their circumstances, feelings, and temperaments. But their shaping of their relationships constitutes mere variations on socially recognized themes. That is inescapable with all 'dense' social relations, ones involving a wide range of complex interactions and mutual expectations. Their density means that they cannot be entirely created by the people involved in them. Rather the people know the social form, and rely on it while adapting it.[17]

It is typical of the social practices that create the possibility of various relationships that they endow some actions with symbolic meaning relevant to the conduct of such a relationship: they signify a desire to form it, express a commitment to its continuation, show the degree to which one finds it important, that one desires to reduce its intensity or to end it, that one feels that the other has failed to live up to its requirements, and so on. These actions sometimes express their meaning whether intentionally or not, but typically they will be performed to express their meaning—and such actions are actions where the relationship, the friendship in our example, provides a reason, or part of the reason for the action. Valuing as we do our friendships, caring about them, and about our friends, it is natural that we have reason to express these facts, not only to reassure our friends, but out of the need to express how we feel, to make plain or reaffirm how we feel. But even though much of what we do within a friendship has that expressive value, and can, and often is, done partly to express our attitudes to our friends and friendships, this is not yet the central case, nor perhaps the most troublesome case.

The key to the way in which friendships give reasons lies in the fact that they are social products: constituted by complex interweaving practices. They determine what conduct is or is not appropriate between friends, and the appropriate ways in which we recognize and respect friendships among others. As I mentioned the socially determined patterns of conduct and expectations are malleable, and adapted by people in building their own friendships (though the degree to which deviation from the socially determined factors is permissible varies among societies). But even the private, individual shaping of one's relationships is done against the backdrop of those social practices. They form the point of departure, the baseline that endows variations with their meaning by the very fact that they are variations. The background of social practices is essential. It enables people to know how to conduct themselves within friendships, and what to expect from their friends.

Now we can see the complex pattern that attachments generate: friends act towards each other in the knowledge of what is appropriate or expected, and that of course allows considerable freedom for both the social practices and their personal modifications to determine types of appropriate actions,

[17] I discussed this matter in some detail in Raz, *The Morality of Freedom*, Chap. 12.

allowing various degrees of freedom in choosing the specific act one would perform. That choice is informed by any number of other reasons, not necessarily to do with one's relations to the friend (people follow their professional or other interests partly in common with their friends). The friendship is part of the reason for such action, the part that says that the action is appropriate in the context of the relationship. Sometimes, however, one has no other reason for taking the action, nor is one emotionally moved to take it. One may even be reluctant to take the action, and take it unwillingly with various degrees of reserve or resentment, simply because one knows (or believes) that one owes it to one's friend.

3.3 Have We Solved the Puzzle?

You will remember the puzzle I set out to solve. In Herman's words:

> When I attend specially to the needs of my children and friends because I am partial to them, either I have acted as I ought not (morality requires that I count their needs no more than others'), or I have done what I ought to do, because there are obligations to one's children and friends, but I have done it the wrong way: my actions were expressions of my partiality, not of my moral understanding and commitments. (776)

Or, for those unworried about the distinctness of moral reasons: If we have reasons to act with or for our children because of the value of the parent-child relationship, does it not follow that when acting for reasons that express my attachment to my children I am acting for invalid reasons? I am not acting to promote the value of parental relations. I am expressing my partiality, not my adherence to value.

That worry, I implied, is generated by a mistaken view of the way attachments provide reasons. Attachments provide non-instrumental reasons only when they are the fostering of a valuable relationship. Valuable relationships consist in dense patterns of interactions, expectations recognized by those in the relationship and by others. That means that they are constituted by a web of duties and other practical reasons, the basic pattern of which is underpinned by social practices, which people are familiar with, and which they modify to suit their personalities and circumstances. The relationships provide reasons because they are constituted by those reasons. People act for those reasons because these are the actions that express the relationships, but they are not necessarily motivated by those reasons. Typically, people are motivated by their feelings about and attitudes towards their children, or friends, etc. The fondness for their friends, children etc. moves them to act in ways which would express their feeling, and the relationships with the other people identify which actions do express them, which actions express the fondness of parents for their children, and which express the fondness among friends, or professional colleagues, etc. One takes the action for these reasons, given one's motivation. This, as we saw, is one of the ways in which actions motivated by concern for someone are also actions taken for reasons of friendship, or of parental relations, meaning that those reasons determine what action would express the feelings friends have towards their friends, or parents towards their children.

That is, however, merely a description of the simple case. Often the reasons and motivations will be more complicated—one may have reason to reassure the other of one's commitment to the relationship; one may feel a need to rekindle in oneself the emotions that one thinks one ought or one wants to have towards the other; one may simply be aware that given the relationship one owes this or that to the other, and do so reluctantly—and the complexity of human life and of human emotions guarantees an indefinite number of more complex reasons and motivations.

4. Conflict and Aggregation

Some may feel that I have not yet confronted the main difficulty. It is often discussed through examples: May I save my friend, rather than any of the others, just because she is my friend? Or suppose that three are at risk, and I can choose between saving the two on the left and saving the one on the right, and the one is my friend, or my mother, or child. May I save the one rather than the two, just because of my attachment to her? Or, indeed, may I not do so? Is it permissible to save the two rather than my mother?

That possession of other evaluative qualities provides reasons independently of being a person, does not in itself entail that the strength of the reasons they provide is greater than the strength of the stronger reason among them. It is possible that the reason not to kill Jane because she is a person is as strong as the reasons not to kill her due to the combined facts that she is a gifted musician and a person. But unless one assumes that none of the other evaluative qualities of persons makes a difference to way one should conduct oneself towards them the question is one of detail: a question of when favouring is justified rather than whether it can be (non-instrumentally) justified.

A value-based account is one according to which reasons are provided by the value of things, by the fact that certain actions, people, events, and more possess value properties of a variety of kinds. As we saw, evaluative properties are 'impartial' in being universal. Given that being persons endows people with value, inasmuch as people count because they are persons they all count just the same. But they possess other non-instrumental value properties, and these differentiate between people. Inasmuch as they differ in their evaluative features we have different reasons to behave differently to different people.

5. Partiality to Oneself

It is frequently assumed that whatever one's verdict about other partialities, partiality to oneself must be justified for it is inevitable, or rather it can be avoided only by suppressing powerful natural motivational dispositions, and by distorting one's existence as an agent. I believe that partiality to oneself is never justified and that it is often thought to be justified because it is confused with agential asymmetry. As this is an important point I will take some time to explain it.

Every person is both the agent of his own actions, and in some cases, one of their objects, one of those affected by them. Other people are merely the objects of his actions (though joint action is another important category, with mixed roles for others). That is the obvious, but nonetheless the basic asymmetry. It explains some of the phenomena that are often mistaken for partiality for self. Agents are sometimes affected by a variety of motivational dispositions a few of which can be confused with a disposition to be partial to oneself. Take, to start with, the common belief that people are naturally partial to themselves in that they are liable to choose the action that, they believe, will better serve their own interest, even when aware that the alternative is supported by better impartial reasons. It is at best only partially true, and to the extent that it is, that is for reasons other than those assumed by those who hold it.

It is not clear, for example, to what degree serving one's self-interest shows partiality to oneself. What is in one's interest, or self-interest, to do or have is—normally—that which will secure the means or the preconditions for the realization of one's ends, or will realize a constitutive part or aspect of one's ends, assuming that they are worth pursuing.[18] Thus it is in one's interest to have adequate accommodation, more money, good health, and the like. Some of these would be of non-instrumental value as well. But it is inappropriate to describe whatever is of intrinsic value only as being in one's interest. Listening to a Bach Cantata, listening to it for no ulterior, no further reason or end, is not something that could properly be said to be in my interest, though having a ticket to its performance is. To say that listening to it is in my interest implies an ulterior purpose that will be served by my doing so. It may impress my new friend, or it may advance my goal of listening to all Bach's Cantatas, etc. Given that actions whose value to their agents is purely intrinsic are not properly described as being in their interest, we can conclude that what makes something be in the interest of the agent is not its intrinsic value.

To simplify let us concentrate on those actions that are in the agents' interest because they are instrumentally valuable in serving the agents' (worthwhile) goals. There is no general reason to think that these goals are or will all be self-regarding, that they are or will be the pursuit of pleasure by the agent, or the pursuit of knowledge by him, etc. At least some of them may be other-regarding goals like looking after one's children, contributing to political causes, studying to become a doctor in order to have a socially useful job, etc. Whether or not preferring one's interests displays partiality to oneself appears to depend, at least to a degree, on what one's goals are. It may do so if the goals are self-regarding, but not otherwise. Of course, if one's goals show partiality to one's children or others, then one's preference for doing what serves one's interest, while not manifesting partiality to oneself, may be infected by partiality to one's children.[19]

A disposition to prefer one's interests does not amount to a disposition to favour oneself. Possibly, however, action that serves one's interests may be due to a different disposition, one that can more properly be described as a disposition to favour oneself. Agents sometimes have a preference for being active, and for being in control. Imagine a simplified situation: we can either

[18] I am putting the point crudely without due qualifications and refinements.

[19] Here another complication comes into play. Reference to interest is at home when the action supposed to be in one's interest either serves a self-regarding end (getting a ticket to the performance of the Bach cantata) or serves an unspecific end, as most self-interested actions do. These actions serve or will serve unspecific goals which one has or will come to have: one saves money now to have the means for whatever one would want to do in 20 years' time, etc. That is, when the self-interested action is taken, it is not taken to serve a specific end; that it will advance the end that it will, in the event, serve is not the reason for taking the action. Suppose I borrow a car to be able to take my neighbour's child to school. It would be odd to say that it was in my interest to borrow the car. Though agreeing to have my friend's car for my own use next week may well be in my interest. I will find ways to make use of it. Its possession may even lead me to adopt ends I would otherwise not be able (i.e. rationally able) to adopt.

achieve a certain result by our own action, or let someone else secure the same result, perhaps getting him to secure it by paying him to do so. Not infrequently one has a preference for achieving the result oneself, and such preferences may lead one to take the wrong action, that is, to try to secure the result oneself rather than get someone else to do so, when the latter would be better. More indirectly, the preference for being in control may lead to action, sometimes unjustified action, furthering one's own interests. As we saw, successfully furthering one's own interests is empowering. It enhances one's ability to achieve one's goals. But it is important not to confuse the preference to favour one's interests that results from a preference for being active and in control with taking oneself, implicitly or explicitly, as deserving special favours, or as counting for more than others.

The preference for being in control is but one of the motivational malformations that may afflict agents. It is paralleled by an opposite preference, also often to be found, namely the preference to avoid responsibility, a preference for not being in charge or in control, but letting others deal with the matter at hand. That preference, when allowed to dictate one's choices, will lead one to try to achieve one's goals by getting others to do so, rather than doing it oneself. A single person may well display both conflicting preferences on different occasions, or even at the same time. Neither of them constitutes favouring oneself, both being simply examples of the large number of motivational or executive malformations to which agents are susceptible. The distortions and wrong actions to which these preferences lead do not necessarily favour the agent. Often enough they affect agents when choosing between different ways of pursuing moral objectives where neither option favours the agent. Yet the motivational malformations, either the preference for being in control, or for avoiding direct involvement and responsibility, may well determine the agent's choice. When the choice is between an option that favours the agent and one that does not, the malformations may well lead agents to make choices that disfavour them. Thus it would be a mistake to think of these motivational preferences as dispositions to favour oneself.

Favouring one's interests and favouring being in control and active can be colloquially described as displaying partiality to oneself. But they do not show the ethically suspect partiality. What exactly is the ethically suspect or interesting partiality to oneself? One obvious answer identifies this partiality with favouring the advancement of one's own well-being over other ends that, on the relevant occasion, one believes oneself to have a better reason to pursue. I have argued that normally, advancing or safeguarding one's own well-being is not a reason for the agent concerned.[20] But partiality to oneself need not manifest itself in giving undue weight to an alleged reason to serve one's own well-being. It could consist simply in choosing an option that favours one's well-being when whatever reasons support that option are defeated by reasons for an alternative and incompatible one.[21]

If so then partiality to self has to be treated as a motivational malformation. But why assume that it is unjustified? Why not assume that one should, or may, be partial to oneself? Because that way of understanding the partiality is inconsistent with the combination of (a) the view that agents do not have a reason to promote their own well-being, and (b) the view that partiality to self consists in favouring one's own well-being. Without rehearsing the full argument for (a) it may be helpful to lift the veil and look at its main presupposition, which is that our well-being consists in the whole-hearted and successful pursuit of worthwhile ends—to repeat the sound bite I repeated many times before. One's well-being may consist in alleviating poverty, treating the ill, defending the oppressed, just as it may consist in going on wine tasting holidays, textile tours of South-West China, or other self-regarding activities and pursuits. It all depends on what one's goals are.

The result is that one cannot choose one's non-instrumental goals to serve one's well-being. Rather one chooses one's goals for their merit, in light of one's tastes and inclinations, and they determine what one's well-being consists in and thereby also what serves it, what is in one's interest. It also follows that partiality to self, understood as favouring one's own well-being, need not mean preferring self-regarding activities and goals over other, for example over moral goals. Whether it does depends on each person's ends in life.

Perhaps we should understand partiality to self as a tendency to favour self-regarding ends. For all I know some people may well have such a tendency. But I do not know of an account that suggests that such a tendency may be justified. Nor do I know of an account that gives such a tendency the appearance of plausibility that would warrant attributing belief in its justification to anyone. There are, no doubt, other possible ways of understanding partiality to self. It may, for example, be a tendency to keep with the pursuit of one's well-established ends, rather than deviate from them when weighty considerations point to an overriding case for doing so. A person settled in his

[20] See Chapter 9 above.

[21] Alternatively the partiality could be action taken because one falsely believes that one has a reason to pursue one's well-being. Such false belief does not itself manifest any partiality. Mistakes manifest partiality only when they are the result of partiality, i.e. if they are caused by one's partiality. And that brings us back to the considerations discussed in the text above.

work, with his family and other pursuits, may well not respond to the need to help others afflicted by an earthquake or a flood, or whose plight is not sudden but is now pressed upon him. So understood partiality to self becomes a conservative tendency, a tendency to stay with the familiar, a disinclination to change course when there is good reason to do so. Yet again, such a tendency is probably fairly widespread, and yet again it need not lead to action that favours one's well-being. A doctor looking after AIDs patients in Uganda may feel the same reluctance to disrupt his moral activities in order to improve his education, or in order to keep up a romantic relationship with someone back home, in Denmark, even though his contribution to his patients in Uganda is now minimal and the better reason is to take the more self-regarding options. As with other ways of understanding the so-called partiality to oneself, it is more appropriately understood as an agential distortion, as motivational malformation.

Some writings express the fear that unless there are limits to the demands of morality one's life as an agent is cramped and distorted. One is merely a device for converting moral inputs into moral output, and one does not have a life one can call one's own. A certain partiality to self is a consequence of the fact that 'concerns and commitments are *naturally* generated from a person's point of view quite independently of the weight of those concerns in an impersonal ranking of overall states of affairs'.[22] This is a way of understanding Bernard Williams' integrity objection[23] and it may well constitute a valid objection to some moral theories. But it does not justify partiality to self. Our concerns and commitments do arise out of the belief that they are valuable, and drives and desires that are entirely '*natural*' and not sensitive to our view of what reason there may be (e.g. hunger, urge to move one's limbs, need to be alert to one's environment) are rational, for while they are not as sensitive to reasons as our appreciation of literature, their biological sources and role mean that there are reasons to satisfy them.

I conclude that the phenomena normally identified as partiality to self are motivational biases, and I assume that there are various kinds of them, and that they do not necessarily manifest themselves in choices that favour the agent's own well-being, nor are they due to belief that one counts more than others do.[24]

[22] S. Scheffler, *The Rejection of Consequentialism* (Oxford: OUP, 1982, rev. edn. 1994) 56. I use Scheffler's formulation to identify a concern, using it in a way that is somewhat different from his, and against a target different from his.

[23] J. J. C. Smart and B. Williams, *Utilitarianism For and Against* (Cambridge: CUP 1973) 116.

[24] Though confused people may think that they presuppose belief that one counts for more than others.

11
Identity and Social Bonds

It is not my habit to offer advice about what we should do; how we should behave. I do have views about how one should behave…at least sometimes. But I do not believe that my professional training and expertise, such as they are, give my views any special weight. I do not believe that philosophy is a discipline that qualifies one to—as we say—preach any particular moral views. True, the time may come when things are so bad that anyone with decent views should never pass an opportunity to air them, for they are so badly needed. But I do not think that that is so for me here.

I intended to explain why philosophy should not preach morality. Or, at least I intended to explain why political philosophy should not do so. But, instead I will offer an explanation which falls within a domain in which philosophy can be helpful. I will reflect on why social identity may bind. That belongs with explaining how to think about moral matters, or about practical issues more generally. While the conclusions of such explanations, if correct, should guide us in thinking about what we should do, how we should behave, it is a long way from having a guide, to having answers to practical questions. Most importantly, the answers depend on much additional knowledge of human life and human societies, which philosophy may help us think about but does not itself provide.

1. Justifying Attachments and Social Bonds

My topic belongs within a large problem in practical philosophy, often identified as the question of the possibility of justified partiality.[1] But as Chapter 10 explained the problem is misunderstood when presented in that way, suggesting that impartiality is the standard case, and only deviations from it are problematic. There are two contexts in which we tend to invoke

[1] See for a wide-ranging discussion of identity K. Appiah, *The Ethics of Identity* (Princeton: Princeton UP, 2007). He identifies the fact that being a member of a group is taken to be a reason to favour other members as typical of group identities.

The Roots of Normativity. Joseph Raz, Edited with an Introduction by Ulrike Heuer, Oxford University Press.
 DOI: 10.1093/oso/9780192847003.003.0012

the need for impartiality. One is to underline the importance of following reasons rather than some unjustified inclinations (such as to prefer one's cousin when there is no good reason to do so). The other context is almost the precise opposite. Certain office holders have to be impartial and to act impartially, meaning that there is a range of good reasons that they should ignore when acting in their office, though they are valid reasons that should guide them in other cases. For example, it may happen that a thoroughly immoral and unprincipled person holds high office. Other officials have reason to ignore that he is immoral and should not hold the office he has. They, other officials, have reason to treat him as though he is worthy of his high office. Though, of course, when acting as private individuals they should express the same attitudes that we should all do. My uncle, a teacher, once taught a class which included his son. As teacher he had to act impartially and ignore various reasons that should have guided him in relations with his son when he was not acting as his teacher.

When impartiality is a matter of following reasons, it draws no distinction between reasons that favour few or many. Invocation of impartiality has special force when it is an exceptional need to ignore certain otherwise valid and relevant reasons. In such contexts there is the problem of how to justify impartiality. Partiality as such is never a problem.

The issue we are discussing, it turns out, is not the justifiability of partiality but the justifiability of reasons that people may have in virtue of special bonds they have with other people or groups. It is a normal philosophical task to explain how it is that we can have reasons of a certain type. Our type is important and problematic in certain respects, which is why we are looking at it. I dubbed it 'the reasons we have in virtue of our social bonds' because I know of no good name for it. What I, and everyone who reflects on it, have in mind is a narrower class than the name may imply. Any reasons whose existence presupposes a culture of some kind or another involve social bonds. The kinds of social bonds I have in mind are those that identify us as members of an identity-forming group: You know the usual suspects: members of the same gender, sexual orientation, same racial, ethnic, religious group, and so on. I am gesturing towards something vaguely familiar. I will not try to identify it in a way that minimizes the vagueness, for arguably the vagueness is an important part of our thinking about these matters. This means that while it may be useful to call them 'identity-forming bonds', the term is useful only in virtue of some of its common associations. Nothing that I will say will draw on the meaning of 'identity', beyond that being a member of one of these groups *may* be significant to the way one thinks of oneself or is thought of by others. So is the fact that one dislikes living in a basement apartment, though that is unlikely to be thought of as constituting an identity-forming group, and my reflections are not very relevant to it.

Let me introduce my question through two examples, which I borrow from John Skorupski's comment on a lecture by Scanlon.[2]

> To start from a very stock example, suppose I have a choice between rescuing my mother from a shipwreck or a blaze, and rescuing another person. Is not the fact that I am her son in and of itself a specific reason to rescue her? Does this reason have to be derived from other reasons? On the face of it, it makes no sense even to ask about reasons to 'accept' or 'reject' the identity of being her son. However, this is perhaps not obvious. Suppose, though I know that she is my biological mother, I also know that she abandoned me at birth, that as a result we hardly know each other etc. Doesn't it make sense, in those circumstances, to ask whether I should adopt the identity 'her son'? Couldn't I answer in the negative? 'I don't think of myself as her son,' I might say. But another view finds this response evasive, or self-deluding. Even in the described circumstances the brute fact that I am her son gives me a reason—though one much weaker than the overall reason I would have if in fact she had spent time, feeling and effort bringing me up, as a result of which we were emotionally close.... Next, suppose I am a successful asylum seeker, established in Britain having fled some oppressive regime. Out of the blue, the son of a cousin turns up on my doorstep seeking support. Of course, there may be [...]reasons to aid anyone in that situation who requests aid. But should I regard the family relationship itself, which of course I did not choose, as a reason to provide help? Could I not say 'I'm sorry, but I no longer think of myself as a refugee, with an extended family in ***—I'm trying to lead a new life'. Someone from the same culture might answer 'I'm sorry, too, but how you think of yourself is not really the point. The fact is that you are a member of the family, and that itself gives you responsibilities'.[3]

One mistaken tendency that Skorupski points to is to think that whether a relationship or membership of a group provides reasons for action or feelings, etc. depends on one's choice, here and elsewhere often described as a choice of

[2] T. M. Scanlon's 'Ideas of Identity and their Normative Status', available at https://www.kcl.ac.uk/law/c-ppl/news-events/ppl-annual-lecture-thomas-scanlon-ideas-of-identity-updated-2.pdf.

[3] https://www.kcl.ac.uk/law/c-ppl/news-events/ppl-annual-lecture-skorupski-comment-on-scanlon-on-identity.pdf, 3–4.

one's identity. Given that 'identity' is used in so many quite diverse contexts for so many different purposes I will avoid the term, but will not—I hope—evade the problems Scanlon, Skorupski, and many others debate. For the sake of a more natural flowing explanation I will often refer to 'duties' rather than reasons as I have done so far, without stopping to consider when reasons we have are duties and when not. Both reasons and duties are *pro tanto*, and can be overridden by conflicting considerations.

It is far from clear why anyone should think that relationships and membership in groups provide reasons or impose duties only if undertaken or maintained by choice. Of course, some people may think that all duties, including the duty not to murder, are based on choice or consent. I will disregard that view. But, if some duties do not depend on our choices, why do those which come with relationships and group membership?

2. Voluntary Associations and the Duties of Members

Voluntary associations, whatever else they are, are sets of inter-related practices, establishing the purposes and modes of operation of the association. Members are subject to those practices, having rights and duties as determined by them. So, the question is: how could it be that a social practice, a sociological fact as many call it, can establish rights and duties that people would not have independently of it? The choice-based answer is that people have it because they choose to. After all the rights and duties apply only to and among members of the associations and by definition they are members because they choose to be.

A simple understanding of the choice-based view takes it to regard the practices as a contingent fact of nature. There could be different practices, different voluntary associations, just as there could be different rivers in one's country, and one takes advantage of them or avoids their hazards as one wills. The will binds, and once one is part of an association one is bound by the duties its practices constitute or impose, as they change from time to time, whether one would agree to them or not. One is able to leave the association, but so long as one is in it, its duties bind one because of one's choice to join. Why one's choice, or will or consent, binds is a mystery. The mystery is not why one can do what one chooses—sometimes one can and that is not a normative question. The mystery is why one is bound to act as one does not want to because of a past choice that does not prevent one from acting as one wants, but makes it wrong to do so. The mystery is deepened by the addition of exceptions to the principle that one's choice binds one: choosing to join Murder Inc. does not bind. Choosing to join a legitimate association does not mean that one would be bound by duties it may impose to act immorally. Choices of the very young do not bind them. Finally, choosing to make oneself a slave, that is, to wholly subject oneself to the will of another person or association on all matters, is not binding.

In saying that these appear mysterious I do not mean that these views are mistaken, only that the more one examines them the more they appear to be an assembly of unrelated and unexplained ideas. My suggested explanation, meant to provide a framework for thinking about such duties, is that there can be value in people having the power to join, and thus bind themselves by the rules of, voluntary associations of certain kinds. When there is such value the rules bind them. There is, my example was, no value in the very young having that power to bind themselves, which is why they do not have it, and there is no value in any person choosing to become a murderer, which is why they are not bound by rules of Murder Inc., etc. You may dispute any of my examples. Indeed, I may do so myself. The proposed principle frames considerations of these and other cases. It explains why sometimes choice to join a voluntary association binds and sometimes it does not, thus setting the mode of reasoning about these issues.

It is not the only relevant principle. It explains why sometimes choice provides no case for thinking that one is bound at all. Other principles explain why even though the choice is a case for being bound that case is overridden by other considerations, like the impact of one's choice on other people. A somewhat over-simplistic account has it that the interest of the chooser determines whether his choice is a reason for him to be bound. The interest of others may defeat the force of that reason and lead to the conclusion that he is not bound after all.

There are three points to highlight:

Value: First, people will be sceptical at my liberal use of 'value' left, right, and centre. I plead guilty as charged: I am using the term in a wider meaning than its standard meaning. I use it as a common term for anything that makes something worthwhile, gives an action a point, makes it contribute some meaning to a pattern in our life, makes it good to some degree in some way. I use it that way because there is no single word or brief phrase that does that job. The charge can be made that the result is a term that is too general in application and disguises the great variety of ways in which things can be good or have a point or be worthwhile. But this charge would be justified only if 'has value' is taken to explain what makes the thing valuable, in what way it is valuable. That is not my suggestion. That something has some value is not an explanation of its value. It means that there is something to explain, and the explanation will bring out the great variety of ways in which things can be of value. And of course, I am not assuming that all value is fungible.

A common and foundational way of explaining how an action, or aspiration, or occupation, or something else, has value is to relate it to a wider context of activities or events in human life, showing how it contributes to the richness or fulfilment of that life. And it can do so in many different ways. So, my point is that choice provides reasons and duties only when it does contribute to life in some way that can be described. It denies that there is magic in choice or consent, or that they always bind. And it suggests a way of determining when they do and when they do not.

The Value of Choosing to Belong: My second point to highlight is the obvious one: the explanation of the value of belonging to voluntary associations moves the focal point from the belonging to the ability to choose whether to belong or not. Of course, there would be no value in that choice if belonging to such groups is never of value. The account I am suggesting presupposes that choosing to belong can be of value: depending on the nature of the association, and the condition of the chooser. But my account allows, as is obvious, that choosing to belong can lack value. It maintains that the ability to choose is itself valuable, and within limits that is true even if the choice is unwise, and the association is not worth belonging to for this person or generally.

It is an inevitable concomitant of the value of choice that where it is valuable its consequences bind even when undesirable—a fundamental starting point to any explanation of why what we choose may bind us even when we no longer want the results of the choice.

The Non-Choice-Dependent Implications of Choices: This brings us to the third point: the relation between wanting to do something and having a reason or a duty to do so. Some people associate duties with restrictions on a person's liberty for the sake of others. More crudely, some think that duties restrict one's pursuit of one's own interest in order to protect the interests of others. While some duties have that rationale, that is a gross distortion of the function and justification of duties generally. They are primarily factors that give shape to various aspects of our life.[4] For example, duties of friendship are part of the constitution of friendship. Friendship is a relationship regulated,

[4] I discussed this aspect of duties at some length in J. Raz, 'Liberating Duties', *Law and Philosophy* 8 (1989) 3 (reprinted in *Ethics in the Public Domain* (Oxford: OUP, 1994)). Cf. also D. Owens, *Shaping the Normative Landscape* (Oxford: OUP, 2012).

in part, by duties regarding friends. We, generally speaking, want to be good friends, and observing the duties of friendship is an important part of being good friends. The thought is that when we wish to express our friendship we need guidance. What will express it? Should we go around telling people how wonderful our friends are? Or, should we enter their homes and clean them? Some unsocialized people may be swept by feelings of friendship to do things like that. But those who understand friendship know that such conduct could be offensive. The duties of friendship are part of the guidance of what friends should do to express their friendship. It goes without saying that when reasons and duties fulfil this function, when their role and contribution is to guide our will, their existence is not conditioned by our desire to perform the act they are a reason to perform. In some cases, whatever is the good of following such reasons is diminished or altogether negated, when they are followed reluctantly, unwillingly. In such cases the reason is not only a reason to act in a certain way, but to do so willingly. But even then, the reason is there even when the will is not. Failure to desire to follow the reason is a rational failure as much as failure to act as the reason directs.

In conclusion, when the friendship is good, fulfilling its duties is also good for us, for it is a manifestation of the friendship. It is the same with the duties of voluntary associations generally.

3. Non-voluntary Relationships and Group Membership

Why am I talking about voluntary groups when my aim is to discuss the possibility of duties of group membership that is independent of our will? Many people are inclined to accept that we have duties in virtue of belonging to voluntary associations and having voluntary relationships. They may attribute this to the magic of choice, but perhaps they can be persuaded that the value-based account I suggested explains both why and within what limits choice matters. Regarding non-voluntary groups and relationships doubts may make some people think that that membership does not impose duties because membership is not freely agreed to. My hope is that they may revise this view if they accept that the normative impact of choice requires explanation, and that such an explanation can be provided by reflection on the value of choice and its limits. If value can explain the duties resulting from voluntary membership perhaps it can also provide the key to reflection on the normative impact of non-voluntary groups. The distinction between the two kinds of groups and relationships is not sharp: most children do not choose their parents, but some are adopted when old enough to express their consent. Most people do not consider the possibility of changing their gender but some do change it. The same goes for nationality, religion, and many other non-voluntary belongings, though even when change occurs and even when it is motivated by choice it tends to be considerably more complex and gradual than change of friendship or voluntary associations.

Duties of belonging presuppose belonging. And the group to which one belongs exists only if it is socially recognized as a distinct group. Of course, the group may be defined by some natural feature: green-eyed people, for example. But a natural feature does not a group make. It is a group only if it is socially recognized as such. There is no denying that an individual may assign special significance to a feature—being green-eyed—even though no one else does. But it does not have the significance we have in mind when thinking of group membership. Forms of social recognition vary and some are more explicit and publicly known than others. In a country like Germany or the United States with a Zaydi population it may not be generally known that, say, Zaydis are a social group. And of course the group need not employ the concept 'a social group' when thinking of itself. It may classify itself under another concept (religion, etc.). It may even have no general concept to apply to all its members. Social recognition may consist of no more than feeling, when encountering a person with an accent one recognizes, and others generally do not notice, that that person is likely to be more friendly, approachable, interested; that there are possibilities of satisfying or rewarding interaction with him or her, more than with the average stranger.

These groups are of different kinds, but typically they have pervasive historical, cultural, and emotional connotations, meaning that their members share common knowledge, common traditions, and emotional ties. And in virtue of ties they share they have expectations of one another. These too may vary. Normally they are that the common ties have left a mark on fellow members, which are manifested in their life and in their attitudes. I started this discussion with the possibility that special help, that a favouring, relative to one's treatment of strangers, is expected. That is true of many social groups, but need not be true of all. It depends on their own traditions and they may even reject the appropriateness of favouring members over non-members.

Social groups share a history, a culture, and emotional connotations. But not all their members do, many may not, or may share such ties only to limited degree. Moreover, some, often significant numbers, dislike what they share, feel alienated, and would prefer not to be members of the group. Significantly, however, members know, if only implicitly, that such sharing of ties is common, and expected. Those who dislike it often feel guilty about their attitude, even while they approve of it. Cases where one belongs to such a group and it means nothing to one are more familiar from stories, including self-deceiving stories, than from life.

So, here is the one feature of these situations I wanted to highlight: on the one hand, not only one's membership, but the very existence of groups of this kind is contingent. Ethnic groups and their significance, religions, genders are all historically contingent. Yet those that exist and to which we belong are not passive factors, indifferent to our life and membership, as the weather or climate are. Groups, through their members, acknowledge (or doubt) our membership, and have expectations of us as members, or non-members. We live in dynamic interactive relations with these groups and their members.

All this is just an observation of their character, complementing the observation we started from, namely that membership is not voluntary. One consequential difference between these and voluntary groupings is that while there is more to voluntary associations than their formal constitution and the rules by which they are governed, they also have an ethos, a culture (broadly understood) of their organization, as their formal rules, with the rights and duties they prescribe, and the committee structure that governs them, predominate. Not so with social groups. Whatever formal structure some of them have tends to be but one aspect of what makes them what they are. The pervasive sharing of culture and history with their connotations tends to prevail. Hence, while so long as one is a member of a voluntary grouping one is subject to duties one may no longer wish to be subject to, or even duties one never wanted to be subject to, each of the duties of voluntary associations can be individually changed, that is, without changing the others. Sometimes individuals have the power to exempt themselves from some duties, but in general the committees, etc. that run the groups can do so. Not so with non-voluntary groups and relationships. Their existence and rules depend, as we saw, on pervasive common understanding of their history and a sharing of culture. To be sure, these change over time, partly in response to pressure for change, and besides they often allow for individual variations in one's understanding of membership and its duties. But, it is nevertheless true that they apply in bulk, with no possibility of individuals picking and choosing which to endorse and which to be exempt from.

I am sure that you see where I am leading: The existence of, and membership in, such a group may be morally valuable to its members, without being morally objectionable from the point of view of non-members. It can be enriching and meaningful for its members, framing much of their life, providing them with support and sources of fulfilment and achievement. When this is the case, happily acculturated members do have duties arising out of the membership, and while occasionally resenting or regretting that they have this or that duty, in general they are content with the situation. Note that nothing I say implies that they should be punished by law for failing to conform with their duties. Whether and when this or other punishments are appropriate is a completely separate issue, not one I discuss here.

Needless to say, the happy situation I delineated is not the only one. And we should be warned off too simplistic an understanding of the value approach.

For example, we may be tempted to say that:

(1) membership provides reasons when it is good for a member to belong to the group, and
(2) it is good for a person to belong to the group only if the existence of the group, its continued existence, is valuable, only if it is—as we may say briefly—a good group.

Both propositions are false. Membership may be good for a person even if the group he belongs to is greatly defective. His loyalty to it may make him a campaigner for reform which he could be only as an insider, only as a member. And this is but one example. The complications are more far-reaching. They are mostly due to the differences between voluntary associations and groups like religious, ethnic, national, groups or one's gender or sexual orientation, etc. Most clearly, the value of choosing membership does not dominate. The focus is on the value of the existence of associations of this kind, and the value of opportunities and relationships whose existence depends on the existence of the group. The existence of such groups generally depends less, if at all, on practices and conventions of required or appropriate behaviour, and more on complex webs of beliefs, attitudes, emotions, and traditions. The practices, traditions, and patterns of expectation that constitute the group and those that presuppose the group's existence tend to affect many aspects of the life of members (they affect non-members as well, but I ignore that here). It becomes difficult to pass judgement on the group and its ways as a whole. They all have more and less valuable aspects and various that are outright unacceptable. They also provide a framework for many practices that while not constitutive of the identity of the group depend on its existence.

The result of the richness, variety of aspects, and depth of emotional resonance of group membership is that, commonly, different members are attached to different aspects of it. The variety of value also breeds ambiguities in attitudes and feelings about belonging.

Aspects of the practices associated with the group, some of which may be firmly taken to be essential to its identity, may be, or may have become over time, morally unacceptable. They may and should generate disputes and conflicts within the group, a desire by some members to exit it, and more critical attitudes from outsiders towards members. Can one ignore and disobey just the objectionable practices? Should one follow even objectionable practices, trying to mitigate their unacceptable aspects? Or, should one reject the group as a whole? etc. I will not try to delineate here the myriad situations in which people may find themselves as a result of real or believed unacceptable aspects of such groups. What is important is that these ambiguities and conflicting emotions are the result of, are made possible by, the fact that we have reasons that are there independently of our choosing, and which create the framework of attitudes and the opportunities for actions and feelings, which make these groups such a potent force in our lives.

I wanted to outline a framework for deliberation on these issues. It shows how non-voluntary membership can give rise to duties. It explains why these come in bulk and cannot readily be negotiated singly, independent of the others, while the duties of voluntary associations can be. And it explains why it is that whatever the moral case for one way of dealing with one's group or another, all those that involve critical attitudes towards aspects of the group's practices, or towards its very existence, are likely to find us conflicted and agonized. The very richness of the groups, their very potential to shape and contribute so much to our life, guarantees that no certitude about one's correct response to their deficiencies will absolve one from feeling conflicted, and ambiguous about much of one's own and other people's situation regarding the groups, and responses to them.

12
Normativity and the Other

1. The Question

Many writers think that normative truths, or truths in some normative domains,[1] are true only if they meet a condition that does not apply to non-normative truths. A good number of different arguments have been offered for the existence of some form of such a condition, and the advocated conditions differ in content, though they form a family. This chapter considers the case for conditions that belong to that family, challenging some of the ideas offered in their support. I will call them participatory conditions. To simplify, let me focus on truths about the practical reasons that apply to a certain person, namely on the practical reasons that person has. If the view, held by some, that normative reasons feature in the explanation of all normative truths is correct, then a thesis about practical reasons would have far reaching implications regarding normative truths. The distinctive constitutive element of participatory conditions is that conduct or attitudes, actual or hypothetical, of people other than those who have a reason, which express approval or the absence of disapproval of the reason in question, are a condition for the existence of practical reasons, or of large classes of them.[2]

The chapter, while not establishing that no participatory conditions exist, offers arguments doubting their existence. Arguably, the advocacy of participatory conditions can be traced back to Rousseau and Kant. Contractualism is perhaps the most influential family of theories claiming that a participatory condition applies to all, or to the central cases, of moral

[1] I will be concerned only with practical normativity. Similar issues regarding epistemic normativity, if there are such, are not considered here.

[2] There is no doubt that the existence of some reasons depends on a participatory condition. E.g. some believe that a promise is binding only if it is accepted by the promisee. This, like all examples, is controversial. This chapter does not examine participatory conditions that apply in some special circumstances. It addresses claims that such conditions apply to all or to large classes of practical reasons. One undisputed special case is that of joint activities, like two friends going on holiday together, where the reasons each has depend on an appropriate attitude in the other. Philosophical inflation may lead people to think of everything one does, or nearly everything, as a joint activity with others, perhaps the rest of humanity. I will not examine the mistaken analogies that lead to such exaggerations.

The Roots of Normativity. Joseph Raz, Edited with an Introduction by Ulrike Heuer, Oxford University Press.
 DOI: 10.1093/oso/9780192847003.003.0013

reasons. I will not examine the history of the idea, nor the views of anyone favouring one or another version of a participatory condition. Not only is that a task for libraries of writings; showing that each of those theories is flawed does not advance the case against the existence of participatory conditions.[3] Instead I examine three of the sources favouring such conditions, aiming to undermine their force. Regarding one of them, examined in Section 2, I argue that it fails to account for the nature of practical reasons, illustrating the point by sketching a simple picture of normativity. The following sections develop some aspects of the simple picture by commenting on other ideas that are inspired by one argument of Rawls, where the participatory condition (along with some other of his ideas in the theory of justice) is justified by being the only possible alternative to two approaches, both of which are unacceptable: intuitionism and consequentialism.

His argument is that consequentialism while presenting itself as a theory concerned with the good of people (or of sentient beings) and nothing else, is not concerned with the good of people at all, because its aim is maximizing (or some other function on) pleasure or desire satisfaction, regarding people as mere containers of pleasure or desires, whose fate does not matter because their individuality is not recognized. It turns out that the simple picture of normativity is also inconsistent with consequentialism as Rawls understands it. As I proceed to illustrate, stage after stage, how the simple normative picture recognizes people's individuality, I join Rawls in highlighting some of the defects of the consequentialism that he rejects,[4] while at the same time undermining his case for participatory conditions by illustrating the existence of additional possible accounts of practical reasons.

The rest of the chapter examines the thought that given that one person's reasons affect or may affect others[5] they are valid only if those others have a role in their creation. This thesis may be motivated by the thought that there is a limit to the ways in which we may, normatively speaking, affect others, and that limit is constituted by a participatory condition. Section 3 explores the ways in which concern for the well-being of others is accounted for without such a condition, and suggests that, contrary to the expectations of

[3] Though a brief appendix disputes Scanlon's contractualism. It illustrates how an argument against a particular view differs from arguments against claims that a participatory condition applies to central classes of reasons.

[4] J. Rawls, *A Theory of Justice* (Oxford: Oxford University Press, 1971, revised edn. 1999) Section 5. Whether anyone was ever committed to it is not our question. I think that Rawls is at least right to pinpoint some popular utilitarian arguments that appear to be guilty as he charges them.

[5] The expression is meant to cover two distinct cases: (a) the very existence of the reason affects others and (b) conduct influenced by awareness of the reason affects others.

some, the participatory condition will reduce rather than enhance the normative concern[6] for their well-being.

Section 4 begins an exploration of a different rationale of the participatory condition, based on the recognition principle, as I shall call it. It claims that normative concern for others is not exhausted by a concern for their well-being that is manifested in the reasons that their well-being provides. Understanding normative concern for others to be so exhausted offends. It equates the way we should relate to others to the way we should relate to other non-instrumental goods such as works of art, objects of natural beauty, and animals of species that have no or very limited rational powers. Others, in the sense meant all along, are beings with rational powers, and relations with them require recognition of the fact. The participatory condition, it is sometimes claimed, expresses that recognition. Section 5 considers the suggestion that a participatory condition is required to acknowledge that people have views not only regarding the reasons we have, but also about what reasons are. The final section acknowledges the recognition principle but denies that it justifies the participatory condition. What is essential to the success of my argument is that the simple normative picture that I rely on is established on independent grounds. It is not an ad hoc invention devised in order to dispute the need for participatory conditions. The chapter cannot and does not establish the justification of this picture. Its achievement is, at most, much more modest: to show that if the ideas I explore are the ones that motivate acceptance of the participatory conditions, then those conditions are not needed, and contribute nothing, as the ideas are fully included in the normative principles I rely on. I also suggest various reasons why participatory conditions can distort our understanding of our normative concern for others.

2. The Accountability to Others Thesis

The participatory condition marks normative truths as unlike other truths. One view sees practical reasons as essentially how a person's thoughts, plans, and actions are justifiable to others. Roughly speaking, the suggestion is that a fact p is a reason for me to perform an action[7] iff my performing the action for the reason that p will make others acknowledge, in real life or

6 By 'normative concern' I mean concern about the ways normative considerations affect others.
7 When referring to actions, omissions and activities should be understood to be included.

hypothetically,[8] that my action is right, appropriate, justified, etc. This is a radical view of the nature of normativity. But its radical character makes it a convenient starting point.

Doubts about it are nourished by familiar features of our existence. One traditional way to describe what I have in mind is to point to what is sometimes taken to be a duality in human nature: our nature is part animal, part rational. The mistake in this thought is the assumed duality. We are animals that have rational powers. Members of various, though not all, animal species have rational powers, and those that have them do not necessarily have the same rational powers. Nor do all humans who have rational powers have all of them or all of them to the same extent. Our rational powers enable us to conduct ourselves in ways that are appropriate to the circumstances we are in. This requires the power to appreciate, at least to a degree, what those circumstances are, and to discriminate between desirable, welcome, aspects of the situation and others that are unwelcome or undesirable. Our rational powers do not assure us of success in making our thoughts and actions appropriate to our circumstances. They do, however, make it possible to do that, to match our ways of being to the world we inhabit. They enable us, for example, to realize that we need rest and to seek it, or to realize that we would enjoy company and to join it, to realize that we would better understand the world if we knew physics and to study it. Sometimes we fail, either to recognize our circumstances or what is appropriate given how they are, or how to achieve it. But success is not random. These are reasonably reliable ways, which can improve with experience and attention, to adjust our thoughts and conduct to our circumstances. If they were not reasonably reliable, they would not constitute the use of rational powers.

There are other beneficial ways in which humans and other animals respond to their environment, ways that do not require recognition of the conditions in which they are, or choice of responses to those conditions. We speak endlessly these days of the ability of our immune system to protect us from threats to our health and existence, doing so without our knowledge or choices contributing to the process. We flinch if we touch a hot object, thus avoiding burns. And we are aware that these processes can fail, and even aggravate threats to our health.

These two ways of reacting to our circumstances are interwoven, and interdependent. When I see a car approaching at speed and decide to jump in

[8] Roughly meaning that they would acknowledge that the action is right if asked under suitable conditions.

order to escape its impact, I manage to jump because my autonomous nervous system responds automatically, accelerating my heart and lungs in the ways required for my jumping. The fact that I am one organism, and my thoughts and actions depend on integrated activities in different parts of the organism, does not undermine the value of drawing distinctions between different ways we respond to conditions, and in particular those that depend on our rational capacities recognizing what the conditions are, identifying their desirable and undesirable aspects, leading to choices to pursue the former and avoid the latter.[9]

The preceding few paragraphs described what I take to be generally known facts, stated without using any technical or philosophical terms, in order to avoid commitment to any systemic account of these facts. I belong with those writers who rely on two main concepts in offering a systemic account of these phenomena. Features of the world that are desirable are valuable, and valuable features that meet certain conditions constitute reasons that agents are to be guided by in their thoughts and actions.[10] From now on I will refer to the facts described above using these two concepts. But for the argument of this chapter nothing depends on whether my account of values or reasons is along the right lines, or whether different concepts must be invoked in accounting for the facts described above. Nothing depends on them because the only point relevant is that these facts lay the foundation for an account of normativity, as involving our rational powers, namely the powers to discern which aspects of our situation are valuable and which are not, and to identify what reasons for thoughts and actions those values provide. They show how normativity, namely the guidelines for the use of our rational powers, is pervasive, and is the precondition of reasoning and of actions for a purpose.

That appears sufficient to establish that even if there is only one person in the world, there are at least some normative truths, truths about values and reasons, and at least some of them are accessible to that person. The people to whom they apply can know them and be guided by them, regardless of how many other people exist. Moreover, given that they are likely to be capable of

[9] The preceding descriptions should be understood to presuppose that our activities change features of the world that are desirable and undesirable, as well as our rational capacities to identify them. Some readers may be inclined to think that I am assuming that the desirable features are those conducive to the survival of and to increasing the power of the agent. That is far from the truth. Such features are sometimes desirable, but not always, and they are not the only ones. In previous writings I cast doubt on the common understanding of self-interest and emphasized the cultural origins of many of the desirable and undesirable features. But these matters cannot be examined here.

[10] Are not reasons mostly facts that are not valuable, e.g. that it is raining being a reason to take an umbrella? The reason to take the umbrella is that given the rain doing so will protect one's health, and that is valuable. That it is raining is part of the reason, mentioned to refer to the reason as a whole.

communicating with other people, they will be able to communicate such truths to them. It may not always be appropriate to do so. Possibly, they should not wake up other people in the middle of the night to tell such truths, etc. But the existence of some normative facts appears to be independent of the ability to communicate them or of the appropriateness of doing so, and therefore, it also appears to be independent of the agreement of others.

Do these appearances mislead? In one way they do. They may suggest that our capacities for action, for discriminating perception and for judgement can be acquired and maintained in solitude, independently of any social learning and acculturation. Given the kind of animals we are, this cannot happen. But the simplified narration of the appearances helps us separate the sources of our ability to be normatively guided from the content and function of normativity. Given the social sources of our abilities, other members of the society in which these abilities were formed and trained are themselves capable, given adequate information, of understanding why we behave the way we do when we are guided by reasons, as we see them. But that does not mean that the aim or role of normativity is to make us understood, or to secure approval of our conduct.

To illustrate, imagine that in the current situation I have three options, A_1, A_2, A_3, each supported by a different reason, R_1, R_2, R_3, and that all other people agree to my pursuing any of them for the related reasons. If so, given that other people do not approve of any of the reasons more than any of the others, I have no reason to prefer one option over the others. Whatever I will do will be justified in the eyes of others, and therefore, there cannot be additional reasons for any of them. Alternatively, if others agree that I am justified in choosing the first option but neither of the others, then I must choose that option—my reasons are those that would justify me in the eyes of others, and only through doing so are they reasons for me to choose one option or another.

This is the result of the justifiability to others thesis, and no doubt its supporters may bite the bullet and accept the result. The illustration assumes that many people, including all those who would agree that sometimes there is no reason to prefer any of three options, will doubt that the mere fact that the reasons for them are approved by others can establish that conclusion. I think that they are right, namely that there could be in such a case additional reasons, not approved by others but valid nevertheless. After all, people are liable to make mistakes, and it is implausible that they be mistaken about what reasons they have, but not about what reasons other people have. The justifiability to others thesis fails to account adequately for our fallibility about reasons.

Still, some people who are attracted to the view that practical reasons are subject to a participatory condition may say that the justification to others thesis misidentifies the case for the participatory condition that it leads to. Some of them may support what I will call the validation thesis: it says that a participatory condition is necessary for the validity of practical reasons for without it one is not entitled to trust one's judgement that the reason is valid. Approval by others validates one's judgement. However, this validation thesis encounters the same objection as the justification to others thesis: It fails to acknowledge that others are fallible, and that it is wrong to take their validation as decisive. Needless to say, responsible agents take note of disagreements with their views, and when needed take steps to make sure that they are right, or modify their views to make them more likely to be true or closer to the truth. Such epistemic considerations cannot require a participatory condition (again: except in some special cases).

As these observations suggest, these are mistaken accounts of reasons not necessarily because validation or justification are totally irrelevant to practical reasons, but because they find nothing else in practical reasons, thereby failing to identify their essential character.[11]

3. The Protection of Others

Some people feel that the simple picture of normativity (as I will refer to it) I painted above is nevertheless too simple. It contains some truth and succeeds in refuting the 'accountability to others' and the validation theories of practical reasons. But it leaves out the dependence of values on the existence of beings for whom what is valuable is good, and for whom values may constitute reasons. Anything of value is or at least can be (i.e. will be under certain conditions) good for some being, and only beings who have rational powers, and thus are able to recognize what is of value, can have reasons for thought and action. We should be careful. It does not follow that were beings for whom some things can be good to disappear there would be nothing good in the universe. It merely follows that when we contemplate such a universe, we are unlikely to have an interest in the fact that some of its features are of

[11] I suspect that even though occasionally a desire, or a need, to be understood or approved of do provide reasons, they have no general role to play in explaining reasons or normativity.

value, as they are of no use to anyone, and no reasons apply to anyone in that universe.

However, returning to our own universe, we, generally speaking, have reasons to act in ways that are good for or can be good for, ourselves and other beings, and we have reasons to prevent and or avoid actions that would be bad for us or others. I will not commit to or discuss any view about the extent of such reasons. I will also ignore without argument various popular mistakes about what reasons are, and when we have reasons to act for the good of others.[12] Our interest is with normative protection others enjoy in circumstances in which my conduct or that of other people can affect them, possibly adversely. One consideration that may establish that the participatory condition applies in those circumstances is that it is needed to protect the interests of people who are or may be affected by agents acting for reasons. Perhaps, when this is the case, reasons for actions that will or may affect others are valid only if the others consent to them, or if they do not object to those reasons, or if any objections they may make do not meet conditions that are required for them to invalidate those reasons.

Such versions of the participatory condition can come in various shapes. Does it apply to everyone who may be affected by our actions? If so, then arguably the condition applies to everyone regarding any action. For possibly, at least in principle, any action of ours may affect, directly or indirectly, anyone else. People sympathetic to this view will think that if the rationale for the participatory condition is to protect others from being affected by our actions then it applies to all actions and to all people (except those no longer alive).[13] In this form the condition implies many conclusions that are widely rejected. This is evidence against it. But the deviation from common views can perhaps be mitigated, and in any case, those views may be mistaken. Another way to argue against this version of the condition is that its motivating thought—that people be protected from actions of others—does not support the condition. I will explore this possibility.

Assuming that the good of others has a bearing on our reasons, let us examine what bearing it has. Naturally, there will be reasons not to kill or maim, etc. people, and to prevent some harms to them, etc., these being

[12] Given that many who endorse mistaken views about reasons, are motivated to accept a participatory condition in order to avoid some of their misguided implications, it is tempting to expose those mistakes, e.g. that only the agent's attitudes can be reasons for him, that pleasure or desire satisfaction or well-being are the only reasons, or that they are the metrics by which the strength of reasons are determined. But it would be impossible to do so here.

[13] It may apply also to those no longer alive regarding the more restricted categories of actions that can still affect them.

reasons similar to those we have regarding anything of value, or at least everything that is, as we say, non-instrumentally valuable. The question we need to address is what reason we have regarding others when:

(1) 'the good of others' concerns the good of beings having rational powers, broadly the same rational powers that human adults typically have, and
(2) what is good for them is determined, in part, by their ability to do what they have reason to do.

To repeat, I will ignore contested questions regarding the degree to which my reasons include reasons to act for the good of others, and whether all such reasons or only some of them depend on what reasons those others have. Instead, I will focus on those cases in which my reasons to act for the good of others apply, and where the good of others is determined by their choices, and by the reasons that they have, namely the cases in which their good is served by their complying with the reasons that apply to them. In such cases, at least up to a point, my reasons to act for their good make their reasons mine, and they are mine because conformity to them is good for those others, those whose good I have reason to protect or pursue.[14] I will call these second-level reasons.

As usual I am not interested in drawing boundaries, or providing necessary and sufficient conditions, but in identifying central cases, and the lessons we learn from them. An example: If I have reason to look after my grandchildren, then it is good for me to be able to do so. If others have reason to protect or advance what is good for me, they have reason to enable me to look after my grandchildren. Note that they do not have a reason (at least not one derived from mine) to look after my grandchildren. Why not? Naturally because my reason is for me, myself, to look after my grandchildren, the point of which is to cultivate a relationship of a certain character with them, a relationship that in itself and in its consequences is, on balance, good for them and good for me.[15] So, take another example. I have reason to have a bottle of milk at home

[14] I formulate the thought in this way to acknowledge its Kantian origins, but I will not be concerned with interpreting Kant on the subject, nor to clarify how far I deviate from him. It seems plausible that second-level reasons apply also regarding animals of some other species, even when their choices are the result of a pursuit of rationally endorsed goals. To determine the issue requires an extensive examination of the rational powers typical of various animal species. But when confronted with an animal whose actions placed it in peril I have a *pro tanto* reason to help it out, regardless of how it came to place itself in peril. If so then only level three reasons apply only to rational beings.

[15] Possibly I also have reason to favour the outcome of my looking after my grandchildren, i.e. to see to it that my grandchildren will be well looked after, regardless of my intervention or contribution. It is separate from the reason to behave towards them myself in certain ways.

tomorrow. This reason, I am assuming, is not a reason to get the milk, except to the extent that I have an instrumental reason to do so in order to satisfy the core reason of having the milk. Still, if others have some reason to act for my good, they may have a reason to enable me to get the milk, but not, except in special circumstances, reason to get the milk and place it in front of my front door. The explanation of this point (which is of course just another controversial example) is too complex to be undertaken here. Suffice it to say that such assumption of one person's reasons by others is an intrusion that violates his autonomy and is permissible only in some circumstances (to save him from imminent danger, etc. or when they are close friends, etc.).

To complicate matters, what reasons people have at any given time may depend on choices they made previously, for good, bad, or no reasons. For their past choices to determine in the right way what is good for them, those choices had to have been freely made, or freely endorsed by them at a later time. To protect or advance what is good for them one needs to respect and protect their freedom to choose what to do, as that will affect their reasons thereafter.[16] The upshot of this discussion is that the reasons that apply to anyone include reasons to act for the good of others, and those reasons, especially the second-level reasons among them, show comprehensive sensitivity to what constitutes the well-being of others. Does it follow that the reasons to act for the good of others express all the normative protection of the good of others that is normatively required? That may depend on how extensive and how stringent are our reasons to act for the good of others. But arguably, if they are extensive and stringent enough, they leave no room for the participatory condition. They provide adequate protection of the others without it.

Some would say that as people know better than others what is good for them, the participatory condition reduces the mistakes that people make about the reasons they have when acting for the sake of others. That is not obviously true. For example, if Islam is correct then Moslems may know better than non-Moslems what is good for the latter. Besides, people object or refrain from objecting for many reasons, including many that have nothing to do with their own good. Therefore, whatever truth there is in this empirical claim it does not justify the participatory requirement that we are considering.[17]

[16] I am summarizing, inevitably inaccurately, the conclusions of complex arguments that there is no point in repeating here.

[17] It may leave room for more specialized requirements of participation by consent, e.g. for medical procedures, for being used in an experiment, and much more.

4. The Recognition Principle

We have been warned time and again that doing something that is good for X (be it a person, or a dog, or a car, etc.), even doing it because it is good for X, does not establish that we have a correct grasp of the value of X. It is consistent with taking the good of X to be only instrumentally valuable. An example is the view that takes the good of the world to be the ultimate value: people's lives or characters are good because they improve the world. It can be maintained that while the good of people's lives is good because they make the world better, they are also good in themselves, that is, the good of the world is not the only core (i.e. non-derivative) value. Arguably, such a view is possible only if the different values can conflict, and in some circumstances, it would be required to act for the good of someone even when that would involve abandoning a course of action that would have improved the world more.[18]

I do not think that the world is a sort of entity that can be valuable in itself. Reference to the good of the world makes sense only as a short-hand reference to the good of beings in the world whose good matters. Let that be as it may. Of interest for the purpose of this chapter is a somewhat different thought, I will call it the recognition principle, which maintains that even if one acts for the good of a being because one takes the good of that being to be of value in itself (and even if it is not taken to be valuable in any other way), one may still fail to understand and recognize in one's action that the being is valuable in itself.

That is due to the fact that for beings to be of value in themselves more is involved than that it may be reasonable to care about how well they are doing, and more is involved than recognizing that their value is, under appropriate circumstances, a reason to act for their good. To provide an account of what it is to be a being of value in itself, we need an explanation of why it is so valuable, and what it takes to acknowledge that is it of value in itself. One feature of such explanations establishes how it can be that recognizing that a being is of value in itself may justify, or even require acting in ways that are less good for that being rather than in ways that are better for it. This will show (or be a way of showing) that recognition of the value of another

[18] If conflict between the good of a person and the good of the world is impossible the claim that persons have value in themselves, and not only value because their good contributes to the good of the world that is independently valuable, appears to be a verbal thesis with no substance.

requires something other than (or in addition to) acting for the good of that person.

It is sometimes said that that missing element is recognition that at least some beings whose life is valuable in itself have their own view of themselves and of the world around them. That fact has been recognized when it was acknowledged that the good of those beings consists in part in their success in acting for reasons that apply to them, and that their own choices affect what reasons apply to them. That implied that our (second-level) reasons for actions that affect others and must take their good into account, are sensitive to the fact that their choices affect their good, and that our reasons towards them, up to a point, follow their choices. The claim that when relating to rational beings we must recognize that fact denies that the recognition implied by second-level reasons is insufficient. Second-level reasons recognize the effects of other beings' rationality on what makes their lives go better. But they fail to recognize that having rational powers is valuable. More specifically, they fail to recognize that the value of having rational powers is not merely instrumental, or quasi-instrumental, not merely that having these powers improves one's chances of having a fulfilled rewarding life. In part having functioning rational powers is good independently of the results that it enables. That view is manifested, for example when we take it to be better if people's course in life is determined by their choices, rather than if the same life is brought about by luck or generally by factors independent of their choices. The recognition principle asserts that value:

> *Recognition principle:* when we have reasons to act for the good of others, those reasons are not necessarily reasons to make their life better. They include reasons to foster conditions that enable them to pursue reasons that apply to them, and these conditions reflect the fact that they have rational powers.

The recognition principle implies that in many cases we have reason to enable others to pursue goals of their choice, even though their life would be less good than it could have been had they made different choices. By protecting their ability and freedom to choose, rather than getting them to make different, better choices, we allow their life to be worse than it might have been.[19]

[19] My argument divides reasons for the good of others into at least two kinds. One consists in reasons that protect or enhance the quality of their life, and are governed by considerations that

Reasoning along these lines is consistent with taking all reasons to be constituted by values and recognizing that in pursuing reasons for the good of beings who have rational powers, our reasons to act for their good are sensitive to the reasons that they have, including, up to a point, when these reasons are products of choices whose pursuit makes their life worse than it could otherwise have been.

The recognition principle reminds us that we not only have (second-level) reasons to enable people to pursue reasons that they have, partly because of earlier choices they made, but also reasons (which I will call third-level reasons) to enable others to make choices, that is, to enjoy the conditions that make choices meaningful and reason-generating for those who made them.

We have been considering two ways to establish a participatory condition for the validity of reasons for actions that will or may affect others. I have been arguing that neither of them justifies a participatory condition. Both normatively defending others from the consequences of actions that will affect them and normatively recognizing that they are rational beings are fully achieved by the reasons we have to act for the good of others, because they include reasons of the second and third level.

5. The Recognition Principle and Conceptual Mistakes

This section considers a possible case for a participatory condition rooted in the thought that respect for the other must include not interfering with people when they are led by mistaken choices to conduct themselves badly or wrongly. A participatory condition protects people from interference in circumstances identified by the condition, thereby also protecting them from interference when they made mistakes in those circumstances. The question is: does not the toleration of mistakes dictated by epistemic considerations, by the practical necessities of social life, and by the reasons for acting for the good of others that were discussed above suffice to meet the case for

determine how good their life is to them. The other is the value for those beings of having rational powers and of being able to guide their own life using their rational powers (and one may explore other kinds of considerations relating to having other capacities). Some people may claim that these are just two aspects of well-being, or of how good the life is. But that is not the way we normally and rightly treat them. It is wrong to terminate a person's life because his quality of life is poor, even though it may be permissible to terminate the life of a being who has no rational powers because the quality of his life is poor. Many people who would not wish to continue their life once they lost their rational powers do wish to extend their life, even if the quality of their life is poor. These and similar considerations suggest that we are dealing with two radically different kinds of reasons for the good of others.

non-interference in other people's mistaken actions and intentions? One case for a negative reply occurred to me: so far, in looking for ways in which we should act for the good of rational beings, I was relying, hopefully, on a correct understanding of rationality and of reasons, explaining cases in which they require non-interference in the mistakes of others. But people have, or may have, their own ideas about what rationality and reasons are. When these ideas are mistaken, they may yield mistakes about what one has reason to do. Is not the source of those mistakes a reason to tolerate them? That is, does not the value of having rational powers require respecting rational beings' mistakes about the nature of rationality and reasons? And does not that respect require not interfering with people's choices that result from these mistakes? That may mean that we should allow for a participatory condition that will secure such non-interference.

The simple picture of normativity allows that when I examine the nature of reasons I consider the possibility that I am wrong, at least partially wrong, and that other views are correct, or at least partially correct. That is an implication of the very possibility of being mistaken about the nature of reasons. But at the end of the day, I have some views, and inevitably hold some others to be mistaken. If this appears to mean that I favour my view of the nature of reasons over those of others—I do not. I rely on my views not because they are my views, but because, as I see things, they are the correct views. If I am to have any view, there is nothing else I can do. To follow some compromise view, or simply another view, is simply to change my mind about which view is correct. It is not a case of being even-handed between my views and those of others. That is not possible. Supporters of the participatory condition may accept that. Their claim is not about the epistemic implications, it is about the practical-normative implications of the fact that people have their own understanding of what reasons are, and that they may be mistaken.

The recognition principle has taught us that my attitude to other people's mistakes differs from my attitude to my own mistakes. I should always recognize a mistake as a mistake, and correct it, or at least avoid it (if I can). But I do not always have reason to correct others' mistakes the way I have to correct mine. Reasons for the good of others include reasons to respect and support their ability to make choices and follow them, sometimes even when those choices are mistaken. Second-level reasons for acting for the good of others include cases in which other people's mistaken choices generate for them real not mistaken reasons (say a mistaken choice of career leads to studying law in university). Respect for the value of having rational powers means that reasons for the good of others include reasons to protect the freedom of others to act for what they believe to be a reason but is not. Call these reasons of the fourth level. My reasons to uphold the ability of others to make and follow choices, are, at least sometimes, fourth-level reasons not to interfere when they make mistakes. Of course, sometimes we should interfere to make it unlikely that others will make certain mistakes, for example when they deny the freedom of others to make mistakes, and sometimes we should strive to stop them from following their mistaken beliefs into action. This is not the time to trace the boundaries of the tolerance of mistakes. Our concern is merely to point to the disanalogy between our reasons regarding our own mistakes and those of others.

Does this tolerant attitude to many of the mistakes of others extend to mistakes arising out of a misunderstanding of the nature of reasons? I can think of two simple arguments supporting a positive answer. The first, and more radical, argument points out that we respect people's freedom to make mistakes and to lead their life by their mistakes (within whichever boundaries this respect holds) because they have rational powers, and their freedom and its consequences manifest these rational powers. That is true even if the result is a misguided idea of what are reasons and what are values. Given that these mistakes manifest their rational powers they deserve the same response from us as other manifestations of their rational powers.

The second argument, whose implications are perhaps more limited, is that those mistaken about what reasons are, are mistaken in their effort to establish what reasons they have. Put it in other words: both they and I are engaged in the same quest: to establish what reasons we have. Whatever reasons we have to respect people's freedom in the exercise of their rational powers in that quest, apply to that exercise whichever mistakes it leads to.

We should reject the first argument. It is typical of all human powers and abilities that even if they have a function and their proper use is for a purpose, they can also be used in ways removed from their proper function, including in ways that can be said to distort their nature. Such uses need not be bad or reprehensible, though sometimes they are. But their evaluation does not benefit from the respect due to the proper use of these powers. Hence, just the fact that some activity or process involves the use of our rational powers does not establish that it merits the respect that is due to the possession of the rational powers, and their proper use.

Is the second argument more successful? And if it is, can the simple view of normativity accommodate it, or is a participatory condition needed to do that? Let us recap: The fact that some beings have rational powers affects our reasons for thoughts about them and actions affecting them, and the question is how? In part the answer is that we have reason to act in ways that enable them to comply with reasons that apply to them. Noting that the reasons that apply to them, or some of them, are the results of choices they made (if they did not choose to ski in the Alps, they would have no sufficient reason to travel to the Alps) we have to face the fact that some of those choices are mistaken and yet they generate reasons for those who made them. Assume that they chose to ski. It would have been much better not to ski in the Alps but to spend one's holiday helping Meals on Wheels, but given the choice to ski, a good activity and thus in principle choice-worthy, they still have reason to get to the Alps.

The recognition principle directs us (i.e. gives us third-level reasons) to take account of the reasons others have, even when they arise out of mistaken beliefs leading to mistaken choices. However, it does not tell us to take account of the reasons they think they have because they think they have them. Nevertheless, it also directs us to respect and protect the ability of beings with rational powers to choose and to follow their choices. That is why the principle gives us fourth-level reasons to tolerate mistakes, including action on mistaken reasons (i.e. what the agents wrongly believe are reasons). If they are mistaken about what reasons are, should the resulting mistakes also be tolerated? It seems that people with mistaken views about what reasons are often have correct views about what reasons they or others have.[20] Moreover, we have no evidence to think that they make more or worse mistakes about what reasons people have. Possibly this is because their views about what reasons they have are not a result of their mistaken understanding of reasons. However, we have no reason to doubt that sometimes mistakes about the nature of reasons do lead to mistakes about what reasons people have. Does the principle direct us to respect those mistakes?

The second argument says that when mistakes about the nature of reasons occur when people are using their rational powers for the proper end, that is, to determine what reasons apply to them (and to others) their mistakes should be tolerated, exactly as and when their other mistakes about the application of reasons are, that is out of respect for them as beings the success of whose life depends, in part, on the use of their rational powers. That is the lesson of the recognition principle.[21]

[20] For example, philosophers who disagree about what reasons are do not necessarily disagree about what reasons people have.

[21] It is possible to maintain, at least for some cases, that while my understanding of a concept was reached though faulty reasoning, through a mistake that I should not have made, given that I have that understanding now, my having it makes it the correct understanding of the concept. But this is not

It shows that a fundamental way in which what we have reason to do is affected by the existence of beings with their own perspective on themselves and the world, who themselves have reasons, is to enable them to pursue those reasons, to inquire what they are and how to follow them. It shows that up to a point our reasons regarding them are to protect their ability to choose, and to enable them to follow their choices even when their choices are misguided, perhaps because they are based on false beliefs about reasons (namely even when they have better reasons to choose other than the way they do choose) and that in part their subsequent reasons are determined by their earlier choices.

The second argument points out that at least sometimes when people's mistakes about what to do stem from their mistakes about what reasons are, they are engaged in the same enterprise as we are, namely finding out what to do by finding out what reasons we have. Therefore the recognition principle accepts the second argument, and extends respect for beings with rational capacities to respecting them when they make such mistakes in the same way that it extends to tolerating their other mistakes.[22] Here too, it seems that the simple view of normativity leads us to adequately respect the fact that our actions do or may affect beings with rational powers, and no participatory condition is required to enable us to do so.

6. Why Not Participatory as Well?

I argued that the requirement of recognizing that the other is a rational person, and of conducting one's relations with him in accordance with that requirement, is met when we simply follow the reasons that apply to us to act for the sake of other rational beings. These reasons reflect the fact that persons have a subjective perspective on themselves and the world, are guided by it, and what is good for them depends on the way they are so guided. That would involve refraining sometimes from actions that would enhance the well-being of others in order to respect the course they have given to their life by their decisions and choices, and to foster their freedom and ability to use their

true regarding the concept of a reason. On a related matter: some writers think that mistakes that are due to a misunderstanding of the concepts involved cannot be irrational. This view betrays a misunderstanding of the nature of rationality. But this is a different issue, not pursued here.

[22] It is a question not to be pursued here whether it is possible that mistakes about the nature of reasons may have the consequence that those who make them do not engage in the same enterprise at all. I tend to think that that can happen when people's mental processes are seriously affected by chemical disturbances (e.g., by some drugs).

rational powers. Granting that, one may ask: 'would not meeting the participatory condition further enhance the recognition of the value of the other?'

There is a respectable tradition of seeking an appropriate consent condition for the validity of some reasons for actions likely to affect those whose consent is required. Needless to say, consent of the others and their agreement are often required. They are required where people have normative powers to affect our reasons by their consent or agreement. I have in mind cases like the power to make agreements, the requirement of consent to medical treatment, etc.[23]

The case for a participatory condition stems from deeper sources. One may doubt that the recognition principle, or anything like it, can be adequately followed within the framework of the simple view of normativity I sketched. Needless to say, I cannot discern the difficulty. I mean that if, for beings with rational powers, having those powers and the ability to use them is of value, there does not appear to be an obstacle preventing the simple view of normativity identifying and expressing that, by something like the recognition principle.[24]

I sometimes feel that the case for a participatory condition derives from an obscure image that says that the simple normativity view regards others as passive objects, being treated or addressed as reasons prescribe. One misses a normative recognition of the value of the other which gives the other an active role. Of course, the simple view allows for joint activities, reciprocal relationships, and quite commonly makes those the most important part of a successful, fulfilled life. Nor does the simple view conflict with the fact that our relations with others have attitudinal and emotional components whose existence is not a response to reasons (though their existence is compatible with compliance with reasons): love, joy, grief, and so on, are not responses to reasons. And in any case participatory conditions do not contribute to their explanation.

[23] I offered a general account of normative powers in Chapter 7. It denies that there is a case for a general requirement of consent as a means of recognition of the other's standing as a person.

[24] However, it has been said to me, the simple view simply articulates what the participatory conditions require. It does not show that they are redundant. E.g. one may say that it all depends on where one starts. I started with the simple view and it turns out, let us concede, that it shows that what the participatory conditions require is required by it too. Had one started with the argument for the participatory condition one would have been led to the conclusion that what the simple view required is required by the participatory conditions and that the simple view is redundant. However, this argument ignores the fact that the participatory conditions cannot be the starting point or the core of an account of normativity. By their nature they presuppose some other account which they qualify. It turns out, my argument shows, that the qualification is not needed, and leads to mistakes.

In recent times a more popular participatory condition is the No Reasonable Objection condition. It protects those likely to be affected by our actions when they have a reasonable objection to the actions. The condition protects people who do not object, if they could have objected, that is, if there is a reasonable objection they could have raised. But it does not endow every objection with normative force, only those that are reasonable. The no reasonable objection condition, when correctly applied, may or may not lead to results that differ from those the simple view of normativity sanctions. The most likely explanation for a version of the condition that cannot deviate from the conclusions of simple normativity is that the test for reasonableness of objection is that the action would not be justified by the standards of simple normativity. If such a version of the condition is recommended this can only be because the right normative answer is the one provided by simple normativity, but we are more likely to discover it when we use the no reasonable objection as a heuristic device for discovering it. In circumstances where a participatory condition has this advantage I cannot think of an objection to using it. But, and crucially, there is no independent ground for the no reasonable objection condition, unless it can generate the right normative answer by itself, without borrowing it from the simple view. If, however, the condition can deviate from the conclusions of simple normativity, we need an explanation of why, and why it overrides those conclusions. Just saying that it allows a participatory role, or an extended protection, to rational beings will not do.[25] We need an account of why and how it does so. Not knowing of any, my interim conclusion is to reject the participatory condition.

Appendix

Scanlon's 'Contractualism and Justification',[26] his most recent and comprehensive defence of Contractualism, exemplifies the problem. 'Contractualism

[25] By way of an example, consider the claim that the simple view ignores the special wrong of being treated in ways that manifest disrespect. Often there are reasons not to act in ways that manifest lack of respect, just because they are disrespectful. Can a participatory condition help here? One may imagine that the affected person would object to principles that allow disrespect. But disrespect is not always wrong, and even when it is not merited, actions manifesting disrespect are sometimes right on the balance of reasons. It is not obvious how the participatory condition can help in discerning the right response, except by borrowing it from the conclusions of the simple account of normativity.

[26] T.M. Scanlon, 'Contractualism and Justification', in M. Stepanians and M. Frauchiger (eds), *Reason, Justification, and Contractualism: Themes from Scanlon*, Lauener Library of Analytical Philosophy vol. 7 (Berlin/Boston: De Gruyter, 2021) 17.

makes the rightness of an action or policy depend on whether it would be permitted by justifiable principles. And it makes the justifiability of principles depend on the reasons of certain kinds that individuals have to accept or reject them' (17). Explaining 'this action (or policy) is right' as 'this action (or policy) is permitted by a justified principle' seems unpromising. There are many actions that it would not be right to perform even though it is permitted to perform them, even though they are permissible. (Thinking about the matter from a Contractualist point of view: exterminating whales is permitted by Contractualist principles because no one has a personal reason that constitutes a reasonable objection to doing so. But even a Contractualist would hold that that is a wrong thing to do.) Possibly Contractualism can explain what it is for an action to be morally permissible. The example of the whales suggests that it cannot. At best it can explain what is Contractually permissible.

Scanlon allows that there are practical reasons independent of morality. There are objectively good, valuable, or bad and harmful actions and situations. Impersonal value provides impersonal reasons: As the existence of the Grand Canyon is valuable one has reasons to preserve it, and to oppose spoiling it. Those are moral reasons which are beyond the scope of Contractualism. Contractualism establishes what is morally permissible or impermissible by reference to personal reasons people have, but only to the extent that we should care about these reasons independently of any objective value they may serve. Scanlon explains: 'Actions are wrong in the particular way I was concerned with…because of the reasons that individuals have to object to being treated in that way. These cases are quite different from ones in which the reason against acting in a certain way is an impersonal reason, such as the kind of reason that we have not to fill the Grand Canyon with trash, a reason grounded in the value of such natural wonders themselves (and going beyond the personal reasons that individuals have for wanting to be able to experience such natural wonders in their unspoiled state)' (28). These impersonal-value grounded reasons may justify objecting to principles that ignore them. However, though '[f]ailure to respond to these reasons would be a fault and would properly trigger a kind of remorse.…it is different from the kind of remorse that is triggered by the realization that one has treated a person in a way that he or she has personal reason to object to' (29).

Scanlon addresses the objection that all reasons are grounded in some value and taking them into account is just a way of taking account of those values. His reply is not that they are not grounded in impersonal value, but that there is more to them (normatively speaking) than the values that ground them:

> 'It might be said, however, that the fact that the person has a reason to reject a principle permitting a certain action is redundant. If the person has such a reason it is only because the effects of actions of that kind would be bad for him…the badness of these effects is, in itself, a reason not to act in such a way.' (29)

Because this is true, the person has a reason to object to being treated in this way. But to say this adds nothing. All the normative work is done by the reasons why it is a bad thing for the person to be harmed in this way. But, according to Scanlon, the fact that an individual in a certain position has a personal reason to object to being treated in a certain way is a special kind of reason for taking a principle that would permit that kind of treatment to be unjustifiable.

Now, the harm to someone if treated in a certain way is a *pro tanto* reason not to do so. If undefeated, it may show that one ought not to treat that person in that way, and we all have reason to try and avert such treatment. Contractualism converts a *pro tanto* reason (what Scanlon calls an impersonal reason) into an objection that constitutes a veto or a side-constraint on any principle permitting such harm, making it unjustified, and the action wrong. You may say that Contractualism is a device to turn *pro tanto* reasons into a veto. However, not every *pro tanto* reason against the act constitutes such an objection. It has to be reasonable to do so. The question is when is it reasonable? Scanlon's discussion makes clear that that depends on the impact of such a veto on other people (as well as on the objector). The question is whether the test of reasonableness, and I mean Scanlon's own test, is not in fact a view about which reasons are more stringent (according to the simple view of normativity I presented). The impression I have is that he is rightly objecting to a certain understanding of the force and stringency of reasons. But then why not correct it, rather than invent an artificial participatory condition that indirectly reinforces the wrong understanding of reasons and their force by suggesting that only it can avoid the mistakes generated by that wrong understanding?

References

Anscombe, G. E. M., *Intention* (Oxford: Basil Blackwell, 1957).

Appiah, K., *The Ethics of Identity* (Princeton: Princeton UP, 2007).

Bartha, P., 'Analogy and Analogical Reasoning', *The Stanford Encyclopedia of Philosophy* (Spring 2019 Edition), Edward N. Zalta (ed.), URL = <https://plato.stanford.edu/archives/spr2019/entries/reasoning-analogy/>.

Bentham, J., *Introduction to the Principles of Morals and Legislation*, ed. J. H. Burns and H. L. A Hart (Methuen: London and New York, 1970).

Boghossian, P., 'What Is Inference?', *Philosophical Studies* 169/1 (2014) 1–18.

Bratman, M., *Intention, Plans and Practical Reason* (Cambridge, Mass.: Harvard UP, 1987).

Bratman, M., 'Intention, Practical Rationality, and Self-Governance', *Ethics* 119 (2009) 411.

Broome, J., 'Are Intentions Reasons?', in Ripstein and Morris (eds), *Practical Rationality and Preference: Essays for David Gauthier*.

Broome, J., *Rationality Through Reasoning* (Chichester: Wiley-Blackwell, 2013).

Brunero, J., 'Are Intentions Reasons?' *Pacific Philosophical Quarterly* 88 (2007) 424.

Brunero, J., 'Self-Governance, Means-Ends Coherence, and Unalterable Ends', *Ethics* 120 (April 2010) 579.

Castañeda, H.-N., *Thinking and Doing* (Dordrecht: D. Reidel, 1975).

Dancy, J., 'Enticing Reasons', in Wallace, Pettit, Scheffler, and Smith (eds), *Reason and Value*.

Dancy, J., 'From Thought to Action', in R. Shafer-Landau (ed.), *Oxford Studies in Metaethics*, vol. 9 (2014).

Dancy, J., *Practical Shape: A Theory of Practical Reasoning* (Oxford: OUP, 2018).

Darwall, S., *Welfare and Rational Care* (Princeton: Princeton UP, 2002).

Dworkin, R., *Justice for Hedgehogs* (Cambridge: Mass.: Harvard UP, 2011).

Enoch, D., 'Giving Practical Reasons', *Philosophers' Imprint* 11/4 (2011).

Finnis, J., *Fundamentals of Ethics* (Oxford: OUP, 1983).

Frankfurt, H., 'The Problem of Action', in Frankfurt, *The Importance of What We Care About*.

Frankfurt, H., *The Importance of What We Care About* (Cambridge: CUP, 1988).

Gerhold, M., 'The Meaningful Life and the Good Life', unpublished DPhil dissertation, Oxford, 2004.

Gregory, A., 'The Guise of Reasons', *American Philosophical Quarterly* 50/1 (2013) 63.

Hacker, P. M. S., and Raz, J. (eds), *Law, Morality, and Society: Essays in Honour of H. L. A. Hart* (Oxford: Clarendon Press, 1977).

Hart, H. L. A., 'Legal and Moral Obligation', in Melden (ed.) *Essays in Moral Philosophy* 82–107.

Hart, H. L. A., *Essays on Bentham. Jurisprudence and Political Theory* (Oxford: OUP, 1982).

Hawkins, J., 'Desiring the Bad under the Guise of the Good', *Philosophical Quarterly* 58/231 (2008) 244–64.

Herman, B., 'Integrity and Impartiality', *The Monist* 66 (1983) 234.

Herman, B., 'Agency, Attachment, and Difference', *Ethics* 101 (1991) 775.

Heuer, U., 'Intentions and the Reasons for Which We Act', *Proceedings of the Aristotelian Society* 114/3 (2014) 291–315.
Heuer, U., 'Reasons to Intend', in D. Star (ed.), *The Oxford Handbook of Reasons and Normativity* (Oxford: OUP, 2018) chapter 37, 865–90.
Hieronymi, P., 'The Use of Reasons in Thought (and the Use of Earmarks in Arguments)', *Ethics* 124/1 (2013) 114–27.
Hieronymi, P., 'Reflection and Responsibility', *Philosophy and Public Affairs* 42/1 (2014) 3–41.
Holton, R., *Willing, Wanting, Waiting* (Oxford: OUP, 2009).
Holton, R., 'Intention as a Model for Belief', in Vargas and Yaffe (eds), *Rational and Social Agency: Essays on the Philosophy of Michael Bratman*.
Hume, D., *Treatise on Human Nature*, ed. P. H. Nidditch (Oxford: OUP, 1978).
Hursthouse, R., 'Arational Actions', *Journal of Philosophy* 88 (1991) 57.
Kahneman, D., *Thinking, Fast and Slow* (New York: Farrar Straus Giroux, 2011).
Kenny, A., *Action, Emotion and the Will* (London: Routledge & Kegan Paul, 1963).
Kenny, A., *The Metaphysics of Mind* (Oxford: Clarendon Press, 1989).
Kolodny, N., 'Why be Rational?' *Mind* 114 (2005) 509.
Kolodny, N., 'How Does Coherence Matter?' *Proceedings of the Aristotelian Society* 107 (2007) 229.
Kolodny, N., 'The Myth of Practical Consistency', *European Journal of Philosophy* 16 (2008) 36.
Korsgaard, C., *Self-Constitution: Action, Identity and Integrity* (Oxford: OUP, 2009).
McClennen, E., *Rationality and Dynamic Choice* (Cambridge: CUP, 1990).
Markwick, P., 'Law and Content-Independent Reasons', *Oxford Journal of Legal Studies* 20 (2000) 579.
Marmor, A., *Social Conventions: From Language to Law* (Princeton: Princeton UP, 2009).
Melden, A., *Essays in Moral Philosophy* (Seattle: University of Washington Press, 1958).
Monti, E., 'Against Triggering Accounts of Robust Reason-Giving', *Philosophical Studies* 178/11 (2021) 3731.
Monti, E., 'On the Moral Impact Theory of Law', *Oxford Journal of Legal Studies* (2021).
Moran, R., and Stone, M., 'Anscombe on Expression of Intention', in Sandis (ed.) *New Essays on the Explanation of Action*.
Muller, A., 'Radical Subjectivity: Morality v. Utilitarianism', *Ratio* 19/1 (1977) 115–31.
Nozick, R., *Anarchy, State and Utopia* (New York: Basic Books, 1974).
Owens, D., 'The Possibility of Consent', *Ratio* 24 (2011) 402–5.
Owens, D., *Shaping the Normative Landscape* (Oxford: OUP, 2012).
Owens, D., 'Habitual Agency', *Philosophical Explanations* 20 (2017) 93–108.
Paul, E., Miller, F., and Paul, J. (eds), *Cultural Pluralism and Moral Knowledge* (Cambridge: CUP, 1994).
Rawls, J., *A Theory of Justice* (Oxford: OUP, 1971; rev. edn. 1999).
Raz, J., *Practical Reason and Norms* (1975; 3rd edn. Oxford: OUP, 1999).
Raz, J., 'Reasons, Decisions and Norms', *Mind* 84 (1975) 481–99.
Raz, J., 'Promises and Obligations', in Hacker and Raz (eds), *Law, Morality, and Society: Essays in Honour of H.L.A. Hart*.
Raz, J., 'Authority, Law and Morality' *The Monist* 68 (1985) 295–324, reprinted in *Ethics in the Public Domain*.
Raz, J., *The Morality of Freedom* (Oxford: OUP, 1986).
Raz, J., 'Liberating Duties', *Law and Philosophy* 8 (1989) 3, reprinted in *Ethics in the Public Domain*.

Raz, J. 'Facing Up', *Southern California Law Review* 62 (1989) 1153–1236.
Raz, J., *Ethics in the Public Domain* (Oxford: Clarendon Press, 1994).
Raz, J., 'Moral Change and Social Relativism', in Paul, Miller, and Paul (eds), *Cultural Pluralism and Moral Knowledge*.
Raz, J., *Engaging Reason* (Oxford: OUP, 1999).
Raz, J., *Value, Respect and Attachment* (Cambridge: CUP, 2001).
Raz, J., 'The Role of Well-Being', *Philosophical Perspectives* 18 *Ethics* (2004) 269–94.
Raz, J., *Between Authority and Interpretation* (Oxford: OUP, 2009).
Raz, J., *From Normativity to Responsibility* (Oxford: OUP, 2011).
Raz, J., 'A Hedgehog's Unity of Value', in Waluchow and Sciaraffa (eds), *The Legacy of Ronald Dworkin*.
Raz, J., 'On Dancy's Account of Practical Reasoning', *Philosophical Explorations* 23 (2020) 135.
Regan, D., 'Why Am I My Brother's Keeper?' in Wallace, Pettit, Scheffler, and Smith (eds), *Reason and Value*.
Ripstein, A., and Morris, C. (eds), *Practical Rationality and Preference: Essays for David Gauthier* (Cambridge: CUP, 2001).
Robins, M., 'Is it Rational to Carry Out Strategic Intentions?', *Philosophia* (Israel) 25/1–4 (1995) 191–221.
Ryle, G., *The Concept of Mind* (London: Hutchinson, 1949).
Sandis, C. (ed.), *New Essays on the Explanation of Action* (Basingstoke: Palgrave Macmillan, 2009).
Scanlon, T., *What We Owe to Each Other* (Cambridge, Mass.: Harvard UP, 1998).
Scanlon, T., 'Reasons: A Puzzling Duality', in Wallace, Pettit, Scheffler, and Smith (eds), *Reason and Value*.
Scanlon, T., 'Ideas of Identity and their Normative Status', 2018, https://www.kcl.ac.uk/law/c-ppl/news-events/ppl-annual-lecture-thomas-scanlon-ideas-of-identity-updated-2.pdf.
Scanlon, T., 'Contractualism and Justification', in Stepanians and Frauchiger (eds), *Reason, Justification, and Contractualism*.
Scheffler, S., *The Rejection of Consequentialism* (Oxford: OUP, 1982, rev. edn. 1994).
Scheffler, S., 'Valuing', in Scheffler, *Equality and Tradition*.
Scheffler, S., *Equality and Tradition* (Oxford: OUP, 2010).
Sciaraffa, S., 'On Content-Independent Reasons: It's Not in the Name', *Law and Philosophy* 28 (2009) 233.
Setiya, K., *Reasons Without Rationalism* (Princeton: Princeton UP, 2007).
Shafer-Landau, R. (ed.), *Oxford Studies in Metaethics*, vol. 9 (Oxford: OUP, 2014).
Skorupski, J. https://www.kcl.ac.uk/law/c-ppl/news-events/ppl-annual-lecture-skorupski-comment-on-scanlon-on-identity.pdf, 3–4.
Smart, J., and Williams, B., *Utilitarianism For and Against* (Cambridge: CUP, 1973).
Star, D. (ed.), *The Oxford Handbook of Reasons and Normativity* (Oxford: OUP, 2018).
Stepanians, M., and Frauchiger, M. (eds), *Reason, Justification, and Contractualism: Themes from Scanlon*, Lauener Library of Analytical Philosophy vol. 7 (Berlin/Boston: De Gruyter, 2021).
Stocker, M., 'Desiring the Bad—An Essay in Moral Psychology', *Journal of Philosophy* 76/12 (1979), 738–53.
Stocker, M., 'Raz on the Intelligibility of Bad Acts', in Wallace, Pettit, Scheffler, and Smith (eds), *Reason and Value*.
Sussman, D., 'For Badness' Sake', *Journal of Philosophy* 106/11 (2009) 613–28.

Theunissen, N., *The Value of Humanity* (Oxford: OUP, 2020).
Thompson, M., *Life in Action* (Cambridge, Mass.: Harvard UP, 2008).
Vargas, M., and Yaffe, G. (eds), *Rational and Social Agency: Essays on the Philosophy of Michael Bratman* (Oxford: OUP, 2014).
Velleman, D., 'The Guise of the Good', in Velleman (ed.), *The Possibility of Practical Reason.*
Velleman, D. (ed.), *The Possibility of Practical Reason* (New York: OUP, 2002).
Verbeek, B. (ed.), *Reasons and Intentions* (London: Routledge & Kegan Paul, 2016).
von Wright, G., *Norm and Action* (London: Routledge & Kegan Paul, 1963).
Wallace, R., Pettit, P., Scheffler, S., and Smith, M. (eds), *Reason and Value: Themes from the Moral Philosophy of Joseph Raz* (Oxford: Clarendon Press, 2004).
Waluchow, W., and Sciaraffa, S. (eds), *The Legacy of Ronald Dworkin* (Oxford: OUP, 2016).
Zalta, E. (ed.), *Stanford Encyclopedia of Philosophy* (Edward N. Zalta (ed.), URL = https://plato.stanford.edu/archives/spr2019/entries/.

Index

For the benefit of digital users, indexed terms that span two pages (e.g., 52–53) may, on occasion, appear on only one of those pages.